the

search

for

david

# the
# search
# for
# david

## a cosmic journey of love

## GEORGE SCHWIMMER

Unity Library & Archives
1901 NW Blue Parkway
Unity Village, MO 64065

HEARTSFIRE BOOKS

AN IMPRINT OF HAMPTON ROADS PUBLISHING COMPANY

Cover photo by Keith Trider
Cover design by Marjoram Productions

*For information write:*

Heartsfire Books
c/o Hampton Roads Publishing Company, Inc.
134 Burgess Lane
Charlottesville, VA 22902

Or call: (804)296-2772
FAX: (804)296-5096
e-mail: hrpc@mail.hamptonroadspub.com
Web site: http://www.hamptonroadspub.com

If you are unable to order this book from your local
bookseller, you may order directly from the publisher.
Quantity discounts for organizations are available.
Call 1-800-766-8009, toll-free.

ISBN 1-57174-051-1

10 9 8 7 6 5 4 3 2 1

Printed on acid-free paper in Canada

Dedicated to David and to
all those who have helped
me with my search in this
life and in other lives.

# contents

# acknowledgements:

I would like to thank all of the people, named and unnamed, and organizations who took part in the spiritual journey recorded in this narrative. Neither the journey nor the narrative would have come into existence without all of them.

I also want to thank my publisher, Claude Saks, for taking on this project, and my editor, Sara Held, for her guidance in helping me to determine the final shape and content of the book. Thanks as well to Kathy Grotz for her suggestions and corrections and to Keith Trider for his photograph of Baja on the cover.

# preface

Judge nothing before the time, until the Lord
come, who both will bring to light the hidden things
of darkness, and will make manifest the counsels of
the hearts. . . .

*The First Epistle of Paul to the Corinthians 4:5*

And ye also shall bear witness, because ye have
been with me from the beginning.

*John 15:27*

Eighteen years have passed since the phone call that
shattered my life so completely that I've had to change not
only my views of existence, my life-style, my behavior and
my work, but even who I am. The man who I was then
has died as surely as did my younger son David.

The cascade of events that has washed over me since
David's death was put into motion on January 8, 1978,
when David began an Outward Bound kayaking course in
Mexico's Sea of Cortez, paddling with his crew along the
eastern shore of the Baja peninsula. On January 27,
David's nineteenth birthday, I was called and told that
David had been swept out to sea by a violent wind storm.
Although a substantial search was eventually mounted,
the sea stubbornly refused to yield up my son. David did
not appear. His body was never found.

After the search for David ended in Baja, I was confronted by the first of several seemingly unanswerable questions, questions which pushed me back into the darkest corner of my being and then challenged me, like the sphinx in *Oedipus*, to come into the light and answer them. The answers were already there, I discovered, because the questions were there; the universe poses no question until it has first created the answer.

So, in only a few days, David's friend Alice answered my most agonized thought:

Why David? Why take the one who was already aware of Your love on Earth? Why take the one who gave us joy as no one else did, by his emanations of this light and love? Why the scholar, the giver, the one most ready to live life? Because, the answer came back from the faith we both shared, to take away David will force you all to look, some of you very hard, into your own souls to find the light and love that God gives to each. When we find this which we have been made to hunt for, we will each have a part of David for ourselves, the part he would have liked most to give.

I laid aside Alice's letter—I wasn't ready to search my soul then. Yet the inner quest had already begun, although I didn't know it.

Two other questions also surged forward, demanding immediate answers: What happened to David in the storm? and What can I do to keep David's spirit alive?

The sea had taken David's body, but I refused to let it extinguish his flame. There had to be something I could do for David. Within days the answer to the third question came to me: publish David's writing. During his last seven years David had kept personal journals; I had no idea what the journals contained or whether they had any literary value. But when I read them I discovered that David had conducted an unusual inner—as well as outer—search for himself and for the meaning of his life during his teenage years. I was fascinated and impressed by the journals and decided they—along with some of his poems, papers, and fragments of two books—had to be published. Over the next few years I edited David's work. I didn't yet consider writing about my own experiences.

I found the question of what had happened to David in the storm much harder to answer. After the search had ended in Baja, I began another search, this one to find out what had taken place during the last day of David's life. I *had* to discover what had occurred—I couldn't resume a sane life without knowing. When Outward Bound refused to release any details of the tragedy, I threw myself into this new search with enormous energy, but more than three years had to pass before I could unearth everything that had taken place in Baja during Southwest Outward Bound Kayaking Course S-54.

Some of my questions could not be answered through ordinary research, so I turned to reputable mediums. They told me facts about David's life and death which they had no way of knowing; at times their accuracy was stunning. They also recounted unexpected, extraordinary things about David, some of which were confirmed by David's journals. I learned about David's prior lives, his personal symbology, his dreams, his astrological chart, and his life plan. David himself—through many of the psychics—communicated with me, while David's friends and family began to report having sensed, felt, heard, or seen David since his death. As I was given more and more such information, I decided this had to be published as well, so

I began to record it all, and much of that material is included in this book.

But as the number and significance of unusual incidents grew, I found I couldn't merely note these—I had to examine them as well, and as I did so I saw a logical pattern emerge. I realized that what was before me was a demonstration of the mechanics of spiritual life on Earth. David's life and death were a striking allegory of what existence is all about—David had lived a textbook of cosmic truths. And I was being led, item by item, person by person, place by place, along a path which had been laid out long ago with great care by some unseen consciousness.

My search for these hidden facets of spiritual life, however, was hampered by the fact that I was directing my efforts through my intellect only. I saw myself as a researcher of cosmic life, often excited and illuminated by the discovery of how something worked or what something meant, but I was missing the essential point. Although it was continually presented to me, I couldn't understand, couldn't sense, the basic spiritual truth which I was being shown, because I would look only at the outer reality.

I failed to perceive what lay behind the kindness and patience of the members of the spiritual study group which I had joined around the time of David's death. I wasn't aware of what motivated David's friends to speak with me and write to me when I sought them out. I wasn't sensitive to what radiated through the readings of the psychics whom I visited for help. I didn't hear the inner whispers of all who helped me with my outer search. I didn't realize the importance of David's message to me, and I misunderstood what many others brought into my life.

What I was unknowingly searching for and had searched for all of my life, I finally realized, had been given to me at the birth of the universe, but I had always walked blindly past this primal gift. A number of years had to pass before I understood what my search was for.

That search is the search on which we are all embarked, and its destination is one we have always known, since our destination is our starting point—a point which we actually never left. That search is the search for ourselves and who we *really* are.

Come join the search!

# 1

# the search in baja

*Raleigh, North Carolina*
*Friday, January 27, 1978*

The telephone rang shrilly in the next room, and my head turned toward the sound. I had come to the kitchen after my evening bath and was getting a snack before going to bed. I glanced at the stove clock: it was three minutes after midnight. Wrong number, I thought, although both I and my wife Veronica tended to stay up late, and friends and family knew that. The phone rang again. I went into the small sunroom and picked up the receiver.

"Mr. Schwimmer?" a male voice inquired.

"Yes," I replied.

The man identified himself as the director of Southwest Outward Bound. For some reason this didn't alarm me—I don't know why. My calm was shattered a second later.

"Mr. Schwimmer, your son David and two other students have been lost at sea in an accident."

The impact of his words was more violent than if he had struck me. What he'd said created a complete void in my mind: I could find nothing to say, I couldn't even think.

After a moment of silence, I asked him what had happened. He couldn't tell me. He said that only a one-sentence message had been left with Southwest Outward

Bound's answering service in Santa Fe shortly before this call and that he himself was in Florida. He continued to talk, but I heard his words only as meaningless sounds. I finally said goodbye and hung up the receiver dazedly.

Thoughts and images flashed from my mind, as if flung by a cyclotron: a dark sea, waves, David struggling. Questions: What kind of accident could have occurred in the Sea of Cortez? How could David be lost at sea? Where could he be? Was he alive? I struggled to control the storm that raged inside me.

I went into the living room where Veronica was watching television, turned off the sound as I walked by the set, and sat down beside her on the sofa. Then I told her. She burst into tears, and I could only sit there feeling totally unable to help.

A few minutes later I called John Rhoades, associate director of Southwest Outward Bound in Santa Fe. He couldn't give any further information since the only telephone was in Loreto, inside a tire store which had closed for the night and wouldn't open again until 9:00 A.M. Baja time (PST). That telephone was thereafter the only link between Baja, Santa Fe, and us. I asked Rhoades if anyone had called the U.S. Coast Guard, since San Diego was just up the coast and a helicopter could be sent to help with the search. Rhoades answered that he did not believe the Coast Guard had been notified. I asked him to contact them immediately and said I would call him at 9:15 A.M. Baja time. That ended our conversation.

I told Veronica what Rhoades had said, after which we lost ourselves in our own thoughts and prayers. Around 2:00 A.M. Veronica told me to go to bed. I said that was impossible. I couldn't and wouldn't lie in a bed while David was adrift in a dark sea, I thought to myself. All through the night I sat on a small sofa in the dimly lit living room, while Veronica walked tensely around the house.

I mentally listed the reasons David should survive. Each thought was a prayer bead that I clutched with my mind. I thought: David is so resourceful and intelligent, studied outdoor survival so carefully at Duke University, took two endurance swimming courses the past year, trained for cross-country running the previous summer and fall, completed a Red Cross first-aid course recently. I thought: the Outward Bound course is designed to teach him to survive, might have been preparing him for what had occurred; he had to be all right. I had always felt that nothing would ever happen to him—he had always seemed very special. I tried to convince myself that he was safe, but underneath it all I was desperate. My mind held my prayer beads more tightly, but the thread on which they were strung snapped. My thoughts scattered.

I stared into the darkness of the most terrible night I had ever lived, terrified that I might never see David again, that another kind of darkness, a darkness without end, may have slipped into my life and that a critical part of my future had been torn from me.

My mind spun backwards in time.

✦ ✦ ✦

David was our second child, preceded by his brother Eric and followed by his sister Krista. When pregnant with David, my wife was larger than normal, and it seemed as if David would never be born. Veronica insisted—before and after his birth—that David was a ten-month baby, and when he finally arrived, after twenty-four hours of labor, he was not red and wrinkled, but smooth and clear-eyed. He also seemed oddly mature for his age, a trait he would have for the rest of his life.

David had radiant good looks as a child, with translucent skin, hair almost platinum blond, large brown eyes, and a strong, healthy body which he liked to use. I found it hard not to keep looking at him after he was a year and a half old. It also became obvious early that David was a very distinct individual who was constantly at work building his inner and outer personality structures.

If one word can characterize David it is "love." He loved to love people he was attracted to, he tried to love—and often succeeded in loving—people he wasn't attracted to, he loved being in love, and he allowed others to love him. This last trait was perhaps his most important one. For although loving others is often not that easy, *accepting* the love of persons we're not really drawn to can be even more difficult. David, however, permitted "the outcasts"—as he called them—to love him, although he yearned for the love of some of his more popular schoolmates as well. Love, in any case, whether given, received, or denied, dominated David's inner life. Once, I mentioned this characteristic to the girl David had asked to marry him. She sighed and said, "Yes, David was a love essence."

This lovingness showed itself at an early age in the most striking aspect of David's life: his relationships with people. Everyone seemed to love him, even before he was born. Veronica said that giving birth to David had been a wonderful experience: the doctor had been wonderful, the nurses had been wonderful, everyone at the hospital had been loving to David and to her. David's charisma was evident even when he was a young child. During the summer that he was six years old and I was teaching acting at a children's camp, several girls from six to sixteen each sidled up to me to boast that she was engaged to David.

That charisma was not just a matter of looks or personality. From the time he was small to the last time I saw him, there was a shimmering quality to David—invisible, yet present. I had always been aware of this quality, and I was particularly struck by it when he came home one weekend in the fall of his last year.

It was evening, and we went to the dining room to eat. When David came in, Krista immediately started chatting with him, Eric also began talking animatedly to him, then Veronica started discussing something with him. I looked around and thought, "Every time David walks into a room, the place *lights up*." And that was the only way I could describe it. David literally radiated more light—a whole *lot* more light—than anyone I had known before him. I couldn't see this light around him, but I always sensed it was there.

Since people were attracted to his light and the warmth of his personality (although David himself often felt shy), he had to find a way to structure personal relationships. He developed a wonderful capability for interacting with family, friends, teachers, and others through empathy, humor, reason, friendship, charm, and basic good nature. He became an enjoyable companion and an excellent conversationalist and was always good with small children. Observing all this, I felt—from the time he was able to talk—that he would be a very successful person, able to obtain whatever he really wanted in life. Ironically, I always thought he was the child about whom I would never need to worry.

Now, as I wandered into our dining room, all I could see was darkness.

✦ ✦ ✦

When morning finally came, we said nothing to Eric and Krista. It seemed better to wait until we had more information. David might have been found already, after all—there was no point in upsetting them needlessly. They watched us from the corners of their eyes, though—they knew something was wrong. I looked away; they said nothing, ate breakfast, then went off to class—Eric to North Carolina State University, Krista to Broughton High School.

By that time I was completely numb, mentally and emotionally. I didn't realize it, but I was in a deep state of shock. I don't remember how the morning passed, except that my office manager and his wife came by shortly after nine. They had already heard about David, having been called from Dallas by the president of our company, who—oddly—was on the board of directors of Southwest Outward Bound.

The next three hours were an agonizing wait. When 12:15 finally arrived, I called Santa Fe. Rhoades told me that a wind storm had caught David's crew near a point of land called Punta Púlpito. David had been in a double kayak with a girl named Brenda Herman, and she and a third student, Tim Breidegam, were also missing. All the other students were safe. I asked about the U.S. Coast Guard, and Rhoades said that a delay had developed over obtaining diplomatic clearance for a Coast Guard helicopter to enter Mexican air space but that Southwest Outward Bound was trying to get a private helicopter also.

Immediately after talking with Rhoades, I called the office of Duke University President Terry Sanford, since it was public knowledge that he had White House connections. Then I phoned North Carolina Senator Robert Morgan's office to request his help. Assistance was next obtained from California Governor Jerry Brown's office through the office of North Carolina Governor James Hunt. Eventually I was able to speak with two White House aides also, and, as a result of all this contact, I later discovered, considerable pressure was brought to bear on the Coast Guard to dispatch a helicopter. Simultaneously, the State Department—contacted by Terry Sanford—asked Mexico to expedite diplomatic clearance for the helicopter. None of these people who made all this effort knew me or my family, and I was grateful and touched by their concern for a stranger.

Permission for the Coast Guard to enter Mexican air space was finally granted that afternoon, but the helicopter didn't start its sweeps until the following morning. However, a couple of small private planes were searching, and then the San Diego Mountain Rescue team—a volunteer organization which the Coast Guard had contacted because that group needed no diplomatic clearance—flew in at mid-afternoon. A Mexican helicopter also arrived to help at some point that day, but I didn't learn about it until three years later. Despite all this activity, I felt helpless. I desperately wanted to be out in Baja to look for David myself, but I knew that was impossible. I had to stay here.

Duke University Dean of Student Affairs Bill Griffith called; he kept in touch with us every day thereafter. Terry Sanford phoned. The State Department called again. Around 3:30 Eric and Krista came home, and I told them.

"I knew it," Kris said. "I knew something would happen."

"What do you mean?" I asked.

Kris shook her head, stricken. "I don't know. I just knew it."

Since my parents also lived in Raleigh, I went over to their house and broke the news to my mother, then came back home immediately. At 4:20 I contacted Santa Fe once more—still only very sketchy information, although I probably learned then that survivors had reported that Tim was dead. It seemed incredible to me that more facts were not available. I later learned that by this time the survivors had given full accounts, both oral and written, to Outward Bound, but we were unaware of these reports.

I could hardly stand up by now and told Veronica that I would lie down for an hour. I went upstairs and fell into a very uncomfortable sleep. Later I realized that this day was David's birthday and that I had gone to sleep only a few minutes after the time of day when David had been born nineteen years before. When I awoke, it was with a sinking sensation deep inside me: I felt David was gone. But I said nothing about this to anyone.

Sometime that evening, Tim Breidegam's father phoned to ask if there was any news of David. We spoke for a few minutes, and I thanked him for contacting us. Considering that he knew Tim was dead, his thoughtful call was undoubtedly difficult to make.

Just before 9:00 P.M., I checked with Santa Fe for the last time that day. A Coast Guard report, which we obtained much later, stated that by 9:00 A.M. Baja time searchers had found David and Brenda's kayak washed ashore on the northern end of Coronados Island, about twenty miles south of Punta Púlpito. Perhaps Rhodes told me this during our conversation, but I don't remember if he did. The only thing I cared about was that David hadn't been found, and I could do nothing but wait.

Then there was only the darkness once more.

✦ ✦ ✦

Kris had known something would happen. Perhaps I too had been warned but hadn't understood.

I thought back to a moment seventeen years earlier, when I was artistic director of a Texas theater and David was less than eighteen months old. The theater where I worked was on city property, in the middle of a large field of cropped grass, and I had been able to rent a house just across the street from it.

One day Veronica and I took David and Eric, then nearing three, to the field to play. David was dressed in pale blue corduroy pants, jacket, and a kind of bonnet. He could walk, but wasn't able to really run yet. Eric was running around, Veronica was playing with him, and I was watching them. David was to my right, just standing there.

I suddenly felt David staring at me, and when I turned to look into his eyes, I saw something in them that chilled me. A wise, thoughtful, intelligent consciousness was sizing me up, and although I knew this consciousness was David, I also knew I wasn't perceiving the look of an eighteen-month-old child—what I saw was timeless. With great fear I realized that David was calmly deciding whether or not to remain a part of this family, whether or not to continue living. When the meaning of his look hit me, I ran over to him, scooped him up in my arms, hugged him, and kissed him, to make David understand that I wanted him to stay with us.

That's all I remembered, but I never forgot the look. Maybe David was warning me, I don't know—I guess I didn't want to know. I never told anyone about that look. How could I?

*David as a toddler.*

During the same year, David probably saved all our lives. In our house we had a floor heater, which was covered by a piece of rug when not in use. I normally removed the rug from the heater's grate at night, although we rarely needed the heater since the town was quite hot. One evening I forgot to move the rug; the temperature fell during the night, and the heater kicked on around dawn. Veronica awoke to hear David crying and saw our bedroom full of thick brown smoke. She yelled to wake me, and the minute I opened my eyes I knew what had happened. I leaped out of bed, grabbed the piece of burning rug, and flung it out the back door. A few minutes more of that smoke and we might all have been dead.

David terrified me once more when he was eight. We were then living in Raleigh, in an apartment whose living room and kitchen were on the ground floor, and David was playing with some children in our backyard. Suddenly he stumbled in through the back door, unable to breathe. David later said he had been sucking on a small lollipop with a paper handle, which had somehow become lodged in his throat. At that moment I didn't know what had happened, but I could see his face already starting to turn blue. I put two of my fingers into his mouth to determine what was wrong, and with that David swallowed the entire lollipop and was able to breathe again. I was in shock and didn't react then, but two days later I was shaking like a leaf inside.

Now, with David missing, I didn't dare look inside myself.

✦ ✦ ✦

*Saturday*

The morning paper contained a small article about David. It noted that he had been lost on Tuesday, and I assumed "Tuesday" was a misprint. Later in the day we discovered that the students *had* been caught in the wind storm Tuesday morning, around 9:00 A.M. We were stunned once more. The accident had not been reported to Outward Bound offices in Santa Fe until Thursday night, and now more than four days had passed since David was last seen. Any faint hope I still had for David's survival was rapidly ebbing away.

At 12:05 P.M. I called Santa Fe. The news was bad. David had not been found, but the bodies of Tim and

Brenda had washed ashore on the northwest coast of Carmen Island, which was a few miles south of Coronados Island. I felt Rhoades was warning me not to hope. I next phoned the Coast Guard in Long Beach to ask for further information. There was none. I could feel myself beginning to come apart inside.

I hung up the receiver, and as I walked past the living room fireplace a piece of paper on the mantelpiece caught my eye. It had been lying there since Christmas, and I knew that on it were the name and address of a girl David had grown very close to during the past nine months. Although I had never met Preston and knew very little about her, I felt I had to speak with her. I returned to the phone and called her. She was very subdued, having already heard about David. I told her what I knew and promised to call again. For the next ten or twelve days, every day, either I called her or she called me.

A short time later a newspaper reporter called. Friends, David's friends, parents of David's friends called. There were many other calls. I was on the phone much of the day—all that is a blur now. The afternoon paper came with another article about David. I later learned that the young reporter who wrote the story had known David at Duke and that one of our friends was the reporter's editor.

I continued to feel that David was gone, and my thoughts now started to focus on finding his body. Late in the afternoon I began to consider contacting psychics: often they were able to help in locating people. I thought of Irene Hughes, a Chicago psychic to whom I had written years ago, and I also remembered the Psychical Research Foundation in Durham that I had read about somewhere. I finally decided to hold off calling either one.

The day dragged on. It was unbearable, but all I could do was wait. I made my last call to New Mexico at 9:23 P.M. There was no news.

David was still in the Sea of Cortez, and I was completely powerless to help him.

It wasn't chance that led David to Baja. He loved nature as much as he loved people. I always see David in nature: at age three, surrounded by woods on Long Island, sunlight pouring over his head in a golden cascade; at five, standing on the branch of a tree in the overgrown backyard of our rented Illinois house; at seven, running with our dog Clark on the broad grounds of our Raleigh home, tall pines all around him; thirteen, riding and jumping horses on a beloved farm in Ireland, trees everywhere; fifteen, running doggedly along the side of a wooded road in Raleigh, getting in shape for a cross-country meet; eighteen, hiking a heavily forested, snowy North Carolina mountain. Trees, always trees, around David. He was drawn to the ocean, too, and sometimes went there with friends.

He also loved the animals that came into our home: hamsters, birds, cats, dogs—in fact, David was responsible for the coming of many of the animals which lived with us over the years, the last of which was Lord Peter, a cat. David came home one day when he was sixteen, holding the tiniest kitten, which had the most fleas I've ever seen on an animal. Lord Peter became an important part of our family. Everyone could love Lord Peter.

David wasn't here now, but I picked up Lord Peter and held him.

*Sunday*

Another article about David was in the newspaper, but the information was old and incomplete. After breakfast Eric left the house saying, "I still have hope."

I called New Mexico around 2:00. Rhoades told me that David's life jacket—zipped up and tied with its waist cord—had been recovered on the northern end of Carmen Island. Both Brenda's and Tim's bodies had been found with their life jackets on. We subsequently learned that the students' life jackets had all been the same size, and since Brenda had been smaller than David I couldn't understand how David's jacket could have come off while Brenda's had remained on. The zipped and tied life jacket was an enigma. Rhoades couldn't explain how this might have happened, nor could the Coast Guard when I asked.

Rhoades also told me that a young woman in a single kayak had become separated from the group by high waves. When David and Brenda were last seen they were paddling toward her to try and give her help. Rhoades finished his report by saying that the weather in the Sea of Cortez was starting to deteriorate.

Around 4:00 I decided to contact Irene Hughes. I called Chicago but was unable to get Mrs. Hughes' unlisted home number. Her answering service said she would be in her office the next morning. Once again, I could do nothing but wait.

At 5:00 I called the Coast Guard, then Santa Fe. There still was no sign of David. Around 8:30, I received a call from New Mexico, but there was nothing new. A few minutes later, I phoned Dr. Griffith, then Preston. By now my whole life was flowing through the telephone.

Eric came home later in the evening and said that on the bus to Greensboro in the morning he had suddenly had a tremendous feeling of peace. He told us this feeling lasted for just a few minutes, and he couldn't explain it.

Another day was gone, David was still missing, and the darkness I had begun to dread was around me again.

✦ ✦ ✦

David's inner life was more obvious on the surface of his personality before he was three than at any time after. He was very thoughtful and serious as a baby, but these traits were later overshadowed by the outer mask of good nature that he began to develop when he was about two. He soon became very humorous, sometimes mischievous, and often filled with pure joy. One day when he was about sixteen I told him, "I sort of envy you your good temperament." He gave me an odd look and replied, "Yeah, but you don't know how *hard* I have to *work at it* sometimes." He also liked to put himself down and could needle others as well, including me, but he would do it with humor.

His personality seemed to be well balanced at every age. On those occasions when he got into a mood, he normally worked himself out of it, usually in a couple of hours. He was slow to anger, though he could blow his top spectacularly, and he didn't have a mean bone in his body. He possessed leadership qualities of a subtle nature: those being led were often unaware that he was leading. He also was a great supporter of others, cheering even the most obscure team at his high school, where he was elected to the National Honor Society in his junior year, voted most valuable player for his cross country team in his senior year, and earned a three-year grade average of over ninety-four.

David's way of living was open and honest, and he always wanted to be at the cutting edge of life—where the past joins the future. He immersed himself in the moment: he was always alert, always intense and focused, whether writing a paper, running a race, or telling a joke. He also was introspective and sentimental, seeing values in the past.

Most unusual for a teenager was David's consciously directed control of himself and his life. Once, around five A.M. on a Sunday morning during the time David had a newspaper route, I staggered out of bed to drive him to pick up his bundles of papers. David had been sitting silently beside me in the car for a while when he said, "You know, I really don't like delivering these papers, but I think the discipline is good for me. Everyone needs some discipline like this. That's partly why I run, too; it's good discipline, even when it hurts." Considering that David was barely fifteen years old then, I was impressed by his observation. A journal entry he made two years later also typified his response to life: "I am very tired of this day . . . but, yet, the challenge!"

David had some flaws—brashness and impatience were two—and he would hate being considered a paragon of any sort, I knew. He wasn't, but I couldn't think of anything I would change in him.

✦ ✦ ✦

*Monday*

At 10:00 A.M. I reached Irene Hughes at her office and summarized what had happened. She asked for the date and time of David's birth and when and where the accident had occurred. When I told her, she said that January 24 had been a very bad day astrologically for David, and when I next mentioned that he had been in a double kayak with a girl, Mrs. Hughes instantly responded that it would have been "disastrous" for David to have been in the company of a woman that day.

Mrs. Hughes started to say that she would mail her impressions to me but then, apparently sensing that this delay distressed me, asked if we had any hope left that David was alive. I reluctantly answered that I personally felt David was gone, to which Mrs. Hughes replied that although she did not like to give such information over the phone, she would now tell me that David had not survived.

She also told me she perceived that David's body was only about 300 feet from where his accident had occurred, and that he was in an area that jutted out from shore, to his right. David's body was just under the surface of the water but would be difficult to see because he was wearing a green sweater.[1]

"David's head had been injured," Mrs. Hughes continued. "He died soon after the accident, his soul left before death, but he felt no pain or distress, though he had been apprehensive earlier. He had known since last June that he would die, and he also had a premonition of his death three days before the accident. During the previous year, David had been emotionally disturbed. David's life, as all our lives, had been planned at the time of Creation, since we are all co-creators with God. David will be around you, and you will feel his presence in the future," she concluded.

Since Irene Hughes was a nationally respected psychic, I gave credence to what she said; so when our conversation ended, I called John Rhoades and passed on her impressions about David's body. Rhoades agreed to relay the information to his people in Baja, then advised me that the Coast Guard was planning to end its efforts after that day. Distressed by this news, I asked him to put pressure on the officer in charge to keep the helicopter looking for at least another twenty-four hours. He agreed to try.

But when I spoke to Rhoades again that evening, he said that although more Outward Bound personnel had been flown in to help with the search, the Coast Guard had cancelled its operation. I urged him to call the Coast Guard one last time and again request that the search be continued for another day.

Then I rang up the Raleigh area council chairwoman of the A.R.E. (the Association for Research and Enlightenment, the Edgar Cayce organization), whom I had met a few months before, and asked that her local group pray for David. She quickly said they would and also inquired if I would like to talk with Marian, a Charlotte spiritual counselor with psychic abilities whom she had mentioned to me several months before. I asked her when Marian would be in Raleigh and was told a week from that Saturday. That seemed too late to do any good, but I thanked her for the suggestion. (I have no idea why I didn't try to call Marian sometime that week. I apparently wasn't thinking clearly on Monday and then forgot about Marian.)

The day ended, as had the three before, with my feelings of total helplessness.

✦ ✦ ✦

David's love of nature had deepened in 1976, when he left for Duke University. He signed up for Project WILD—an eleven-day outdoor program for incoming Duke freshmen—so as to make the transition from home to college in the wilderness. By then David had become firmly committed to the outdoors, and he—as I—felt that the Project WILD concept was a good idea. He was out among trees again. His continued involvement with Project WILD over the next year led to his taking the Southwest Outward Bound kayaking course.

*David during his first semester at Duke.*

David had lost his focus at Duke, and his grades had slipped badly in his third semester. He felt he needed to get away for a while. I had mixed feelings about David going to Baja. It seemed like a big step for an eighteen-year-old recently out of the family nest, but I finally concluded it might be good for him to be on his own for a short time. David requested and was granted a leave of absence from Duke for the 1978 spring semester, and he found a ride to California with a Duke divinity professor. After the kayaking course, David planned to work, think, and write, either in San Francisco or Boston. Since David had relatives in San Francisco and friends in Boston, I thought his plans were reasonable. He said he would return to his studies at Duke the following summer.

✦ ✦ ✦

*Tuesday*

I called Irene Hughes at 10:00 A.M. and asked whether she could get more precise impressions if she had a detailed chart of the area where David was lost. Mrs. Hughes replied that she *could* be more exact with a chart, and she also said she felt David's body had moved and was now more accessible. I phoned Rhoades, and when I learned he had charts of the area, I asked him to send them by Express Mail to Mrs. Hughes. He agreed to do so at once.

The rest of my day was spent calling Senator Morgan's Washington office, the White House, the State Department, the Long Beach Coast Guard Headquarters, and finally the Chief of Coast Guard Operations in Washington, either to ask for help or to pressure the Coast Guard to resume its search. Although these calls had some effect—Coast Guard logs record that the White House office of Hamilton Jordan called Long Beach at 2:00 P.M.—the Coast Guard adamantly refused to resume looking for David. "We don't do body searches," was the cold response of the Washington admiral whom I called. I was enraged, but could do nothing.

I spoke with Rhoades several times more during the day and was told that although a fresh crew of Outward Bound instructors was on the scene searching, nothing new had been found.

David was still missing, and much of my life seemed to be slipping away with him.

✦ ✦ ✦

When the 1977 fall semester ended, David came home, and on Christmas Eve he and his friend Alice went to midnight mass at St. Michael's Episcopal Church, then came back and talked with Veronica for a while.

David left for Baja on December 26. He had gone to bed early the night before but came back downstairs later, apparently sensing that his mother was worried. He stopped in the entranceway of the living room—Veronica later told me—and said, "Don't worry, Momma. I'm coming home."

David and I got up about 6:30 the next morning, in order to be in Durham by 8:30 for his ride to California. I helped David pack his gear into our station wagon, and he then went upstairs to say goodbye to his mother. He kissed her, turned to go, then came back and kissed her again. During the drive to Durham, David and I hardly spoke, but I felt we were communicating somehow.

When we arrived, I pulled into the sloping driveway of the professor's house and helped David unload his gear, which he began to carry down to the truck that would take him west. When he returned, we said goodbye awkwardly—it is a family curse to be undemonstrative, physically or verbally. I felt like hugging David and always regret that I didn't. I then backed the car onto the road and drove off, looking back at David over my right shoulder as he trudged down the driveway with the last of his belongings. I had no conscious foreboding of danger, but I felt empty and a little lonely.

✦ ✦ ✦

*Wednesday*

David had taken his Duke and Project WILD journals with him to Baja, and Veronica and I were afraid these also had been lost in the storm. I had seen David writing in his journals for years and knew he had put so much of himself into them that their loss would have been like another part of David dying. And almost from the start I had had the feeling that recovering David's Duke journal was very important, although at that time I didn't know why. So when I talked with Rhoades Wednesday morning, I asked him if the journal had been found. He said he didn't know but would check into it.

I called Irene Hughes at 2:00, but she had not received the charts. I immediately phoned Santa Fe, and Rhoades told me he had sent the charts by air express and gave me the name of the company that he had used. I contacted the air express office in Chicago—the charts had arrived but couldn't be found anywhere. I called Mrs. Hughes once more and asked her to check with the air express office the next day. She said she would.

In the evening, my father and mother came to see us. They looked ravaged. My parents were from Hungary and most of their closest relatives and friends had died during or shortly after World War II. In addition, my father's youngest brother had died at the age of twenty-one. Now my parents had to endure the death of a grandchild.

A short time after arriving, my father motioned me out into the front hallway, handed me a thick envelope, and said, "Get another helicopter." After my parents had gone, I looked in the envelope and found $5,000 in cash. During the following day, however, it became obvious that getting a helicopter wasn't possible, so when I next saw my father I returned the money.

His offer would be the only outer sign I'd ever see of my father's feelings about David's disappearance.

✦ ✦ ✦

I was born into a dysfunctional family but didn't know it, since this condition had not been identified then and the word "dysfunctional" had not been coined. It wasn't until around 1989 that I learned I was dysfunctional and co-dependent and began to read about these behaviors.

The worst dysfunctional rule was the code of silence. Not only was one not supposed to show one's emotions, but one did not talk about one's feelings or personal issues, either. When my mother did, my father would ridicule her—or my sister Kathie, or me. All family skeletons and problems had to be kept secret. Misfortunes, once past, were never referred to again. My father and mother almost never mentioned their dead parents, brothers, or sisters. After David died, my father never spoke of him again. The dead buried the dead.

This code of silence was the most unfortunate bequest I received from my father, for it affected how I responded to the world and to all my personal relationships. Once learned, it was a behavior that was incredibly difficult to unlearn. You stuffed your thoughts, you stuffed your emotions, and you stuffed the words that went with them. I managed to escape into activities and jobs which broke the silence and forced me to speak. Acting, especially, also allowed me to feel. But the code of silence functioned rigidly within my family. Only David seemed to shake off the curse partially, by forcing himself to be outgoing and by writing his thoughts and feelings in his journals.

Now the code of silence hung like a shroud over my family's tragedy. No one spoke.

✦ ✦ ✦

*Thursday*

Nine days had passed since David had last been seen, but my mind shut out that fact. My entire emotional system had closed down. Veronica, Eric, Krista, and my parents were all devastated emotionally, and I believed it was up to me to stay calm and centered to prevent my family from disintegrating psychologically. I couldn't afford to have any feelings, so I buried them, very consciously, as deep inside myself as I could.

I phoned Mrs. Hughes at 10:00 A.M. The charts still hadn't been located—she said she'd call as soon as they were found. The morning dragged on, but the phone never rang. I became even more desperate: I *had* to help David. At 1:30 P.M. I called the Psychical Research Foundation in Durham and asked about any psychics who might be able to locate David. I was given the names of Don Hudson, of Charlotte, and Karen Getsla, who lived somewhere in Illinois.

I called Don and explained what had happened. There was a long pause as Don allowed the scene to form in his mind, then he told me that David's body was in a "dugout cove" about a mile north of where the body of Brenda had been found. There was a sharp cliff above David, rocks north of him, and a lot of debris and underbrush around him. Further north of that cove was a more pronounced cove which cut deeply into Carmen Island (See chart, page 59). Don ended by saying that David's body was out of the water, with his legs pulled up in a fetal position.

I thanked Don for his assistance and phoned Santa Fe at once. Rhoades agreed to give this new information to his search party. I wondered what Rhoades thought of my using psychics, but he never resisted the information which I gave him. I next attempted to contact Karen Getsla. I tracked her to a Midwest college where she was lecturing and left a message.

Later in the afternoon, the Duke chaplain called to say that David's friends at the university were going to hold a memorial service for David on Tuesday evening, and he invited me and Veronica to attend. Preston was to speak at the service, and the chaplain asked if I also would like to address David's friends. I wasn't sure if I was up to that, but I told the chaplain I'd think about it and tell him the next day.

Rhoades probably called us that evening, but I don't know what we talked about. Time had become nothing but a blur, with only David in focus. My life had shattered.

✦ ✦ ✦

My marriage to Veronica was probably doomed from the start, as she also came from a dysfunctional family. Veronica was even more unwilling than I to communicate what was inside her, and I—trained in the code of silence—did not press her to talk. Year by year, both of us became more and more entombed in this prison of silence. By 1978 our marriage had disintegrated—only the children kept us together. Now, the hub of the wheel, David, was missing.

✦ ✦ ✦

*Friday*

Mrs. Hughes was on the phone around 11:00 A.M. to say she had finally received the charts, and she gave me directions for locating David's body. My notes of this call are fragmentary and unclear now: "Near Pt. de la Lancha . . . from Tintorera . . . Cholla . . . on the north end of Carmen Island." I eventually learned that Cholla is a tiny island off the northwest corner of Carmen Island. According to Outward Bound records, obtained much later, David's blue life jacket was found two-thirds of the distance from Cholla to the first big point on the north side of Carmen (Pt. Tintorera). This was the same quadrant of the island about which Don Hudson had spoken.

I called Rhoades, and he told me that the last formal search would be held that day and that the Outward Bound staff would leave Baja on Tuesday. I gave Mrs. Hughes' new information to him and asked him to have the searchers check the area that Mrs. Hughes had indicated, then work their way south along the western coast of Carmen. If David were not found there, I felt he never would be. Rhoades agreed to have his team do as I asked.

Karen Getsla contacted me at around 2:00 P.M. She told me she could not help because her psychic abilities work primarily on the scene. She said she could take me to the spot where David's body was, but she couldn't visualize it or give me directions. I nevertheless described the sea-horse shape of Carmen Island and asked Karen if she had any impression of David's location. Karen replied that she felt David's body was in the curve of the neck of the sea horse, which I later discovered was almost the identical spot that Don Hudson had described (see chart on page 59).

Karen then suggested I contact a Los Angeles psychic, a friend of hers who was better able to visualize a distant scene. Her friend's name, Karen said, was Audrey Mankoff. Startled, I asked Karen if Mrs. Mankoff had recently lived in Raleigh, and Karen replied that she had.

I had met Audrey Mankoff briefly at two spiritual meetings which she had helped to sponsor in Raleigh. The group had presented lectures, discussions, films, guest speakers, and local psychics—one of whom was a man named Howard Granger. I had not known that Mrs. Mankoff had developed psychically herself or that she had left Raleigh. I immediately called her Los Angeles office and was startled again, this time by a secretary's routine response which indicated that Mrs. Mankoff was now working for a psychical research organization with which I had corresponded twelve years earlier. When Mrs. Mankoff came on the line, I told her what had happened, and she said she would call me the next day with her impressions.

I then phoned the Duke chaplain and told him I would speak at the service. He invited me and Veronica to have dinner with him before the service and said that Preston and Dr. Griffith would also be there. We agreed to meet at the chapel.

Around 8:00 P.M. Mrs. Mankoff phoned with her impressions. When she finished, I asked whether David's body would be found. She replied, "I get the number three. I feel this means that if you don't find his body in three days, he will not be recovered."

I thanked her for taking the time to help, and when Rhoades called later, I passed on Mrs. Mankoff's impressions to him. Rhoades then briefed me on what had been done that day and repeated that the searchers would stop their efforts on Monday. I had no answer for that, and our conversation ended there.

Only the ocean knew where David was.

✦ ✦ ✦

I was in Ireland in 1973, writing my doctoral dissertation in theater, when my father was hospitalized for surgery. He had just begun to manufacture pillows in Raleigh and he asked me to help him carry out his first pillow contract with the Department of Defense. He wrote that if I didn't come, he would not be granted the contract, which I knew he needed badly. I flew back to the U.S.; Veronica and the kids followed by boat.

After we had been in Raleigh a few months, David, who had just started high school, came up to me and said, jokingly but serious, "You will not move from Raleigh until I've graduated from high school." I understood what he was saying, as I had moved our family six times in the past ten years and had myself been uprooted as a child five times, once halfway through high school. I told David I would stay put till he, Eric, and Krista had started college.

When the government contract ended, I got a job selling life insurance, occasionally taught private classes in acting, and had been working, for the year before David was lost, to establish a regional theater in Raleigh. My income from insurance sales had become adequate, and with a V.A. loan I had bought a large old house that we were fixing up.

For once, things were starting to go well.

✦ ✦ ✦

*Saturday*

We received a note from the mother of David's friend Lisa. With it came a book, *Baja California and the Geography of Hope,* and a letter from Lisa:

> David is the kind of person who just can't die. He's too intense—he gets into living too much—and even if something has happened to the physical David, I can't help but feel he's going to be popping up for a long time: in trees, and squirrels, and even in the air. David's like that. Even when he's not here, he's here. . . .

Little did I know how prescient Lisa would turn out to be.

Although I expected no news from Santa Fe, I still waited all day for it. But the phone never rang, and time seemed to move only backwards.

✦ ✦ ✦

My family was Jewish, but I had always had a deep and abiding distrust of religion, any religion. When I reached thirteen, I told my father I would have nothing more to do with religion, and I didn't. For the next fifteen years I was an agnostic, shunning atheism also, since I felt that was as questionable as religion. I was quite suspicious of any absolutes or of any authority, and the field of religion seemed rife with both.

At college, being an agnostic became uncomfortable for me. I was both envious and incredulous of friends who had firm religious convictions while I was floundering in an inexplicable universe. My prime concern, of course, was what—if anything—would happen to my consciousness, my identity, when I died. Having rejected traditional religious thought, I had no answer for this troubling issue. And I don't recall even considering the possibility that my consciousness had existed before I was born.

I did have one experience in college which I found odd and surprising, however. The final question in my last exam for an ethics course instructed me to compare my personal ethics with those of any man I had studied. I chose Jesus; I don't know why, but I plunged into writing the comparison. When I finished and reviewed what I'd done, I discovered that my ethics and those of Jesus were almost identical. I was quite shocked. I had never thought of having *any* affinity with Jesus, and here we had the same views. However, this was just ethics—it dealt with life, not death, so I put the experience aside.

✦ ✦ ✦

*Sunday*

I seem to recall that there were storms in the Sea of Cortez this day, so we may have been called by Rhoades; but if we were, I don't remember it.

My life had become surreal. There was an opaque film between my consciousness and reality. Mundane activities—washing, shaving, dressing, eating, looking at the newspaper—seemed totally unimportant, irrelevant; it felt bizarre that I could manage to keep doing ordinary things. I can recall nothing of my daily life then, nor do I remember any significant conversations with anyone in my family. Each of them was shut off in his or her own inner space, to which I had no access. I didn't know how anyone was dealing with what had happened, and—trapped in the code of silence—I was afraid to ask. But I could wander through my own inner space.

✦ ✦ ✦

I didn't really trouble myself much about death until I was twenty-three. Death was too far away, I thought. However, halfway through my army stint the problem turned critical when I learned that the girl I had dated during my senior year in college, Carol Davis, had been killed in an automobile accident. I was tremendously upset by her death, not only because Carol had been a very nice person, but also because she was only about twenty-one when she died, her death had been violent, and I had no sense of her continuing existence in spirit. It took me many months to recover from this trauma, and I eventually had to sit down and write a short story to come to terms with her death.

I continued as an agnostic, though, until my late twenties, when I discovered the work of Edgar Cayce, who in trance had repeatedly spoken of and illustrated the concept of reincarnation. What he said made complete sense to me and convinced me that the universe was indeed rational and orderly and that the human spirit exists before birth and after death. But until David's death my convictions had not been tried.

Now, in the first week of February 1978, although I felt that David still existed somewhere, his death was testing all of my beliefs to their furthest limits. I wasn't certain I would pass this test.

✦ ✦ ✦

*Monday*

In a morning conversation with Santa Fe I was told that the searchers had gone to check one last spot on Carmen Island before ending their efforts. I asked the director of Southwest Outward Bound for the names and addresses of the instructors and surviving students, so that we could write to them to find out how David had spent his last three weeks. I was assured that the list of names would be sent shortly.

Late in the afternoon, Rhoades called to say that David's personal effects, including two journals, had been recovered from his beached kayak and would be sent to us. However, the Outward Bound searchers were leaving Baja. When I hung up the receiver, I leaned my head against a door frame and cried for the first time. David had disappeared, and part of me disappeared with him.

The search for David's body was over.

# 2

# david remembered

After dinner that evening I went to my desk and began to organize my thoughts for the Duke service the following night. I was reluctant to speak since I was not a churchgoer and felt uncomfortable during any formal service, but I sensed that David's friends needed help. I knew that the service was to be an expression of their love and respect for David, but I also knew that at deeper levels David's friends were in distress. Most of them would feel as lost and as helpless as I had been when I had been faced with Carol's death, and I wanted to offer them a framework of concepts which might give them some support, a support which I had not had at their age.

Musing over Irene Hughes' impressions about David, I began to wonder what sort of work David would do in spirit. I had read enough on this subject to know that David was too much of an activist to remain idle. As soon as this thought crossed my mind, another thought flashed in: "*Catcher in the Rye*—Holden Caulfield." I gropingly seemed to remember Holden wanting to be at the foot of a cliff to catch children who fell from it.[2] I interpreted this thought to mean that David's work in spirit would involve helping children who had died.

A few minutes later, Veronica told me she had been looking for quotations that could be used at the service and had remembered that both she and David had always liked Zoe Akins' "The Wanderer." She handed me a copy of Bartlett's *Familiar Quotations* opened to the Akins entry. I read:

> So much do I love wandering,
> So much I love the sea and sky,
> That it will be a piteous thing
> In one small grave to lie.[3]

As soon as I read these lines, I knew that David's body would never be recovered, was not meant to be recovered. Veronica thinking of this poem was not chance: it was a message from David, telling us not to look for him on Earth any longer. However, since Veronica was still clutching the hope that David might have survived somehow, I said only that I would use the poem at Duke, then returned to my desk.

I don't recall when it started, but I had begun to have mental conversations with David. They were limited in scope, consisting mainly of short replies in David's voice to thoughts in my mind, but his voice was very distinct, very clear, and very intense. Although I knew that it *could* be David communicating with me, I found this dialogue suspect. I felt I was talking to myself and tried to discount it, supposing I was somehow trying to comfort myself by hearing David's voice. Yet this phenomenon continued clearly for many months, even years, and if I would ask, for example, "David, are you there?" I'd hear his voice answer, "Yes, Daddy."

I apparently created a mental block, however, to unrequested communication. Since I suspected the process, I refused to consider the possibility of very factual or unexpected messages. I seemed to be willing only to accept *responses* to what I was thinking, although sometimes certain thoughts—such as "Holden Caulfield" or, later, the title of David's book, *DAVID: leaves from the journal of a soul*—would just drop into my head. And I use the word "drop" deliberately, because that's how it felt when such a thought came—as if someone had dropped a penny into a piggy bank: plop!

That evening, having completed my notes for the service and read them over, I suddenly had doubts. Everything I intended to speak about seemed so fantastic on paper, even to me: the pre-existence of the soul, life patterns, clairvoyance, life after death, reincarnation. These concepts felt so right in the privacy of my own thoughts, but how could I get up in the pulpit of the staid Duke chapel and talk about them? How would the Duke students and others who would attend the service react to those ideas? I started to feel shaky inside myself. Then I thought, "David believed in these concepts. What would he say if I didn't discuss them with his friends?" Instantly, I heard David's voice inside my head, as bright and clear as ever, saying, "Oh, shit!"

I had my answer. That was what David would say if I told him I had lost my nerve—what he apparently *did* say. The response had been instantaneous, unexpected, and powerful. I felt that if I didn't speak at Duke, then, in the moment after my own death, David would appear, look me in the eye, and caustically say, "You chicken!" Still, was that really David speaking in my thoughts? I didn't know, but I decided to address the students at the service. And in my mind I could see David grinning.

✦ ✦ ✦

The next evening around 5:30 Veronica and I met the chaplain in the lobby of the Duke chapel. With him were the associate chaplain, the head resident of David's dormitory, Dr. Griffith, and an attractive young woman who was introduced as Preston.

I was immediately drawn to Preston. There was an intensity about her, an electric quality flowing from her—focused especially in her eyes—that was very similar to the energy which David had always radiated. It's hard to gauge the energies any person projects, but Preston was one of only a handful of people who have had an immediate effect on me when I first came into their presence—as if a relationship existed between us before we had ever met, as if we already were old friends. I liked Preston at once, very much. She greeted Veronica and me, then impulsively stepped forward and kissed Veronica on the cheek, then kissed me on the cheek also.

At dinner I was seated opposite Preston and so was able to observe her. All I knew about her then was that David had met her in May on Project WILD, that she was a pre-med student, and that—Veronica had told me—David had been very fond of her. As we talked, I found her to be sensitive, perceptive, and very intelligent; it was obvious why David had been attracted to her. The previous autumn David had hinted at marriage, and I had no doubt now that Preston was the one he had wanted to marry.

I had been avoiding eye contact with those at the dinner, since I wasn't capable of revealing my inner state to anyone. Yet halfway through the meal something made me look into Preston's eyes. There I saw the most agonized pain, and from an endless darkness in her eyes an almost mortally wounded being looked out at me. I was torn all over again, this time by my inability to help her. I was afraid to look at Veronica beside me because I knew I'd see the same darkness in her eyes.

When dinner ended, we returned to the Duke chapel. As I entered the chapel and walked to the back of the center aisle, I thought I perceived David—with some inner vision, not my eyes—to my right and facing me, sitting on a railing that separated the congregation from the chancel. David appeared to be dressed, as usual, in a sloppy T-shirt and shorts. Then I saw David grin and wave animatedly to me, and the thought "Hiya, Daddy" came into my mind. At the time I couldn't accept that I was really seeing David. I thought it was just my imagination, and I never told anyone about this impression. But looking back, I now feel I *did* see David psychically that evening.

Everyone who had come to attend the service was already seated, mostly on the left-hand side, since the pulpit was placed at the left. I walked down the center aisle with Veronica, and when we arrived at the front of the nave, the chaplain asked me to sit with Preston in a pew behind the pulpit, since she and I were to speak. I took a seat to the left of Preston, while Dr. Griffith guided Veronica to a place in the first row and then sat beside her.

The service began with a prelude of classical guitar pieces performed by three young men from David's dormitory, Wilson House. The music was peaceful and beautiful, and I thought that David would like it very much. After scriptural readings, an invocation, and the singing of "Morning Has Broken," Preston rose to speak:

Hi.

I met David last May on a backpacking trip, and since that time he's touched my mind, my heart, and my soul. I would like to share David with you.

David is a giver. He gave energy, love; he gave time—a valuable and rare gift. While on a trail hiking, setting up camp, or relaxing around a fire, his laughter, his exuberance penetrated the hearts of everyone. We wanted to clone a dozen Davids and send them on every crew, because he had made our experience so enjoyable, so real, so alive. At Duke, he gave to people: he gave his time as a listener; he gave his energy as a cross-country runner and as a folk dancer; he gave his mind as an intellectual, a writer, a librarian; he gave his love and sensitivities as a friend.

David always took the high road: he never stepped back from a challenge out of fear or from a namby-pamby attitude. It was David's determination, strength of will, and strong desire that convinced every other member of our May crew to climb to the top of Pilot Mountain, rather than walk around it. When we got to the top, I looked over miles and miles of rolling hills and green pine trees, and I knew why David had fought so hard to be there. It was what he wanted out of life: simplicity, love, peace.

David was not always highly disciplined, but he was searching for his niche in society. He wanted to be able to live out of a backpack, stripped from attachments of material possessions. But, how would he support his twenty-five children? Well, he's supporting more than twenty-five children now.

David is continuing to teach me the value of time in my life: the importance of sharing experiences, frustrations, dreams and oneself with others. He gave and he took in trust. David is teaching *all* of us about life, about beauty—and its process of growth. He's teaching me the beauty of friendship, the commitment to make it work. He would want us to exult the living, rather than mourn a loss.

Preston finished by quoting a passage from *Jonathan Livingston Seagull*, then returned to her seat beside me. I rose and took her place at the pulpit. Although I was nervous, I felt *right* being there and began to speak. I mentioned my fears of death when young, how my present views might perhaps help someone tonight. I said that David exists now, existed before birth, planned his life before birth—including the time of his death—and that he carried through those plans on Earth. I stated that the universe is rational; that God exists; that—as mystics such as Emerson and Edgar Cayce have told us—everything in matter is first created in spirit, all of life is structured, and we all reincarnate. I discussed the shortness of David's life, but how he had illuminated that life.

I recounted what I knew of how David had been lost in the Sea of Cortez while trying to help a member of his crew. I said I believed that David was present tonight, enjoying this service, and that his friends would feel David around them at times in the future. I concluded:

> Let's wish him well on his outward bound adventure, and when our turn comes he'll be there to greet us, excited, happy, full of all the new things he has learned on the other side, impatient to tell us about it all. And we will then once again enjoy the pleasure of his company.

I returned to my seat beside Preston, who took my right hand and held it for a time.

When the service ended, many of David's friends came to greet us: people from Project WILD, from Wilson House, from the university library where David had worked, and David's roommate Dale. Alice, from Raleigh, along with another of David's Raleigh friends, Debbie, and

Debbie's mother were also there. I spoke for a few minutes with Susan, David's library supervisor, who told me, "You know, it was the strangest thing. When David came to say goodbye in December, I blurted out, 'Be sure to come back alive.' I don't know *what* made me *say* that. I could have bitten my tongue off."

After most of the people had gone, Preston came to me and hesitantly said that she had felt David's presence the Sunday after he was lost, felt he had returned to comfort her, and that before David had left Duke he had told her—very firmly—that he did not expect to return from the trip alive. I asked Preston to tell me about this in detail at a later time, and she agreed that she would.

When the last of David's friends had left, Veronica and I thanked the two ministers and left the chapel. Dr. Griffith, thoughtful as always, accompanied us to our car and said goodbye. We drove home on the dark road to Raleigh saying nothing, each of us immersed completely in our own thoughts.

I later reviewed in my mind the concepts that I had spoken of at the service. What had the listeners thought, I wondered. "It doesn't matter what they thought." The words floated through my mind. "They heard what you said . . . and they will never forget it."

Two days later, Veronica received a letter from Alice:

> I just want you to know the ways David was part of my life. David and I met during our junior year in high school. In that year a group of firm friends came together, known loosely as the folk dancers. I was (and have continued to be) impressed by David's scholarship. We both were studying Latin. When David and I went for the Angier B. Duke Scholarship interviews, David

showed up wearing an old Mickey Mouse button "to add a little levity to the proceedings," he said.

David always amazed me for his ability to be so close and caring with his friends, without ever giving cheaply what should be held dear—friendships were to be made close and sacred, never to be used for one's own advantage or for one's own excitement. How did he keep going this way when I seemed to fall down and fail so many times?

David had so many places in the world. The hole looms large in the dance circles for Mayim or Haroah Haktana or Dodi Li or twenty of his other favorite dances. [The dance of life being his greatest favorite, I hear in my mind from David.] But if everybody takes their little piece of David and puts it there, maybe we can someday heal the wound. All that's left to be afraid of is that we won't make the effort, and the circle may scatter and the rhythm will never be recaptured.

David and I were looking forward to seeing Israel someday. Now I am sure David sees it better than anyone. For him Jerusalem is now a city shining without the shadows of war and strife.[4]

*He has truly been*

חבר נחמד

*chever  nechmad*

*a lovely companion.*

*All my love,*

*Alice*

Daniel, a Duke student who had become friends with David in the previous semester, also wrote:

> When I met David . . . I saw a unique individual [and] I immediately took a liking to him. David was cheerful, open, spontaneous and devoid of all pretense. . . .
>
> I am grateful to have shared time and experience with him. David was also, by inadvertent example, a teacher. Mr. Schwimmer, you were right, he developed himself in mind, body and spirit, and that is inspiration for me. . . .
>
> I will remember him fondly, try not to mourn for him, and do my best to keep learning from him. . . .

During these rending weeks and for months afterwards, I kept hearing three popular songs over and over again on the radio. It seemed as if nothing else were being played. The titles and lyrics finally penetrated my consciousness:

### YOU LIGHT UP MY LIFE
So many nights I'd sit by my window,
Waiting for someone to sing me this song,
So many dreams I kept deep inside me,
Alone in the dark, but now you've come along.
And you light up my life.
You give me hope, to carry on.
You light up my days
And fill my nights with song.
Rollin' at sea, adrift on the waters,
Could it be fin'lly, I'm turning for home.
Fin'lly a chance to say, "Hey! I love you."
Never again to be all alone.
And you light up my life.[5]

The second song was "Candle on the Water"[6] and described a person who was "lost and drifting" and whom "a cold and friendless tide" had found, but who was told not to give up—that the person had somewhere to turn, that the clouds were lifting, and that the person would soon see a stream of light.

The third song was "What a Difference You've Made in My Life,"[7] and kept repeating its title throughout the song, as well as stating that the one being sung about was "my sunshine day and night."

The lyrics of these songs seemed to have been written about the circumstances of David's death and that just as God had lit up David's life and had made such a difference to him, so David had lit up the lives of all who had known him and had made a difference to them. All three songs used images of light, which had loomed large in David's mind and writing. When I later read David's journals, I found the correspondence between the lyrics and David's life even more significant. The songs spoke to me and affected me a great deal.

The next day, Saturday, brought a note from Dale:

> . . . I was one of the fortunate ones to get close to David. We shared good times and bad but knew behind it all that our similar beliefs in reincarnation and spiritu-ality would pull us through. Mr. Schwimmer's talk at the service was reassuring.
>
> But it is only human to mourn the loss of a friend. We mourn the loss because we won't be able to learn more from the person. I feel David taught me a lot. . . .

In the afternoon I suddenly remembered that Marian, the spiritual counselor, was to be in town that evening. I called the A.R.E. area council chairwoman and got directions to Marian's meeting. I didn't really know why I was going or what I expected from Marian. I think I was still hoping that she could tell me something about the physical David—a sad and desperate sort of hope, but all I had left.

Few memories remain of that evening. I recall only that Marian spoke and that later the group stood in a circle holding hands and singing several spiritually oriented songs, including "Morning Has Broken," which had been sung at the Duke service. While we sang, tears often slipped down my face, for I remembered how much David had loved songs and music. To this day, I can't sing "Morning Has Broken" without having tears come to my eyes.

After the meeting I asked Marian if she would do a reading about David. When she learned that David had died, however, she said she didn't like to give posthumous readings. Then she stopped in mid-sentence, as if she had heard something, and asked me David's name, date of birth, and where he had died. When I told her, she closed her eyes for a moment, then opened them again and said strongly, almost with relief it seemed to me, "He's all right. Make an appointment for next month. He's all right. Bring a picture of him." I understood that she didn't mean that David was safe physically, but that he was safe in spirit.

I wasn't happy with having to wait until March, since I didn't see what she could tell me that would help one month from now, but I felt I had no choice. I signed the appointment sheet and left. I didn't know what I had been looking for that night but felt I hadn't found it. I was wrong, of course, since Marian's monthly meetings helped me to restore and rebuild my spiritual structures, and I attended most of her meetings until I moved from Raleigh.

The following Monday, Veronica and I began to plan a memorial service for David in Raleigh. Almost no one in town had known of the Duke service, and we wanted to allow those who had been close to David in high school to have an opportunity to participate in a ceremony for him. I felt it was also very important for Eric and Krista to have this experience, since we had not taken them to the Duke service. Remembering that David had gone to Christmas mass at St. Michael's Episcopal Church for three years, we decided that David would want the service held there.

I asked the priest who would conduct the service to mention "the New Jerusalem," since David had spoken of it several times, and Veronica requested the prayer of Saint Francis to be read, as David had liked that very much.[8] After I spoke with the priest, I called Brian, David's friend from his high school cross-country team, and Mrs. Muriel Allison, David's high school English teacher, and asked them to say a few words about David at the service. Both said they would.

A week later I came home from work mid-afternoon and found Veronica crying on the floor beside a large open cardboard box in the living room. In the carton were those of David's belongings which had been recovered in Baja.

"I didn't want to get them," Veronica sobbed.

I could find nothing to say. I just helped her up from the floor and took the box upstairs to David's room.

That evening I checked the contents of the carton. In addition to David's clothing and gear, I found his Duke and Project WILD/Outward Bound journals, his Bible, letters he had begun writing to us and to Preston, a letter Preston had written to him, some Mexican documents, and his birth certificate. Between layers of David's clothing were a four-inch-high brown and white stuffed bear (named Boswell) and a well-worn ten-inch orange hand-puppet with the face of a monkey.

I glanced through David's clothing and saw his light blue swimming suit with white stripes down its sides. I remembered one of Mrs. Mankoff's impressions that "David is wearing royal blue trunks with gold stripes up the sides," and Veronica's comment at the time that this impression was wrong, since she had bought David this light blue suit just before he had left for Baja and that he must have had it on. What *had* David been wearing on January 24, then? I suddenly remembered that last summer David had bought running shorts to train in and that they had been dark blue with gold stripes down the sides. Those were what he must have had on, as Mrs. Mankoff had perceived.

Tuesday morning we received a letter from Brian's mother:

> . . . We will miss David terribly, as we and the world have lost a delightful, friendly, compassionate person of highest integrity. . . .

Wednesday evening I decided to begin reading David's Duke journal to see if it could be published. I read a few pages and then left the journal lying open on my desk. Veronica came through the room, noticed the journal, and said, "Read the earlier journals first. David told me last November that he was gay. He was going to tell you when he came back."

This revelation caused no reaction at all in me. Why, I wondered. No surprise, no shock, no dismay—nothing. Yet it had never occurred to me that David might be gay—on the contrary. However, when I later read David's December 18, 1977, dream entry, I found a possible explanation:

> A lot of hope in me tonight. I dream again of strong, honest men. I am talking to my sister and tell her I'm gay. I tell my father. I laugh in California. . . .

Mystics claim we all meet in our sleep on the astral plane. If so, then David had already told me—two months earlier, in my sleep—that he was gay. That was why I wasn't surprised.

Thursday evening I was back at my desk, thinking about the service at St. Michael's on Sunday. I was reluctant to speak, yet felt that something was needed. A thought suddenly came to me, and I started to type. At times I felt as if David were writing with me. I wrote:

> To David's friends:
> I had contemplated saying a few words to you, but then the thought came to me of having David speak instead. So I have tried to listen to what David is saying. I seem to hear:
> "Now, don't be sad about me.
> I came *when* I planned to come on Earth,
> I did *what* I came to do,
> I left *when* I planned to leave
> And *where* I planned to leave.
> Every minute of this Earth life was great,
> Including the pains and disappointments—
> They made me grow,
> Made me search myself and the world around me—
> And I learned a lot.
> All of you who knew me helped me to grow,
> Even if you didn't know you were helping—

You were all very important to me.
Some of us knew each other in previous lives,
And some of us will know each other again in future
    lives,
Because I and you existed before time began,
And we will exist when time ends.
I exist now—
I'm here with you today—
But I'm in a higher school of learning now.
It's a sort of work-study program,
So I may be allowed to help you sometimes,
Even if you don't know that I'm helping,
Though you might feel my presence around you.
Meantime, if you're out running—give that extra
    kick for me.
If you're dancing, think of me and I'll dance with you.
If you're studying or writing, push a little harder.
If you see a flower, smell it.
If you hear church bells, stop and listen.
If you see a stray cat, pet it and feed it.
If someone's frowning, smile at them.
If someone's crying, hold them.
And just remember,
I love you all,
I love you,
And I always will.
See you later."
This is what David asks me to tell you.
        George Schwimmer


Everyone who came to the service was given a copy, and
later I also mailed copies to those of David's friends who
hadn't been able to attend.

The service on Sunday began with an organ prelude and
various readings,[9] then Mrs. Allison rose to speak. Her

eulogy was a beautiful picture of David as she knew him, and I include a small part of it here:

> He threw the sand against the wind,
> And every grain became a gem.
> And every gem became a star.
> A morning star.
> The complete shaper of his destiny, David developed the stamina for life. As the North Star has directed generations, so did David guide his teammates. A beacon, David was a star with brilliance and beauty. . . .
> And every star became a light.
> Each generation fosters those rare souls who fashion and apply beautiful ideas and who make the difference between the fame and the glory, the agony and the ecstasy, the emotion and the response, the conception and the creation, the idea and the reality, the mundane and the ethereal! And what a *difference* David made! David, I shall see you lying on the sand with the wind playing in your hair!
> He threw the sand against the wind,
> And the wind blew it back again!

When Mrs. Allison left the pulpit, Brian took her place and said, in part:

> It was through running that I really came to know David. Running was something special for David—he was really *good* at it. I think it was because he enjoyed it so much that he was such a determined runner. He didn't just *run* up a hill—he *charged* up a hill. I've never seen anybody else run up a hill the way he did.
> I also remember him in the Conference Cross-Country meet, when he was a senior. It was a very muddy day, and David lost a shoe about halfway through the race. Instead of returning to pick it up and lose his position in

the race, he continued to run. He ran over gravel, through mud, across hard asphalt, and still managed to become an all-conference cross-country runner. . . .

What was *really* special about David, though, was that he was just so much fun to be with—running with him was so much fun. He was a team leader, too. He would, instead of beating us and going on—since he was the better runner—he would stay back with the rest of the team and encourage us verbally, and just *be* with us—encouraging us.

That demonstrates the kind of person David was—he was thoughtful and determined. I will miss David.

After the service had concluded, Veronica and I spoke individually with everyone who had attended, then drove home silently through the grey winter afternoon. Although a memorial service is meant to create closure, I didn't know how I would ever be able to accept that I wouldn't see David alive again.

A few days later, one of David's high school teachers, Dorothy Hege, wrote:

> . . . David's presence in my homeroom on Wednesday mornings was one of the brightest spots in every week. He had a wonderful sense of humor. . . .
>
> It did not surprise me to see the A's on his final report, but I knew that the marks were incidental to the pleasure he took in mastering his studies. He was apparently not so much involved in competition with his fellow man as in a daily challenge to himself to be a better person than he had been the day before.
>
> His every activity seemed to be a celebration of life, from the first time I saw him with his nose in a book, to the last, when I watched him dance the Salty Dog Rag with my daughter.

He was such a beautiful spirit. Thank you for the privilege of knowing David. . . .

*David, age seventeen.*

# 3

# struggle in the storm

A month had passed since I had last spoken with anyone from Outward Bound, and I had not received the names and addresses of the instructors and surviving students as I had been promised, so I phoned the director of Southwest Outward Bound. He said he could not give me any addresses, or even names, since he had been instructed by Outward Bound's insurance company and attorneys to release no information whatever about David's death. I was shocked by what he was saying and finally told him very bluntly that his refusal was futile, as I would get all of the facts some way—by court action, if necessary. His response was, "Well, you won't get it from me."

I was enraged and slammed the phone receiver down on its cradle. How dare Outward Bound withhold any facts about David's death? How dare they play games with the feelings and lives of David's family and friends? And did they believe I would do nothing? Their stonewalling was the worst thing they could have done, both for us and for themselves. I hadn't learned a lot from my father, but I had learned to fight for myself, so if they wanted a fight, they'd get one.

By this time I had obtained—from Tim Breidegam's father—the phone number of Brenda Herman's brother-in-law, Barry, and I had a long telephone conversation with Barry. Barry told me that Brenda's journal also had been recovered and that it contained the names, addresses, and telephone numbers of Brenda and David's crew. Barry promised to send this list, and we received it a short time later. We never again heard from Outward Bound, never heard from David's instructors.

During the following four weeks, either I or Veronica called each of the surviving members of David's crew, as well as two members of a second crew who had been on the trip. From their reports (augmented by letters they sent us, court depositions made by them and others, and Outward Bound records later subpoenaed), we were able to reconstruct most of what had happened on January 24 and during the previous sixteen days. We were shocked by much of what we were told by the students. Veronica was often in tears, since it became obvious early on that O.B. Kayaking Course S-54 had been designed with reckless disregard for the students' safety.

The other members of David, Brenda and Tim's crew—or "tribe," in O.B.'s terminology—were Keith (the elected student crew leader), Catherine (Tim's boatmate), Jana, DelRene, BeeBee, and David R. The two members of the second crew to whom we spoke were Susan and Pamela.

There were unexpected linkages in David's group. DelRene had been acquainted with Jana prior to this course, since they both had attended the same college for two years and both had been on the same boating crew in DelRene's first year there. However, DelRene had found out only by chance about Jana signing up for the Baja course, when a mutual friend mentioned it to DelRene. Catherine noted a second linkage: Brenda was attending Bennington College, where Catherine had taught for several years. "We knew various people in common, which was an amazing coincidence," Catherine wrote us. "I didn't expect to run into such a connection." After that, Catherine formed a close relationship with Brenda and adopted a protective attitude toward her.

A few glimpses of David were offered by DelRene:

> David and I were the "singers" of the group. He knew a lot of songs, and we loved to sing! . . . Aside from music, we both enjoyed running. Dave was really built like a runner—long and wiry—and he really ran well. Another thing Dave really liked was fishing off the rocky points—he usually caught something, too! Dave also quickly rose to any challenge. . . .

BeeBee mentioned that David had become a very proficient kayaker on the trip. He and Brenda had seemed to get quite close as the course progressed, had formed a strong intellectual bond, and had talked together for hours at a time. DelRene said that David and Brenda had sometimes spoken to each other in Hebrew (which David had learned in a course at Duke) and that they had had a good relationship with Tim, the three of them tending to pick up the spirits of their crew.

The Outward Bound course involved catching fish and other seafood, cooking, making camp, acquiring knowledge of the sea, snorkeling, becoming proficient at kayaking, and learning to survive in a wilderness environment. Although the area appeared to be basically friendly, the element of danger always lurked under the surface calm. During the sixth night, for example, some of the kayaks washed away during a high tide, and one kayak was smashed up on nearby rocks. The following day the students had to sit on the beach while a strong northern wind kicked up a high sea.

Pamela estimated that everyone on the course had lost an average of ten pounds of body weight during the trip. David had weighed 143 pounds when he had left home. Pamela said that David and Tim had looked very thin, due to their diet and their physical activity (and probably diarrhea, which David had had during the course). Consequently, David and others in his crew were in a weakened physical condition even before the solo experience and final exercise.

Just before the crew's solo, DelRene had been taking pictures and had one frame left. As she was wondering what to photograph with this last bit of film, she saw David, Brenda, and Tim together on the beach and took their picture. DelRene later thought this was an odd coincidence. In any case, the look in David's eyes in that photograph—which was recovered undamaged—I find quite unusual. Thinking back, in fact, that look reminds me very much of the look David gave me when he was eighteen months old.

*David, Brenda, and Tim just before their crew's solo.*

The solo had always been a major element in all Outward Bound courses, and this course was no exception. Four days prior to their final exercise, the Baja students were sent on a three-day solo, each alone, although each was within earshot of another student, and the instructors—all men—checked on them once a day.

Chart A. Coastline of eastern shore of Baja California.

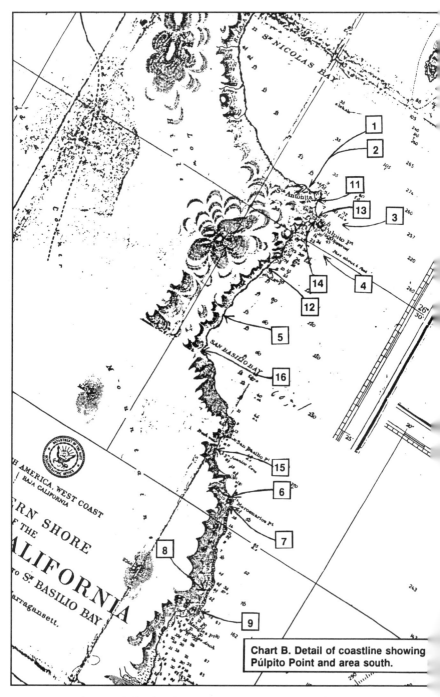

**Chart B.** Detail of coastline showing Púlpito Point and area south.

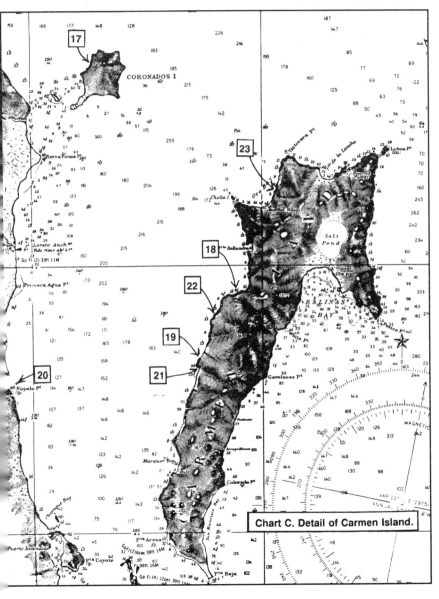

**Chart C. Detail of Carmen Island.**

# KEY TO CHARTS

1. Start of final expedition, David's tribe.
2. Start of final expedition, Susan's tribe.
3. First capsize, David's tribe.
4. Breakup of rafted kayaks, David's tribe.
5. Jana's landing point.
6. Landing point on Tuesday night of Keith, BeeBee, David R., Catherine and DelRene.
7. Kayak of above group found washed up on this beach.
8. Wednesday night campsite of the five students.
9. Area where the five students were picked up by Mexican fishermen.
10. San Bruno fish camp where the five students were taken (Chart A).
11. Area where Susan's tribe put ashore Tuesday morning.
12. Camp of two instructors Tuesday night.
13. Area of accident of Susan's tribe on Wednesday morning.
14. Area where Susan's tribe awaited rescue after portaging.
15. First checkpoint (Juanico Cove) and where the two instructors spent Wednesday night.
16. Fish camp and road in San Basilio Bay.
17. Area where double kayak of David and Brenda were found.
18. Area where Keith's single kayak was found.
19. Area where DelRene's single kayak was found.
20. Area where Tim and Catherine's double kayak was found.
21. Area where Tim's body was found.
22. Area where Brenda's body was found.
23. Area where David's life jacket was found.

Pamela said that the instructors suggested that each student spend his or her three-day solo in the nude for optimum experience. The instructors also urged the students not to take sleeping bags with them. The students received no food for the solo, only one and a half gallons of water each, and were told to fast during the solo. (In a deposition given later, one instructor testified that "many of the students chose to fast," so it is not clear to me whether the students were clearly told to fast, were encouraged to fast, or chose to fast—or whether all of the students actually did fast.) The students were given a choice of staying on the shore or going inland. David, Brenda, Tim, Keith, and David R. went inland.

David took up the challenge of the solo completely, with great enthusiasm, Catherine reported. Due to the suggestions of the instructors, Jana said, David took with him on the solo no clothes except his canvas shoes. Nor did he take a sleeping bag, only matches for a fire. Around his neck, as all of the students, David hung a whistle with which to signal other students in case of trouble. David consequently spent three days in the wilderness with no food, no clothing, and only a fire to warm himself.

David's crew didn't get back from solo until about 4:00 or 5:00 P.M. on Monday, January 23, and they were very tired, Pamela said. Jana reported that when David returned he was black with soot from having stayed close to his fire, and DelRene added that after the solo David was pretty filthy from having slept nude in the dirt but was in high spirits and feeling good about his accomplishment. After their return, the students were fed a meal of fish chowder.

Both crews camped about one mile west of Santa Antonita Point, off San Nicolás Bay. The following morning, with one night's sleep and two meals after a three-day fast in the wilderness, the students began their final exercise. The course director and two senior instructors departed at dawn in an inflatable motorized boat for the town of Loreto, about thirty miles south, leaving behind two assistant instructors—who were the least experienced or knowledgeable about Baja, the Sea of Cortez, and sea kayaking. None of the instructors accompanied either crew that day, or even monitored them visually from a distance, since the final exercise was designed to be executed strictly by the students themselves.

Susan and Pamela's crew left their camp about 7:15 A.M., and David's crew followed about fifteen minutes later—at around 7:30. These times are estimates, since no one was allowed to carry a watch. No check of the students was scheduled until noon of the next day, at Juanico Cove.

When Susan and Pamela's group rounded Santa Antonita Point, they discovered that the wind and wave conditions were quite rough and potentially dangerous. They beached their boats about one mile south of the point when Pamela refused to continue, and the rest of the crew—obeying a unit rule—followed her to shore, probably saving lives in that group. Susan said she never saw David and his crew pass them.

Pamela and another young woman from her crew then hiked back to their base camp, where they found the assistant instructors and two friends of one instructor who had helped him sail his boat up from Loreto on Sunday. The four were about to launch the boat in preparation for sailing south to the students' first check-point. After Pamela and her friend told the instructors what had happened and expressed their concern about the heavy seas, they returned to their crew.

The instructors and their friends launched their boat, motored it around Santa Antonita Point, and—seeing the wind and wave conditions—put one instructor ashore for twenty or thirty minutes to discuss the situation with Susan's group. The instructors and their friends then sailed through the waters that David and his crew were traversing, probably an hour after David's group encountered the first of a series of mishaps. The instructors never sighted David's crew, however; in fact, they had trouble seeing anything—or even looking—since by now their vessel was sailing through waves that reached almost fifteen feet in height. The owner of the boat later testified that he felt lucky to get around Punta Púlpito without broaching.

Meanwhile, Susan, whose group by now had established a camp, hiked south to the top of Punta Púlpito and saw the instructors' sailboat round the point and almost broach from the wind and turbulent seas. She did not see David and his crew, so they must have drifted south by then.

The instructors later reported that they had assumed that David's crew had paddled safely around Punta Púlpito, despite the condition of the seas. It would have made no difference in any case, since the instructors had no radio, nor—apparently—was the sailboat capable of a rescue mission in such high seas. A sports fishing boat was anchored in the lee of Púlpito Point, but the instructors did not try to communicate with those aboard that vessel. A short time later, the instructors anchored in San Basilio Bay, a sheltered area southwest of Punta Púlpito.

Susan's crew remained at their campsite that day, but on the following morning, Wednesday, decided to try the seas once again. Their attempt resulted in four kayaks being badly smashed up on the rocks between Point Santa

Antonita and Punta Púlpito, but no deaths or serious injuries resulted from these mishaps. Once again, there were no instructors around when these events took place.

Jana begins the narrative of the ordeals endured by David's crew on Tuesday: "We left early [that] morning. . . . We had no trouble getting past the surf. In fact, Catherine and I were fishing (trolling)." After paddling for about an hour or an hour and a half, having rounded Santa Antonita Point and now heading south, the students became aware of a strong northern wind. Jana: "As we continued to paddle, it got rougher and the wind picked up. We felt that once we got around Púlpito Point we would be protected from the wind and could continue on our way."

At this point both David and Tim insisted that the group head for shore because the situation had become too dangerous. Jana also objected to going on, but the rest of the group felt they should continue. When the wind became more severe, eventually turning into a wind storm, the crew finally started paddling toward shore. It was too late.

As they were heading in toward the rocky coast, the double kayak of Tim and Catherine capsized, dumping both of them into approximately 60-degree water. The students pulled all of their boats together into a hand-held "raft"—as they had been taught to do—and simultaneously tried to bail out the capsized kayak by hand. Because of the condition of the seas, three of the boats wound up facing north, with Jana's, Keith's and David/Brenda's kayaks facing south.

The students had some difficulty rafting up around Tim and Catherine's kayak. They managed to turn it over, but bailing was of little use because the waves were filling the kayak with water again. They were unwilling to abandon the boat and felt that the wind would push them past Punta Púlpito, and that once they were out of the wind they could maneuver to shore. The water kept getting rougher, though, and they weren't drifting very fast, so they decided to abandon the boat and have Tim and Catherine swim, hanging on to another kayak.

Eventually, Tim and Catherine were pulled aboard the raft, which the students were still holding together with just their hands. Since it was not possible to hold the raft together and paddle at the same time, the crew allowed the raft to drift south, hoping to float around Punta Púlpito to a sheltered beach which they knew was on the lee (south) side of the point.

As the students reached Punta Púlpito (on their right), with the small sandy beach in sight about a quarter of a mile away, a Mexican fishing boat passed them, crossing their path almost due west. The students tried to signal the boat—which Keith estimated to be about a half a mile south of them—with their paddles, but the boat did not respond and disappeared.

Then a rebounding wave—a wave which hits rocks or cliffs on a shoreline but, unable to release its force by rolling up on the beach, rebounds into the sea—from the point hit the students broadside and broke up their raft. Tim and Catherine were thrown back into the water, and Keith's single kayak capsized and sank almost at once. They were going to leave both boats when another wave came and thrust Jana's and David/Brenda's boats away from the raft.

David and Brenda's double kayak, plus Jana's single, were pushed toward the coast and southward, Jana's boat somewhat south of David and Brenda's, according to Keith. Their double and Jana's single kayak remained afloat, however. David R. remembered that David was in the back of his red double kayak, operating the rudder foot-pedals, with Brenda in the front cockpit.

Keith said David looked back toward the main group, as if trying to return to it. Keith: "I just hollered at them to stay with Jana, stay together and head to the shore, not worry about trying to get back to us or anything like that. . . . David and Brenda were handling their craft well. He had trouble with his rudder—that was probably why he couldn't stick with us—but he knew how to handle the boat. . . ." Keith also shouted to David that he should try to get ashore and summon help from the instructors. At this time, Keith estimated, David and Brenda were about a quarter mile from shore, paddling west-southwest.

BeeBee said she last saw David when he turned his head to look back after the rebounding wave had separated them, and that David had "the saddest look" on his face. David and Brenda, still afloat and apparently paddling after Jana, then disappeared behind huge waves. They were never seen alive again by anyone. Jana felt that no matter what ultimately happened to David and Brenda, David would have made every effort to stay with Brenda.

After the breakup of the raft, Jana was not aware that David and Brenda were behind her in the storm. Jana's kayak, being a single, remained higher above the water than David and Brenda's double kayak, and the winds and waves consequently separated her from David and Brenda almost at once. In a few moments they and the rest of her crew were out of Jana's sight and hearing.

As she rounded the point, Jana saw that it offered little protection from the wind. Jana: "I looked for a place to land my boat, but as far as I could see there were only rock cliffs." In addition, the steering mechanism of her kayak had slipped off its track, so her ability to steer was limited. Nevertheless, she managed to stay afloat and about two hours later was able to land her boat four or five miles down the coast. Jana: "I know God was very close to all of us that day. . . . I knew I might die at any time, . . . [but] the prospect of death was not frightening to me."

The other six students stayed with the only—half-afloat—double kayak that remained. BeeBee and David R. sat in the kayak, submerged to their waists in water, while Keith, Catherine, Tim, and DelRene hung on to the swamped boat any way they could. By now, Catherine reported, the waves were ten to fifteen feet high. Once the group was trapped on the water, there was no hope of rescue, and the only reason the remaining kayak remained partially afloat was that there were empty water bottles in the front and back of the boat, which seemingly helped somewhat with flotation.

After struggling in the water for about twelve hours, Tim died, around 9:00 P.M., apparently from hypothermia. Bee-Bee later testified, "When [Keith and David R.] told me that Tim had died . . . I didn't believe he was dead. . . . I could feel his presence still there, but sort of like above where he had been." Tim's body was eventually allowed to drift away in its life jacket. The other students were in the water for three more hours before they finally were able to reach a spot near Mercenarios Point and crawled ashore. If they hadn't managed to land there, one student told me, they would have been swept out to sea and would have died.

The next day, Wednesday, the five began to hike south, and on Thursday they sighted Mexican fishermen who drove them into Loreto in the afternoon. Jana was found the same morning by an Outward Bound instructor. Bee-Bee recounted that during their fifty-hour ordeal she had told the others in her crew to keep thinking of their expedition leader who was in Loreto, and these thoughts must have reached that individual, for he wrote in his daily log on January 26, "Felt uneasy, got up at 3:30 A.M. . . . couldn't figure out why I wanted to drive out."

When David's surviving crewmates arrived in Loreto, they were fed, clothed, debriefed orally, and wrote out individual, detailed accounts of their ordeal. They were told by Outward Bound personnel that copies of these would be sent to the families of David, Brenda, and Tim. Then, BeeBee later recorded: "We had a little ceremony on the beach, a friend of mine and I. We made a fire at sunrise for our friends who had died in the ocean. That same ocean that had given us so much had taken some away."

Weeks afterwards, DelRene wrote: "Dave was very much into living and was the adventurous type. I really enjoyed him—he had such a zest for trying new things. . . . He gave a lot to people. When he died he was doing something he wanted to do—something that was important to him. . . . What saddens me is knowing Dave really felt he had a lot more to do—he often spoke of future plans . . ."

And BeeBee added: "It always amazed me how David would come through when it seemed no one else could. . . . If his life was lost, it was in an effort to help those who weren't as capable as himself . . . David, Brenda, and Tim were, in my opinion, the finest people on the trip. I miss them terribly, probably more than anyone will ever understand."

I had learned what I had wanted to know about David's life in Baja and had discovered much that had been deliberately hidden by Outward Bound—but I still didn't know how David had died.

# 4

# another dimension opens

"We must all follow our Vision Quest
to discover ourselves"[10]

I now see that David's death and Outward Bound's surly stonewalling were really the sound of an ancient trumpet calling me to a quest. I wouldn't have expressed it like that in 1978, yet I had an inkling of what was to come, all the same. Four months after David disappeared, I wrote in my journal, "I know this is the start of something long and complicated, years and years of it, so I must develop patience for it."

Guidance from spirit is very subtle and artful, though, so there was no ancient trumpet, no summons for a quest, no hint I was about to go on a journey of a thousand miles, not even a command to take the first step. Spirit does not work that way. Instead, I was offered sly challenges. "Are you going to take that crap from Outward Bound?" came one inner whisper. "Do you want to see more people killed like David?" came another. "You can't rest until you know what happened to David," a third insisted. "David's gone—what are you going to do for him?" "Aren't you going to find out who David really was?" "Do you have the guts for what you need to do?" Spirit knew I liked a good fight. I couldn't refuse the challenges.

Four weeks after David was lost in the Sea of Cortez, I took up one challenge. Every night after dinner I went to my desk and read David's journals. Some of the entries were charming, some were dark, some were ecstatic, some were beautiful, some were agonized, some were deeply spiritual. I discovered parts of David I had never even glimpsed. Years before I had read that it's not possible to really know another person while we're in the flesh, but I was getting to know David because he had spread much of his heart, mind, and soul across the pages of his journals. It was an extraordinary experience—a very special opportunity—to see inside David. For the next two years I read, typed up, and edited his writing.

The second challenge—obtaining the accounts of the surviving kayaking students—was met quickly, but a third challenge arose even before the previous one had been resolved. Two or three weeks after David was lost, we received a phone call from Mrs. Louise Ross. Her daughter Sonya had also died in an Outward Bound incident, and Mrs. Ross told us that at least three other Outward Bound students also had been killed in outdoor mishaps. I became concerned, since David had told us, "Outward Bound has never lost anyone."[11] Mrs. Ross soon sent us copies of newspaper clippings about these deaths.

I then began to research Outward Bound at the N.C. State University library. I pored over indexes, magazines, and newspapers for the previous sixteen years, and I found evidence of other Outward Bound fatalities. As I uncovered such material, I passed it on to my attorney, Tom Erwin, along with copies of what David's crewmates had recounted or mailed to us. All my spare time went to reading David's journals, to talking with the surviving students, and to investigating Outward Bound.

Meanwhile everyday life had to continue. Krista and Eric had to go to school, Veronica had to manage the house, I had to sell life insurance. But I found it almost impossible to sell life insurance now. It had become excruciating to talk about death to young men, and I often would sit in my office and just stare at the telephone, unable to pick it up to call anyone. My income started to plunge, and I abandoned my efforts to create the regional theater. What little inner energy and will I possessed all went to honoring David's life and death. Perhaps it was my way to work out my grief. I don't really know, because I couldn't *feel* any grief. I was still numb.

On Friday, March 3, I discovered that I had no work to do, so I ate a leisurely breakfast and read most of the morning newspaper, which I very rarely did. Then, although I virtually never looked at the personal advertisements, I felt an impulse to turn to that column. The third notice stated that the psychic Howard Granger was in town and was available for readings. I had tried to reach Granger during the week of the search, but his phone had been disconnected. Now this notice was in the paper. I decided to get a reading. I called and was given an appointment for the following day. The man I spoke with told me Granger lived in Atlanta now and came to Raleigh only a few times a year.

I had my reading from Granger the next morning. Although I had read books and articles about a few psychics, I had never been to one before, so I wasn't sure of what to expect. Granger first gave me his impressions about my health and future work, and when he finished asked if I had any questions. I told him that my son David had recently died and had left a journal which I was thinking of publishing. Granger asked to hold a photograph of David, then said, "A *good* person." He went on to tell me that during the four months before David's death David's behavior had begun to change.

"It's the strangest impression I've ever had," Granger noted. "On the upper left-hand side of the brain—right here [Granger pointed.]—he had a tremendous amount of pressure." During David's last year he had written several times in his journal that he had had a headache, so that was a fit, I thought. "He had a premonition," Granger continued. "He knew *why*, or he knew what was coming. He identified in some way with the pressure [in his head]. He knew he was going young. Somewhere around the age of fourteen it was already beginning to show up in his consciousness. And if you get the journal, all those years . . . it will show it."

David's journals did indeed show it. For example, in January of 1972, when David was thirteen: "Do you believe in signs? I mean from God. In the form of directing the future for you? . . . I think I would be glad to go to heaven if what I am to do was done."

I then told Granger that David had been writing a fictionalized account of some personal problems, with his protagonist narrating the story after the character's death. I asked whether David—through mediums—might want to work on his novel from the other side. "No, I think it's all there," Granger replied. "See, he wrote this basically after his death—he knew at fourteen that he was going, so he *had* to take it from *his* perspective. So, although he was [physically] alive, he knew he was dead. Do you follow me?"

I suddenly realized Granger was saying David had intuitively written from a perspective of looking *back* over a completed life, even though he was physically alive during those seven years, since he subconsciously knew what those seven years would bring. This tied in with the belief that all time is simultaneous, so David simply knew what his "future" would be. Some of David's writing reflected this clearly.

From *The Wilderness* (1976):

> A Novel. About a boy, written by himself and seen in the writing.
>
> Danny died today. He was dead, and was damned well going to stay that way.
>
> Danny is dead—who is speaking?
>
> Danny's spirit.
>
> I dream of prisons. There is no life left. I fear death, for this is only a beginning, and I must pass. Yet I must keep living. Are the people grieving yet?
>
> Oh my God, I am afraid to sleep! That is my dream! Being far from home and alone, and you know how to get home, but you can't, 'cause there just isn't enough time left in the dream. But then, then, there is enough time, but I . . . just don't know about it in the dream. I mean, I know that the time is there, but it isn't there for me. It's only there for the waking me.

Even knowing what I knew, however, Granger's impression struck me as being one of the most extraordinary concepts I had ever come across. Yet I was convinced that he was right. The image of death had been all through David's journals, starting on the first page, when he was twelve. David *had* known he would die young, from a very early age.

"So he wrote it from the *viewpoint* of a dead person," Granger went on. "From that perspective, it's *there*. Many people know—five, ten, fifteen, twenty, thirty years in advance—what day, what night, what hour they will die. He knew at fourteen—he knew almost to the day what day he was going, but he also knew there was no way he could explain to anyone."

On the drive home from Granger's reading, I mused on premonitions. Kris had had one, so had Susan. Then there was Veronica. I had always felt she was quite intuitive, but she had always brushed aside the idea. Still, she was David's mother and had a close relationship with him, so her psychic links with David had to be strong. Events had proven this true.

About two months after David's fourteenth birthday, when we were living in Ireland, Veronica suddenly said to me that she felt David would be in some sort of physical danger during the next couple of years and that she would have to be on her guard about this. Her warning slipped from my conscious mind, however, until after David had died, when I found a notation about this premonition among some of my papers. Veronica had never said anything similar about Kris or Eric.

There were three other incidents, as well. Veronica told me about another foreboding she had felt just prior to David's trip. The night before he was to leave, David went to bed early but later came downstairs to talk with his mother. When I afterwards questioned Veronica about this, she said, "I was very worried—because I felt he wasn't going to come back."

Next, on the evening that David was lost at sea, Veronica was watching a television movie about World War II. Part of the film, she discovered, had been shot in Baja California. Sometime between 12:00 and 12:30 (9:00 and 9:30 P.M. Baja time)—while she was watching the film, she later recounted—she suddenly "felt terrible" and switched off the television set. This feeling lasted throughout the next day, she said.

Finally, several months after David was lost, when I asked her why David had left us Preston's name and address, Veronica answered that *she* had obtained it by copying it from the wrapper of David's Christmas present for Preston, which had been lying on a table in our living room just before Christmas. "I don't know *why*," she said, "but I felt I had to have Preston's address."

A veiled premonition had surfaced in Baja also, I now remembered. One day David's crew had a discussion on a beach after approaching bad weather had caused them to turn back while crossing to an offshore island. BeeBee later testified, "We were sitting in a circle, and I asked everybody to hold hands. I said that I loved everyone there very much, and that if anything ever happened to any of these people, it would hurt me very much and make me very sad." I wondered what David had thought of that.

I recalled Irene Hughes' comment that David had known since last June that he would die. That statement had not struck me as significant, until I read David's Duke journal, where I found:

> Lord, if anything were to happen to me, I hope my parents wouldn't see these journals . . . Oh, Lord, if I die suddenly, let Preston get my journals. [June 1, 1977]
> Then my sudden fear for life today. Such a gift, and what am I giving back? [June 22, 1977]

Suddenly I realized that I had had a premonition too, but had misinterpreted it, since no one had indicated any serious concern to me about David's safety prior to his leaving for Baja. One evening, either in October or November, I went out on a business matter. Going toward my car in front of our house, three words suddenly dropped into my mind: "We're losing David." I stopped walking and wondered, "What does that mean?" I decided it meant he was growing up, leaving the family nest, making a new life for himself at Duke. I had no conscious awareness that this thought was related to the kayaking course, nor did I feel any apprehension.

Yet when David began preparing for the trip to Baja and announced he would hitchhike to California, I felt considerable concern since I believed hitching rides could be dangerous and certainly would be tiring before the kayaking course. I asked him to abandon that plan, but David stubbornly said he would hitchhike, and his plan became an issue between us. I finally sent him a letter early in December, writing that I had done him a great many favors during his life and I wanted a favor in return: that he not hitchhike. I offered to pay his air fare to the West Coast. David never answered my letter, but he soon found his ride to California.

During our talks about hitchhiking, David said that he didn't care about longevity and wasn't concerned about dying. This struck me as unusual for someone his age, but I didn't consider it any further. In retrospect, it seems strange that I didn't connect any of David's statements and behavior with the thought that David might be heading for danger in Baja. But I believed the risk for him was the trip to California, since on the kayaking course he would be traveling with a number of people, including several experienced instructors.

Still, there were other signs. For weeks David had been giving away various belongings to friends. Kris told me afterwards that David had even tried to give her his dictionary and thesaurus just before he left, but she had refused to take them. Veronica had finally commented to David, "You know, you act like you're not coming back." David had just dismissed his behavior with a joke. Yet, although he had been planning to spend time during the next few months working on his novel, *The Wilderness,* he had packed only some of his papers and books, not his typewriter. I didn't learn about most of this until much later, however.

David knew he wouldn't come back. Veronica knew. Kris knew. Susan knew. I knew. Who else knew?

I had my reading with Marian on March 11, at the home of one of her Raleigh friends, Betty. I had no idea why I was there or what I expected, and for a few moments it seemed as if Marian had forgotten who I was. Then she suddenly said, "Oh, you're here about your son. Did you bring his picture?" I handed her three photographs of David.

She asked if his body had been recovered, and when I said it hadn't, she told me it never would be. Although I had come to the same conclusion myself, hearing this from Marian struck an emotional chord in me.

"This happened off the coast of Baja California, didn't it?" she continued. "Yes, I can see that. The impression I am getting is of a tremendous wave or of a tremendous storm—energy—coming, and it was like 'whoosh'—something going under—and then that was it. I very much feel something being capsized."

Marian said she saw a girl with David in the storm. "Was she killed also?" I replied she was. "I don't like the word 'death,'" Marian went on, "because David never experienced a single moment of death. There was an impact, and then David was immediately out of the body. Instantaneous—one moment he was in his body and the next he was out.

"There was a tremendous impact, and I don't even know what happened. I just know: impact, and I feel like being dragged down, down, into the water. But I do *not* see him in that body that went under—he was not in his body, nor was she in her body. Both of them were above, looking down on what was happening. And at that point they were holding hands, literally observing, as if looking at something that was in a puppet show below."

I had read other accounts like this, channeled through mediums, which indicate that the soul often leaves before the physical death of the body in order to avoid undue pain or trauma prior to the process of transition. And thousands of people have described near-death experiences in which they all say that their consciousness was floating in the air above their dead or dying bodies. I felt comforted to know that David and Brenda had not had to suffer as they died.

Then Marian said something which I had never heard before: "David was the one who helped Tim out of the body, and it was he who helped the girl [out of her body], too. He helped them to make the transition." That certainly fit David's character, I thought, and it also fit the chronology of the events in Baja, since Tim had lived several hours longer than David, a fact Marian had no way of knowing. Marian added a last, significant impression about David's passage: "And it was important that David die in water, because there is a great, great purification—returning to pure spirit.

"The girl I see with him—they're like soul mates, standing side by side, working together," Marian went on. I told her this was Brenda, and Marian replied, "It's not the name she has now. But he still carries the name David. It's his cosmic name in this solar system. He's from far beyond—both he and the girl. He had not known her long, had he, on this plane?" David had just met her in Baja, I answered.

"She came *for him*, to help free him. She was from the angelic kingdom. She came to help. Her function on this Earth was to release him from the physical body, so that he could begin his greater work. She came because their patterns [on Earth] were to be released at the same time. He rendered assistance to her; she rendered assistance to him. And they just stepped out [of their bodies] together."

I asked Marian about her comment that David was from far beyond. "Yes—far beyond this solar system. Not only does he come from another kingdom, another dimension, I think he comes from beyond our solar system. But he's so universal now that I can't pin him down. I just know—I have that feeling of expansion—a tremendous soul. . . . I feel your son is not in the same place he was a month ago. He is now on the fifth plane and has already begun work with individuals who have also left the Earth plane under very traumatic circumstances."

I later read: "Man . . . passes into the fourth dimension at physical death, unless he has become so highly evolved spiritually that he will not need to rest there. . . . In the fifth dimension . . . Man is learning to project his thoughts, his wisdom, to an almost limitless extent into lower dimensions."[12]

I had mentioned David's journal, and Marian now told me, "It's funny that he kept a journal here, because he's very much involved with keeping records, particularly opening the records for those who are leaving the Earth under very traumatic circumstances—especially *young* people who suddenly find themselves outside of the physical body. I can see him pulling the big volumes off the shelf and opening the record, showing the one who's newly made transition: 'This is where you are, and this is what has happened, and this is what's going to happen.' Then making his entry and putting the volume back on the shelf."

This description of David's work in spirit startled me because of my own impression the previous month that David was helping children who had passed over suddenly. Then there had been David's job in the Duke Library Records Section and David's output as a journalist, a keeper of records. In addition, David had been researching and planning to write a history of Wilson House, his dormitory. David's life certainly supported Marian's insights.

"David was a very pure spirit. He had not been on Earth for some time, and he came into this lifetime to find out what our social problems were, what the vernacular was, what—how—the people were thinking, in order to establish communication lines, to open channels with certain individuals, including you. He needed to be released from Earth. And he will be working from the fifth plane as a guide and teacher for many, including you.

"Don't look for him here, because he is more alive than you and I will be for a very long time. But he is very active now—and *very* much alive. Be extremely happy that you were fortunate enough to have shared time and space with this one, because, literally, he changes your life." I thought of the song "What a Difference You've Made in My Life" and of Mrs. Allison's words at the memorial service. I told Marian that David had made an impression on everyone. "He very definitely established a communication with you," Marian responded. "He opened something in you that will never be able to be closed down again, even if it took shock to do it."

I wanted to know if David had been on Earth before. "David was a follower of Buddha, when Gautama lived," Marian replied, "and he also was very instrumental at the time of—with Abraham and again with Moses. It seems like every time a Christ spirit appeared on Earth, David had a way of making an appearance. And he came in again during the time of Jesus."

David's Duke journal seemed to validate Marian's last impression:

> I went to sleep last night in one of my peaceful moods, thinking that perhaps I could dream of a time when I was with Jesus in Galilee. [November 1976]
>
> Sometimes I go to sleep with You, Christ. Last night you were on the Sea of Galilee, with your arms back, your hair blowing, and the salt air whipping your robe around. So happy. [December 1976]
>
> It was dark in Galilee tonight. The wind tore at the white robe until it rose, higher and higher in the swirling throw of a maddened dance. The man flung back his arms to embrace the wind and sea and stars, until they filled him so fully that he had to fling his laughter in with the raging wind and moving black sea. And then the wind rises once more, firm and strong, and with a taste of sand and sea I am sitting on my warm porch, I am here. [June 1977]

When I subsequently read *Baja California and the Geography of Hope*, I had to wonder:

> For spiritual renewal, the recognition of identity, the birth of awe . . . [Baja] is a lovely and terrible wilderness, such a wilderness as Christ and the prophets went out into. . . . Looking down the cliffs, . . . [one] can also look as deeply into [oneself]. . . . Baja California is one island of hope. . . .[13]

Marian had much more to say about David's past lives: "David was also very closely tied with Jeremiah, so there was a part of him that was not always joyous, a part that had some tendency—I would imagine that came across in his journal, too—kind of doomsday, the dismal part. That's Jeremiah's influence." Once again, Marian was right on target. In his journals, David would go from pure joy to despair, and he once had quoted Jeremiah in his high school journal. "David again made an appearance about the time of the Spanish Inquisitions. And he was very much a crusader for human rights. He always had been a revolutionary. Always had a cause." David had causes in this life, too, I thought.

"You were with David at the time of Exodus," Marian went on. "The two of you were very much involved with Aaron in leading the people out. You were also with David again at the time of Jesus. You were of the Pharisee class at that time, and you definitely did not see eye to eye with this crazy young man who insisted on following this 'madman' Jesus from out of the desert. But before that lifetime had finished, you yourself had become a believer."

Marian asked what kinds of things David had written in his journal, and I told her that what I found extraordinary was David's love of God, although we had not raised him in any religion, since my family had been Jewish, Veronica's Catholic.

"He came to teach you universality—not to be Christian, or Jew, or Catholic, or Baptist, or Buddhist, or [follow] any one 'ism' or dogma, but to become instead a universal person, a universal brother belonging only to the brotherhood of man. He was born into this family because you had the *perfect* circumstances to teach—for him to develop universally himself—because you were from two different directions. It was like you were taking the East and West and bringing them together—a proving ground for him." I remembered that the Old and the New Testaments had been equally important to David.

"But David was puzzled by his human self. He was puzzled by many things," Marian continued. "He was not a terribly sexual person. He had a great need for companionship, and the rapport with the opposite sex, but he had just as much need to have rapport with males." I was reminded of an entry in David's journals: "I can't help being homosexual. Or help liking girls! They're both in me." Marian went on, "He was like a universal. He was not a saint in this life, but he was saintly within himself." Again, a very subtle but correct impression of David, which his journals clearly reflect.

"And he had no *personal* karma. He carried a very heavy load of planetary karma for the race of men as a whole. But the karma that he worked through was not *his*, but rather what he was helping with on behalf of *his* master—helping to work through while he was down here. It was like he was doing somebody else's dirty work. I have to tell you, though, that he had been a—was like—he *was* a Zen Master. He was just a Zen Master. You are in *very* close contact with him, when you let him in."

Marian continued talking—non-stop, as she always did, I later discovered. When she had finished with David, she channeled information about me, Veronica, Krista, and Eric. Almost everything Marian mentioned—and she spoke about a number of things—was either factually correct or, if unprovable, was consistent with our lives and personalities. What she had said about David raised a number of questions, though, and I had to mentally grapple with some of her more unusual impressions.

Yet when I got home and told Veronica what Marian had said about David and the time of Exodus, Veronica responded that of all the books in the Old Testament David had liked Exodus the most and that one of his all-time favorite books and movies had been *Exodus*, preferences I had never known about.

Furthermore, I had to recall that although David had never studied or even read the Bible prior to arriving in Ireland, he was given his Irish school's prize for Bible scholarship at the end of his second semester there. After that time, his small plum-colored Bible never left his side—was in his kayak with him in the Sea of Cortez when he was lost—and when we returned to the U.S. from Ireland, David developed, with no encouragement from anyone, a very strong affinity for the state of Israel.

The congruence between Marian's reading and David's life was flawless, leaving me a great deal to think about.

✦ ✦ ✦

One Saturday Veronica, Eric, Krista, and I went to have dinner at my parents' house. As my mother was preparing dinner in the kitchen, she hesitantly told Veronica and me that she had been hearing David talking to her and was afraid she was losing her mind. We of course told her she wasn't. I asked her what David told her, and she replied that he'd say, "I'm all right, Grandma. Don't worry." She also mentioned that last September, in the middle of one night, she had had a premonition about David. I told her not to discuss this any further now because I knew it would excite my father if he heard, but the next Monday afternoon I returned to talk with her.

I asked about the dream she had had about David. "It was not a dream," Mother said. "I was sleeping and woke up with this thought, 'We are going to lose David.' And I got excited and said to myself, 'Don't do that.' And I told myself that I have to get this thought out of my mind, that I cannot tell this to you—I cannot tell this to anybody, and I didn't. But I was very afraid about this trip." I was struck by Mother using the word "lost," just as I had heard in my own thoughts the previous fall.

When I asked her if David actually *talked* to her, Mother replied that he did. Did she really hear him? "It is more in my mind," she told me. I wanted to know when all this had started. "About six weeks ago," she responded. "I'll be going around the house doing something, and all of a sudden I feel that he is talking to me. And he is always telling me, 'I am here.'" Mother said that she heard David's *words*, that a conversation went on, and even when she tried to deny that he was speaking to her, he would come back strongly to affirm what he was saying and to insist that he was present with her. Conversely, when she tried to evoke his voice, she could not—he wasn't always around. Once he told her, "I don't have time for you today." On another occasion he said that he can see and hear us in our daily lives, including our thoughts, which was later confirmed for me.

Mother also said that on the previous Sunday evening David had tried very hard to make her put a seventh plate on the table, saying, "I am here, too, Grandma." Mother added, "I was going to sleep one night and again felt his presence, so I said, 'David, don't start to talk to me, I'm very sleepy.' And he said, 'O.K., but when you aren't so tired, wake up and talk to me!' I saw him already, too. I saw him on the street. I feel him so intensely! I can almost touch him. I feel him *so intensely!*"

The following Wednesday Mother saw David again, she later told me. Around noon she had been washing stockings in her bathroom sink, when she suddenly saw the image of David floating before her eyes, as if on a TV screen. She said she saw him lying on a beach, wearing only dark blue swimming trunks, with a relaxed expression on his face. I had to recall Mrs. Mankoff saying that David had been wearing dark blue swimming trunks.

Mother's contacts with David continued. She once told me that David had said to her, "I am not dead," and at a later time she saw him again. Mother had turned off the lights in her bedroom one night, when the room lit up with a blue light, and David was suddenly standing there in the center of this blue light. "Laughing, laughing," Mother said. He did not speak to her this time.

When Mother returned from a vacation in Europe, she recounted that she had seen David twice more, although the images were not clear this time, just outlines. She had been aboard her plane going abroad when she noticed David's shape out of the corner of her eye and heard him say, "Je suis ici, grandma."

"Why are you speaking French, David?" she had responded mentally.

"Because I can't speak German," he quipped in response. David had been a top French student in high school.

The second occasion she had become aware of David's presence was when she was in England visiting my sister Kathie, who had been very fond of David. Mother told Kathie, "David is here," but my sister asked Mother not to discuss it. David then responded, "Just tell Aunt Kathie I love her." Mother also said that after David's death she had been in a state of deep grief, but that since David had come to her she had had a great feeling of peace. Without my questioning her, Mother volunteered that David talking to her was distinctly different from her thinking about him.

David continued communicating with Mother for more than a year, once telling her he was much closer to me now than he had been while he was alive. However, she never saw him again. The final time she mentioned David talking with her, she said that he had asked her to tell me that I should continue with what I was doing. After that she never spoke of other contacts with David, and I never questioned her about this phenomenon again.

David had been a very lively human on Earth and now seemed to be an extremely lively spirit.

# 5

# a different search

My daily life continued to be a blur. The only thing I was really aware of was that Veronica was even more withdrawn than she had been before the tragedy. Her wound was enormous—I couldn't imagine how it would heal. She had been extremely close to David, talking to him for hours when he was home. She once told me I would never understand what losing David meant to her, and, since David's body had not been recovered, she kept hoping—for months—that he might still be alive somewhere. Every night she sobbed herself to sleep. I felt I no longer had any place in her life. Before David's death there had been an invisible barrier between us—now that barrier had been replaced by an immense wall of grief. I saw no sign that she wanted anything from me. I felt blocked, shut out.

I kept on with my search for David, now turning to David's friends. I had read David's journals, but those were very introspective, so I knew little of how the outer David had interacted with his world. David *had* sometimes written about his friends, so I now felt a real need to speak with them. I knew I had to start with Preston, since David's journals showed that she had been closer to David spiritually, emotionally, and mentally than anyone else.

Almost two months to the day that I had been called about David, I went to see Preston at her apartment in Durham. We talked casually at first, and I mentioned a few of the things Granger and Marian had told me. Watching Preston, I had to notice that even in grief she still glowed. Twice during our meeting, Preston said, "I feel so close to you. It's so strange. I feel like I've known you before." I didn't tell her, but I felt very comfortable with *her*, despite the difference in our ages. Like David, she was far more mature than her years. I finally asked her about David.

"My relationship with David was so unique," Preston began, "because I really needed, valued, treasured it—communicating with him was a part of my own being. And I never understood why. It was the first relationship where the friendship was more important than anything else. And from the very beginning it was always close. Why did we both go on Project WILD at the same time; we both were down here all summer; we both were working in the library. We lived about a mile from each other. Then!—in the fall, he moved into Wilson House, and his room was directly across the quad from mine—both on the third floor, and our windows were directly across from each other. Both early risers. Get up and run sometimes in the morning together. We both had breakfast at the same time, generally ate lunch at the same time.

"And it was exactly what I wanted and needed then. I was emotionally and spiritually very close with David. It was always very open: giving, never having to play a game. I never once felt inhibited to give, to ask, to seek, to share. I never felt like it would be taken and used to pull me closer. And that's why my friendship with David is so special.

"No matter where I met him or where I saw him, I was always on the next energy level—I was put there as soon as I saw him, no matter how down I was. We were in the same Organic Chemistry lab, the first time I had ever enjoyed being in a lab. It was incredible, because I'd be so depressed by this lab, but around David I could be just as depressed as I wanted to and it would be O.K.! He'd walk in, and I'd go and give him a hug, give him a kiss, and say, 'Oh, David, it's so horrible to be here.' It was great!—that I could be like that with him. Then there was the time when I hit a low point and I sought him out. We sat outside and I cried, and I cried, and I cried, and I cried. He sat and he listened, and he talked, and listened and talked. That wasn't the only time, either.

"And I always felt that David was a teacher—in many ways. I felt like he was teaching me to draw people into my life, placing people as more of a priority. They always have been—but I made it a functional reality, which will never, never change. I think that was the most important thing he gave me—the realization that *people* are the most important. I admired David's discipline to write, too, and he was also an intellectual teacher for me, literally. Very wise. I would normally go to breakfast and seek him out, see if he was there. Lots of times I'd just go and sit at the Wilson table when he was there, and just listen and watch him, watch how he would move with people, and share his movements and people's reactions with him. It was very stimulating—it was very exciting.

"David asked me to marry him, and I looked at him and said, 'David, I can't. Not right now.' And he said, 'That's O.K. It doesn't have to be this life. It'll be some day.' And I always felt like it would happen, because it never felt like our souls had ever been separated. I'd got so close to him and had trusted him in a way I had never done with any other man before. I felt there was never a time that I had not been with him, and I could never imagine a time not being with him—whether it be this life or the next life or the life after."

Marian had told me that David's last year had been difficult. She had said he was being prepared for his transition during sleep and had troubled dreams. His journals reflected this and also revealed that he had had some homosexual contacts during the fall and that these had disturbed him a great deal. I asked Preston about any change she had seen in David during the time she had known him. She said that David had been all right when the fall semester had started, but then things had seemed to become much harder for him.

"It was so frustrating, sometimes," she recounted. "I always felt like he was *pulling* me—from where I was—to *somewhere*, and I never knew *where* he was pulling me. He never knew where he was pulling me, either. But I always felt like some kind of *energy* was there, that was trying to go on. That's why I would get so frustrated sometimes, because I wanted him to be happy so much, and he was so frustrated and so confused, and so unhappy. Oh, God . . . I mean, I can't even count the number of times he would come and just sit and talk and eventually cry, and I would just hold him.

"David kept saying, 'I don't know what I'm going to do with my life. All I want to do is be happy. I don't know what I want to do—I cannot project myself *at all* ten years from now.'

"And I never felt like I knew what to say, or I never knew what to do, to calm his soul. And that's basically what I thought I was dealing with. I wasn't dealing with a functional reality, because David *was* functional. That wasn't what he was dealing with. It was something beyond now, and here, and where he was. . . . "

I was distressed that David had had such a difficult time during his last five months, but I thought how incredibly lucky he had been to have had Preston during that time. He may have given her a great gift, but she gave him a gift of equal value. They had been there for each other. Now Preston looked hesitantly at me.

"David said—three times before he left, he said, 'You know, I'm never coming back again.'" I asked her when this had taken place. "He specifically sat me down once the week before he was leaving, and I think he said it the night—the last time I saw him. He sat me down and said, 'I'm not coming back.'

"I said, 'David, please don't say that to me.' And he told me, 'You never know, I may fall in love with some beautiful blonde out in California and stay there.' I just looked at him and said, 'David, give me a break!'" Preston laughed, remembering. "But he said, 'I'm not coming back.'

"So I said, 'O.K. All I want to tell you is that time and distance will not affect *how* I love you and the *intensity* of my love. No matter where you go, no matter what you do, I will always love you. Even if I don't see you—for years—I will always love you the way I love you now. If I never see you again, I will always love you the way I love you now.'

"I felt that was about the only comforting thing I could say to him, because it was what I truly believed—and what I felt. And I was also afraid. I was *very* much afraid because I knew he was right. Because I felt it also. And I don't know why I felt it, and I don't know why I knew I had to believe him. And I didn't know why I could have said that to myself, even if he'd never said it to me."

I thought back to David's journals, which revealed his premonitions, many quite clear to me now. For example:

> I am really getting a very strong feeling that I'm not going to be coming back to Duke for quite a while. I look at the streets and trees and buildings carefully when I walk now, because I hear a murmur in the far side of my mind that says, 'This is it for a while, David. This is it.' [December 1977]

I asked Preston to tell me about her impressions of David's return. She said she had found out that David was lost at sea on the Friday afternoon after the accident, when Ruth—who had been in charge of the Project Wild instructor training where David had met Preston—learned that David was missing and told Preston. Then I had called her Saturday, Preston continued, and for the next forty-eight hours "it was hell—mental, emotional, physical hell." She couldn't sleep, didn't eat, couldn't really do anything.

On Sunday afternoon, around 3:00, Preston was sitting at her kitchen table, just looking out a window. She told me, "And I felt like my whole soul was just being twisted into knots." Suddenly she had a sensation—"Like there was something inside me that was *un*twisting, very slowly and gradually"—and she felt as if someone were putting his hands on her shoulders and making her relax, from her head to her toes.

"I looked up," Preston went on, "and I said, 'David, you're here. Thank you for coming. I needed you, and I needed what you're doing for me now. I've been worried that you haven't been all right, but I know that you're O.K. now. Thank you, because I couldn't have taken it much longer.' And I remember I thought, 'Well, if I tell this to anybody, they're going to think I'm really weird.'"

Preston stopped speaking and laughed ruefully for a moment. I was awed by this personal account of David's return. It was one thing to read an account like this; it was another to listen to this bright and rational young scientist tell me about her experience. Some unseen consciousness, I realized, was systematically proving to me that David continued to exist, and proving it in a very touching way.

Preston resumed her account. "But it was as much a part of my reality as any physical act. It was functional, it was mental, it was physical, it was emotional, it was spiritual. It was the most *intense peace* I think I've ever had. I immediately thought of the sea shell, the sand dollar, that David had given me for Christmas and what he'd written to me, 'The sea is one of the most calming places.' And that's exactly what I felt—that he was calming me. It was like the sea—gently rolling, and things were soothing and smoothing, and the sand was coming and going, and things would be all right, because there was a consistency, and a certainty, and a rhythm, and a pattern. And life would go on. . ."

I remembered both Eric and Mother saying they had felt this intense peace. I had little doubt now who had brought that peace to them. I decided to ask Preston about David's roommate, Dale. She predicted that David's death would be one of the most important things that would ever happen to Dale, that it would draw Dale into an emotional, spiritual world. She told me, "Dale had the same sort of experience and called me a day or two after my contact with David, saying, 'I don't know how to tell you this, but I know David is O.K., I know he was here, I know he came to speak with me. You may think I'm crazy or you may have already experienced it yourself—but all I'm doing is calling to tell you that he's O.K. and that I know that. I felt him—I felt him with me, I felt him in the room, I felt him everywhere I was at that moment—just telling me not to worry, not to be upset, that he was O.K., and I had to call you to tell you.'

"And I knew *exactly* what he was telling me! Because I had gone through the same thing! What's amazing is, I've always tended to shut myself off from anything like that—and there was no way I could have shut myself off from the feelings I was getting . . .

"I've just begun to be really functional, but there isn't a day that goes by without my thinking about David. And it doesn't have to be just thinking about David's death.

"I always felt close to him, and I'll always feel close to him. Why? Who can explain it?"

Preston had given me a special gift this day. She had spoken openly and from her heart, allowing herself to be more vulnerable than anyone I had ever met. What she told me about her relationship with David was also extremely important to me. For this was the first time in my life that I had been shown a demonstration of unconditional, spiritual love—her love for David and his love for her. I will always treasure that meeting. Preston is a very special person, with a very special mission in this life. I was certain she would be one of David's spiritual channels.

✦ ✦ ✦

Four weeks later I drove over to Duke and talked to Dale at Wilson House. It was an uncomfortable conversation. For the first time in my life, I felt the gulf between the generations, and Dale seemed ill at ease also. He sidestepped talking about his sense of David's presence the week after David had been lost, mumbling something about being upset back then. I didn't press him further.

He did have a few perplexing things to tell me, though. First he said that of the fifteen residents—all male—in David's first-year dormitory, Z House, eight were Aquarians, a peculiar ratio. Then he told me that a young man in Wilson House named Dan had known Brenda Herman in the seventh grade in Cincinnati and that David's first roommate in Z, Steve, had also been from Cincinnati. I began to wonder what the odds were for all these coincidences.

I told Dale that in reading through David's journals, I had found that David had had premonitions all year. Dale said that David had been undecided about whether he was coming back or not and had asked a few people if they thought he'd return. "I told him I didn't think he was coming back," Dale went on. "He asked some others and then said to me, 'Now it's three *against* me coming back, and two *for*.'"

✦ ✦ ✦

I was starting to be aware that I had been handed a cosmic jigsaw puzzle, which had a great many pieces with quite peculiar shapes and characteristics. Perhaps appropriately, a few of these puzzle pieces were delivered to me by the U.S. Mail. In retrospect, that seems like a cosmic joke: messages from spirit delivered by a physical mailman. (The humor that slid through me as I wrote that thought leads me to believe it came from David, and I hear his quasi-innocent "Who, Moi?" in my mind as well.)

The first letter was addressed to David, sent to his Duke post office box and forwarded to us less than two weeks after the St. Michael's memorial service. It read: "Your name has been submitted . . . as someone who might [wish] information about the Third Order of St. Francis . . . which aims [for] . . . a life-style of self-giving and love sent forth to be a sign of peace, gentleness and simplicity in the world." Since the letter had been sent to David, I felt that he had indeed wanted St. Francis' prayer read at his service.

In April, I received another letter mailed to David at his Duke address. It was from the Psychical Research Foundation, inviting David to join a new organization, Theta Association, which had been formed for the purpose of investigating the possibility of life after death. How did David's name get on their mailing list, I wondered? At any rate, I joined Theta, which eventually led me to every other psychic, almost every organization, almost every person, and almost every event in the rest of this book. Not bad for a simple invitation. But I found a very likely explanation when I read David's dream journals. One entry noted, "Sometime during the dream I put my arms around 'Theta' and asked her to do something important." When I figured that one out, it gave me chills.

But David wasn't finished with the mails. I received a third letter sent to him. It was an announcement of a new magazine, and the promotional copy for it began in the upper left-hand corner of the envelope itself, with the following: "Why dying may not be as unpleasant as you think . . ." When I thought over this obvious message, I had to laugh. Who else but David, with his puckish humor, could be behind this letter? After all, David had done *something* while he was alive for the letter to be sent to us.

Then there were three incidents connected with David's odyssey to Baja. One night I phoned Brenda's brother-in-law Barry, who lived in New Jersey. In the course of our conversation, Barry mentioned that he knew one of the young men who had been in the second kayak crew in Baja with David and Brenda. Now, there are 250 million people in the U.S., only eighteen other students were in Baja with Brenda, and Barry knew one of those students.

Next, David's crew-mate BeeBee recounted a peculiar happening to Veronica. BeeBee, back in college after the Baja tragedy, had gone home to Baltimore for the Easter break and had run into a young man who had been in high school with her and who was unaware that BeeBee had taken Outward Bound Kayaking Course S-54. He first told her that he now attended Duke University and then began describing an experience that he had had at Duke early in February. He said he had been walking by the Duke Chapel and had suddenly remembered that there was to be a service that evening for a Duke student who had died recently. Although BeeBee's friend hadn't known this student, he impulsively decided to enter the chapel and take part in the service. The service had been for David.

Finally, David's friend Debbie called Veronica one afternoon and during their conversation said that she had recently met a young man at North Carolina State University who had told her he had been taking a kayaking course in Baja with the National Outdoor Leadership School when David had been lost. His group and David's had passed each other on the water several times during those two weeks.

Out of 250 million people in the U.S.

One other odd event was reported by BeeBee. She told me she had seen a UFO in Baja, and DelRene later corroborated this: "BeeBee and I both thought we saw a UFO one night [during the solo]. I wasn't saying anything, but then I talked about it, and she said she saw the same thing." Maybe this had no significance, but I found it strange all the same.

✦ ✦ ✦

I continued researching Outward Bound's safety record. I soon was able to document that thirteen students (including David, Brenda, Tim, and Sonya) and two instructors had died in U.S. Outward Bound programs, most of the deaths occurring in a six-and-a-half-year period preceding David's death. There also were other deaths in programs modeling themselves on Outward Bound or set up by Outward Bound consultants, plus deaths in Outward Bound programs in other countries, including Canada. At least seven families of victims charged negligence; at least five families filed law suits.

I also researched Outward Bound schools, courses, instructor training, and safety practices in kayaking and spoke with several kayaking experts. As a result, I discovered numerous kayaking safety violations on Kayaking Course S-54, convincing me that Southwest Outward Bound had seriously neglected the safety of its students in Baja. The bottom line for me was that a group of inexperienced boaters had been placed alone in terrain well known—and documented—to be very unstable and hazardous, without adequate safety equipment or rescue backup in case of life-endangering emergency.

When I finished the research, my attorney told me I had more than enough to go to trial. I sent copies of everything I had found to Tim's father, and the Breidegam family decided to file a suit for wrongful death against Outward Bound. Veronica and I joined the action, as did Brenda's mother. I gave Outward Bound over to the lawyers. I needed to search elsewhere now.

# 6

# on the inner path

David's journal writing had so impressed me that at the end of May I had started keeping a journal myself, although I felt very awkward putting my thoughts and feelings onto paper. Looking back, I can see that this reluctance stemmed—at least in part—from the dysfunctional code: silence at all cost, even in the privacy of my own thoughts. As the years went by, however, and I returned to what I had written, I noticed that some of my entries had come from a much higher level of my mind and were either prophetic, intuitive, or showed me what I needed to know—although at first I often did not truly understand what I was recording. On June 4, I wrote:

> God, how we all live these lives of quiet desperation. No one knows anyone else. This lack of communication is what is killing the world.
>
> I know what it is for me, though. I have blocked myself off from my own soul because I have been so disappointed. I can never build structures—all I do is pitch tents, which the wind constantly blows away. Now it has blown David away, and I really feel lost. I know the lesson—everything is temporal, nothing lasts, so look inside instead. Destroy pride, vanity, ambition: this is one hell of a hard lesson I've set myself to learn.

My life still seemed surrealistic, as if I my mind had slipped off to another dimension and was watching events unfold from there. Everyone in my family was still groping, and silent. I finally got up my nerve and asked Kris how she was dealing with David's death. She said she was handling it better than her friends and David's because of the metaphysical concepts she had heard me talk about for years. I was grateful that this knowledge was now helping her. On June 7, Kris graduated from high school. It was the usual sort of ceremony, but the singing of "America" made me think of what David had wanted for America, and tears came to my eyes and wouldn't stop.

Three evenings later I went to see a woman who had knowledge of psychics in North Carolina. Edna turned out to be a very fine person, and I was at her house for four hours. She told me that David was meant to work on another level, while I needed to work here—exactly what Marian had said. She put on a tape of "Be Still," and I closed my eyes and meditated. As the music played, I perceived an open Grecian style pillared entranceway filled with many colors, and then several more similar open entranceways behind the first one. When I told Edna about these entranceways after my meditation, she said the images meant I had an open door to do what I wanted. She was right, for every spiritual door I walked up to thereafter swung open for me. She suggested some people to see, including Jim Goure and LeRoy Zemke. Edna's presence was soothing, and the evening was very healing for me.

On June 11, I saw Marian for the second time. Since she seemed to have abilities similar to those of Edgar Cayce, I wanted to find out as much as I could from her. In addition, I had spoken with two or three people who also had seen Marian, and they all had told me their readings had been accurate and significant. I felt Marian was a prime source of spiritual research.

I decided to establish a standard for psychic readings, however. First, for me to even consider the validity of what I was told, the psychic *had* to mention some solid factual things about David and me that were indisputable and could in no way have been known by the psychic. Second, I wanted two or more psychics to come up with at least a few identical impressions to validate both the information and the process. I refused to be victimized by charlatans, and I also knew that if any of this material ever found its way into print, I, the psychics, and the impressions would all be examined closely. In addition, Veronica challenged everything I brought home, often saying I was gullible. I was not—I closely scrutinized whatever I was told, and anything I was willing to accept and publish had to be impeccable.

I met Marian at Betty's house again, and we went downstairs to the recreation room. Marian began by "tuning in" to my vibrations through my hands, then told me a few accurate things about myself, ending with, "I feel very strongly that you are meant to make this experience count for something, to help others." I mentioned I was planning to publish David's journals, and she said she felt that David wanted his journals published, that the book would eventually be published, and that it would be of great import. "I feel like this book is something you need to experience, in order to free *yourself*, or *cleanse* yourself, and at the same time help others who are going through a similar experience."

She told me she felt David was present. "I get strong impressions of David standing very strong, tall, and vibrant over you right at this moment. I feel his presence *very* strongly, but I see him as rejoicing, and a lot of gold around him—a lot of yellow—very exuberant colors surrounding him. I sensed his energy when I walked upstairs to meet you—and so I feel, in some way, the two of you have it more together, because there is a oneness between the two of you."

I recounted my mother's experience of seeing David laughing and surrounded by blue light, and Marian's response was, "Well, that's exactly how I feel him now, standing behind you. And it's like he's really joyous, like he's giving everything he possibly has to give you, because you are one of his channels."

When I gave her a photograph of Preston, Marian said that if David had lived, he would have married Preston. I told Marian David *had* asked Preston to marry him, and Marian responded, "That's exactly what I see, because they had been married before. He is also going to work through her. They were soul mates, and he connected with her because she will be a channel."

Marian paused, then told me, "She's been your daughter in another lifetime, in the early days of this country—I see you moving across the frontier. David was present in that lifetime, too, and he was not of your family. She was your daughter, and you were not sure that this young man was good enough for her. It's very interesting that the roles should have been reversed in this lifetime.

"You were super-protective of her, but you were very close to her. You were a teacher, and you taught her to read and to write—you taught her many things that would only have been taught to the male and not the female. So there was a good meeting of minds between you two in that lifetime, although it was a hardship. Your wife died, leaving you with several children, and [Preston] became like the mother—so there was a very close relationship. But you were very antagonistic toward this young man."

Marian's impressions of Preston had at least one parallel in this life. When I had read the letter Preston had sent to David in Baja, I had immediately sensed she had a talent for writing, and at our first meeting I told her I felt that she is a writer. She replied that she had always wanted to be a writer: "I wrote a journal, for years. Then I started writing poetry, extensively. I stopped writing when I came to Duke and started again about two months ago, when David died."

I pretty much forgot about this until a couple of years later, when Preston called to tell me that she was writing a doctoral dissertation, which later became a book. Several months after talking to Preston, I suddenly understood. Marian had said I was Preston's father in a previous life and there I had taught her to read and *write*. Now I meet Preston in this life, and she is *writing* a book. So, the soul continues certain threads—relationships and abilities—through more than one life, developing these further with each successive life.

I next showed Marian a picture of Steve, one of David's teammates on their high school cross-country and track teams, and I mentioned that David had been very fond of him. Marian told me that Steve was devic—also from the angelic kingdom, like David and Brenda. I later came across the following:

> The deva kingdom controls to a large extent the part of life we call Nature, the seas, the winds, the use of the sun. . . . Members of the deva evolution . . . do what they can to help the many who are terrified at the moment of their passing.[14]

When I read this passage, I thought of David's love of nature and Marian's account of David's first job in spirit after his death.

Steve and David had known each other on other planes, Marian went on, had been priests together in Atlantis, and so there was a spiritual bond between them. They also had been lovers in a past life, male and female, and the love bond had been so powerful then that David still felt it very strongly. Just being near Steve, Marian said, would have brought on feelings of love toward Steve in David, as the two were soul mates. David's journals showed the accuracy of Marian's impressions:

> I can't believe how much I love Steve. Every day, more and more real love. If reincarnation is true, I've loved him before, somewhere, sometime.

Marian's comments, including those that follow, came before I told her that David had felt he was gay.

Marian continued her impressions of Steve. "Here again is another of David's channels. But he will act more as a guardian for Steve. This boy is very special. He is going to be a very mystical person and will touch many people's lives in this lifetime. And the love that was necessary for David to have, this great love for him, was for David to be able to establish—to open—the channel. The only way David could establish channels with the people he would work with from the other plane was through a bond of love: the father-love, the love for the girl, the love for the beloved soul mate. I don't feel—if it was a homosexual relationship, I didn't pick that up." I told Marian that David's journals showed that there had definitely been no such relationship, that David and Steve had just been teammates at school. "But David will stand over Steve for a long time to come. Good person, very special. He loved your son, and your son loved him and still does."

I wanted to know more about the angelic kingdom, since angels had always seemed like wishful thinking to me. "We are in the time of the return of the masters," Marian replied, "and many of the angelic force—which is a higher evolution—are stepping down their vibrations to take human embodiment, and have been for a very long time, in order to bring greater light into the Earth. The angels are evolving very slowly, because they're single energy. Where man has twelve aspects, the angels have only one, which is total obedience and service.

"In about the Atlantean period, many of the angels who had evolved as high as they felt they could go did ask, out of impatience, to take human embodiment, so they could step up their evolvement, because the testing is so fast and furious on this plane that they can do, say, in twenty thousand years what would take them a million years to do in their own evolution. Many of these, because of great service, were granted human embodiment, and many of them got caught up karmically in the Earth's pattern. They didn't think they would, but they did. They became, literally, fallen angels. A lot of these are on Earth at this time, as a result of their karma, and have come back to help others. Steve is one of these."

I showed Marian more photographs of people who had been important to David. She said Mrs. Allison had been an Atlantean teacher and philosopher, David her student then as now, and that Mrs. Allison had come back in a black embodiment this time to bridge the gap between the races. From what David and Krista had told me about Mrs. Allison, she has been doing a fabulous job of doing so. Mrs. Winz, David's high school French teacher, had been a priest with David in France long ago, and the two had recognized each other instinctively. Marian said she heard Gregorian chants when she looked at Mrs. Winz's picture. Significantly, David had written in his Duke journal: "I feel a fast pulse that wants to tell me something, but what, what. I raise up images of a Benedictine monastery . . ." Marian concluded, "She is very highly evolved."

I then gave Brian's photograph to Marian, told her that he and David had run cross-country and track together. Marian said Brian had been David's son in a prior life. "David would have been very protective of this boy. I don't know when he had been David's child, although I get the impression possibly in Greece, a very long time ago. But Brian had been a very weak child in that life. David would have been super protective of the boy in this life. Many times Brian would run on David's energy." Sometime afterwards, although I had not yet mentioned any of Marian's impressions about Brian, Veronica said that David always had been very fatherly toward Brian.

This Greek life of David probably was connected to his athletic interests, for when I asked Marian about David's long-distance running, she replied that David had been an Olympic athlete back at the very beginning of the Olympics in Greece, running and throwing the javelin. In his present life, David had thrown javelin and discus while in Ireland. He had dreamed of getting into the Olympics, first in jumping horses when he was around thirteen and later as a long distance runner. David had also made drawings of Greek athletes from pictures of statues in art books when we were in Ireland.

I wondered aloud if there had been karmic connections between David and the people with him in Baja, to which Marian replied, "The strong feeling I'm getting for the entire group is a karmic bondage that goes into Atlantean times and also goes back into the time when the Hebrews were in bondage in Egypt. They were all Hebrew at one time, but not always of a like mind. Most of all, I feel they were all bound together going back to the time of the establishment of the kings of Israel." When I later checked the Bible, I found that the first two kings of Israel had been Saul and David.

I also wondered if David had become one of my spiritual guides. "When I said he was like a Zen Master, I meant he had *complete* control over his destiny—he knew exactly what he was," Marian replied. "He knew where his center was, and he stayed in his center and radiated out from it: he was like the hub of a wheel. He was—*is*—now acting as one of your guides and teachers, and you are in very close contact with him, although earlier you weren't always letting him enter in. Now you're very open and receptive to his vibration."

I had read that a spiritual guide is a discarnate, usually one who lived on Earth before (and commonly one who knew the person or was related to the person in this or other lives), but sometimes one who has never embodied. People are said to have five or more guides, some of whom remain with the person for life and some of whom come for specific purposes for only a set period of time. Each guide normally performs a specific service for each person, such as helping to keep the person healthy or guiding the person spiritually.

I later found the following definition of a "master":

As man evolves along the road that is set before him, he is actually under the control and guidance of a group of adepts, who are perfect men, but who were as you are, countless thousands of years ago. These men have finished the course of lives to be lived at the physical level, for they have learnt all the lessons that the physical world has to teach. Because of their developed love for humanity as a whole, they have elected to remain (at some sacrifice to themselves) in connection with this planet, to help it on and to assist in its development. These adepts are sometimes referred to as masters.[15]

I couldn't say if David was a master, but he certainly radiated.

I was also curious about Marian's provocative statement earlier that David had been serving a spiritual master. I had no idea what she meant, so I asked her who this master was. "I do not know," Marian replied. "I would assume that David probably was working for the Archangel Michael, but that's only conjecture. The reason I say Michael is because of the blue light that has been around David. Today is the first time I have seen him with the gold light—which is wisdom. But I've always seen the blue light, and the blue light usually denotes Michael."

I was really stunned by this information because David had written a poem entitled "Michael Angel," and when I told this to Marian, she said, "O.K. Well, that's his master, then—he worked for Michael." I also had to remember David's attraction to St. Michael's Church in Raleigh and that David had wanted to name one of our cats Michael Angelo.

A major New Age belief is that humans are beings of light and energy, who pre-exist their physical bodies and who come to Earth with specific goals or game plans for their lives. This was heavily underscored by the Edgar Cayce readings. Since the death of any young person, particularly one with talent, always seems such a waste, I had a real need to find out why David had chosen to come to Earth and then had died so young.

Marian had several impressions about David's pre-birth life plans: "David came to stay for only a brief period. He needed to be released from the Earth." There was an echo of this in one entry of David's Duke journal on June 22, 1977: "Oh, Lord, right now I feel as though I've been given the life of a happy boy"—that is, a short life. This was the same month that he had had premonitions.

Having read David's journals by this time—as well as the Edgar Cayce material on homosexuality—I wondered if David had chosen homosexuality prior to birth, as part of his life plan. I consequently told Marian that in the last year of his life David had briefly become involved homosexually with a few people (none of whom are mentioned in this book) and had been having a lot of trouble with that. I asked her what the origin of this issue had been.

"The fact is that he was an androgynous being—totally male-female *within* himself—so that he was reacting—" Marian paused—she appeared to be listening inside herself, then continued, "He's telling me something, and I'm getting something myself—" She stopped again, then came back strongly, "He *had* to go through that experience, on two levels. First of all, he was androgynous himself, so that he sometimes related to people not by what form they were in—as to whether they were masculine or feminine—but by what they were mentally-emotionally-spiritually, so he was led by what they really were within."

Although I had never run across the concept of spiritual androgyny, I later heard and read many times—from both metaphysicians and psychologists—that we all need to fully develop both our male and female psychological aspects. I also found corroboration for spiritual androgyny in a book on reincarnation by Marcia Moore.[16]

Marian continued her impressions of David's life plans: "The other part of David's ministry—and which he will be radiating back here to Earth—is going to deal with homosexuals, and so he himself had to walk a few miles in those shoes, to be able to experience this." That also seemed to be reflected in David's journals:

> We must walk this lonesome valley,
> I have to walk it by myself.
> Oh, nobody else can walk it for me,
> I have to walk it, by myself. [July 1971]

> I will not be a homosexual. I deny that life for myself.
> . . . Pray God, if Thou will, if I am ever well, that I may help others, who, like me, are struggling to find the narrow, long road to Heaven. [November 1976]

David's homosexual relationships in the last year of his life served as spiritual training for him, Marian told me. "There was no *error* in it. This was something he himself had to experience in order to understand it. And so some of such a relationship was: he was led to it, because he, as an androgynous being, was led to those on a soul level—their souls were in harmony with his. But these involvements that he had were a training exercise in making contact, because much of his work, and people who he will work with, will have to do with those who are homosexually bound and who are bound because they have problems within their own consciousness that need to be resolved. David is very clear about this, very clear."

I asked what sort of work from the other side David will be doing with homosexuals. "I feel this is spiritual guidance—I don't feel that he will be working, though, with the homosexuals who are bound by heavy karma, but with those who are very close to a state of androgyny, who are manifesting bisexuality. And I think bisexuality is a better word here than homosexuality. He will be acting as a spiritual guide, helping to give them some kind of direction or feeling of *rightness* about their uniqueness in this particular expression. He will be working with many, trying to help them to rise above purely sensation, or purely sexual expression on this plane, to where there is a greater use or a more *divine* use of their own creative energy.

"David will be trying to work through some to shatter the separation that we have between the sexes—all of these separations that are going to be bridged. We have to tear down all of the barriers, all of the taboos, all of the things that say: 'This is wrong, this is right,' and see only the oneness [of mankind, of souls, of spirit]. Many of those who are approaching androgyny will be angelic beings in human embodiment, who are both male and female within themselves, and David will definitely be working under—I feel very strongly now—the St. Michael energy."

Angelic beings incarnating seemed very foreign to me. However, "chance" led me to another book by Marcia Moore,[17] in which she not only wrote further about bisexual persons but also noted that many bisexuals are angelic beings or devas—the word "deva" meaning "shining one" in Sanskrit. Miss Moore's description of such a human deva painted an astonishingly exact picture of many of David's interests, physical characteristics, and personality traits. I was very surprised by Marian's explanations and Marcia Moore's insights.

My last question for this session was what Marian had meant by planetary karma. She replied that all human beings have both personal and planetary karma, since we are all *one*, and that when a master embodies, he will take on not only his own share of planetary karma but that of several of his initiates also, in an effort to free those individuals. Much that David went through, even at the time of his death, with the group of people he was with—David was doing just that.

Marian's reading had been extraordinary, greatly expanding my ideas about how spirit worked on planet Earth. Especially important for me, of course, were Marian's continuing assurances that David was O.K., was working in spirit to help the planet, and that everything about David's life had been planned. I had read about life plans before, but this was by far the clearest—and most important—life plan I had ever come across. Although my human mind and emotions still grieved for David, my spirit soared from what Marian had told me. I would never again be able to look at existence in the way I had before David's death and Marian's readings.

At the beginning of July, I received a notice from Theta that the well-known English medium Douglas Johnson, an elderly gentleman, would be lecturing and giving readings in Durham at the Psychical Research Foundation. I attended his lecture, then made an appointment to see him the next day, July 11.

When I met Mr. Johnson for the reading, he said he didn't know how well it would go, since a thunderstorm had just passed and his receptivity—and that of all psychics, he claimed—is affected by thunderstorms. This seemed to hold true during my session, at any rate, for Mr. Johnson sometimes took long pauses and told me that he would just get a flash of something, which would then quickly fade.

Before starting, Mr. Johnson held my wrist watch to tune in to my vibrations.[18] I told him I had come about someone who had passed away in the previous year, but Mr. Johnson quickly shot back, "Well, don't tell me anything else," adding, "And one really doesn't know what one's going to get." He obviously was determined to keep his impressions from being colored by anything I said.

He returned my wrist watch and began by saying that I had an ability for writing. "I see manuscripts, and I feel very strongly that this is something which could be positive and progressive. I think you're currently in the middle of some writing, though there's going to be a bit of a delay and a bit of bother." There was more than a bit of bother, and quite a substantial delay—over eighteen years. "But I get a feeling very much of encouragement with the writing. You teach, don't you?" I said I used to. He told me he saw me as a teacher in the future, as had Marian on June 11. "I also think you are quite psychic, very intuitive, and that this could be—later on, possibly—expanded." He noted I had three children.

Mr. Johnson next picked up a discarnate woman, "an old lady," and what he said about her convinced me this was my deceased maternal grandmother. He told me she had someone with her, "a young woman . . . more recent . . . somebody who went *quickly*. This need not be a relative. Did someone have an accident? I really don't like to ask questions, but there's someone here and I can't get at them." I felt Mr. Johnson had picked up David's boatmate Brenda, but I said nothing.

I then gave him David's Bible and stuffed bear Boswell. Mr. Johnson's next comments indicated he was now inside David's mind, almost speaking as David. "I'm feeling breathing, congestion of some kind, and tightness—very much. A very strange feeling in my head. I don't think I was conscious. I'm getting a very funny feeling up here." As he said this, he touched the left side of his head, toward the front of his skull.

Mr. Johnson then told me he was having trouble receiving impressions and finally asked me for questions, hoping to get a smoother flow of information. When I awkwardly began to tell him that my younger son had died at the end of January, Mr. Johnson quickly interjected that he wished I hadn't said that—"I should have warned you to just say something ambiguous." Since he still didn't want any sort of prompting, I became silent and waited.

"I see legal papers," he finally told me. "You're not engaged in something legal, are you?" I replied I was involved in a matter that would result in a law suit. "That's what I mean," he responded. "It's going to hang about, I'm afraid, but you must stick to your guns about it."

Then he suddenly seemed to come alive. "It's about an accident—oh, yes, this is something to do with this boy. I'm getting it now. I felt this old lady back again. She showed me law papers and claims—that's what it is. This poor kid had an accident and got killed—bless his heart—and this claim has to do with that." Mr. Johnson was finally on track. I leaned in and watched his closed eyes, bringing the corded microphone of my tape recorder closer to his face.

"'Oh, he's fine,' the old lady says. 'He's still having a bit of a rest, but he's fine. We met him.' I can feel the boy in the background somewhere," Mr. Johnson continued, "but I don't think he has had enough time to get experienced enough [to communicate]. It seems too new to him. And somebody's trying to act as a transmitter, spokesman for him—perhaps the old lady. But he's bright—it was very tragic—he's quite anxious, through her, to sort of give a feeling that he *is* all right." There was a long pause.

"There's someone concerned with this—an 'ei' sound." Mr. Johnson pronounced the "ei" sound as in "eye," which is a sound in Tim's last name: Brei̇degam. "I think there were three people involved in this," he added. That gave me chills. I could only nod and say, "Yes." Mr. Johnson had picked up all three in his reading. "I'm getting this funny head feeling again," he continued. "I think your boy went on his head." I thought back to Irene Hughes' comment that David's head had been injured, but I couldn't imagine how he could have hurt it in the water.

"I keep getting these words: 'I'm fine. I'm fine. As long as you're all happy, I am.'" There was a pause. "Could he draw?" Mr. Johnson continued. "I feel he had a creative thing and could draw little sketches or caricatures, and you've got some of these at home—something to do with a book." David had drawn some small sketches in his journals and had always liked to draw from the time he could hold a crayon. "Brother and sister . . . he was a talented kid. Very affectionate . . . there were three people involved," Mr. Johnson repeated.

"I am sure that this boy will try again. He's got a good mind, but it takes time to get adjusted. Oh, this is dropping into my mind, 'I knew you were coming today. I was told—we got your thoughts.' He is a lovely boy."

After the reading, I went to the Theta office and asked the secretary if she knew of any other psychics I could contact. "There's going to be a whole bunch in Greensboro with a Spiritual Frontiers Fellowship retreat in August," she said. "We just got the announcement. It's on the bulletin board." I was familiar with S.F.F., having read books about and by Arthur Ford, one of the founders or the organization and the preeminent male medium in the United States for decades. I leafed through the announcement. Among the twenty-two psychics listed were Karen Getsla, Don Hudson, and LeRoy Zemke. Although I really couldn't afford the retreat, I decided to go. Those names were a signal to me—I felt a pull to Greensboro.

Two days later I went to the house of Jim and Judy Carrino for my first meeting with the small A.R.E. group that I would study and meditate with for the next two years. At the end of the meeting, we meditated, and I went fairly deep. Three or four times I felt a wave of energy rise from my toes to the top of my head. I also had the feeling of being filled with energy which had a slight impression of vibration.

The next night I noted in my journal:

> Since David's death, I feel I am being led, step by step, somewhere. I like the process. Much like reading a good book—I guess the best: the Book of Life.
>
> Mrs. Herman called last night. She appears to have had a premonition about Brenda and did not want her to go to Baja. When Brenda arrived in San Diego, a friend also tried to talk her out of going. Brenda said it was something she had to do—the same words David used. When Brenda called her mother from Tijuana, Mrs. Herman again had misgivings and once more asked Brenda not to go. Brenda told her mother that she had to do this.
>
> Brenda had planned to go to Israel to work on a kibbutz after completing the Outward Bound kayaking

course. [David had also wanted to work on a kibbutz in Israel, possibly in 1979.]

I recalled that last March Mrs. Herman had told Veronica that when she, Mrs. Herman, had first been notified that Brenda was missing, Brenda's best friend—speaking with Mrs. Herman over the telephone the Friday after Brenda was lost—had said, when she was told David's name, "Oh, if there's someone named David with Brenda, then it's all right."

My inner path was taking some strange twists and turns.

# 7

# spiritual frontiers

Six months had gone by, but my passage through that time had felt unreal. My inner clock had shattered at 12:03 A.M., January 27. Much of the pain was gone, but the shock, numbness, and disbelief persisted, almost as in the first moment. My world had no niche in it for David dead at eighteen. I didn't know where to put this fact. My mind had no space for it. I could live with it now, but I couldn't integrate it. The fact merely sat outside of me, watching me—it had nowhere to go. Marian had said one of my lessons for this life was patience. Edgar Cayce said, "little by little." I had doubts about my ability to master either concept. However, August was almost here, and I was looking forward to the Spiritual Frontiers Fellowship retreat. Except for Marian's meetings in Raleigh, this would be the first time I had ever attended a metaphysical event.

*Monday, August 14*

I arrived at Guilford College in Greensboro early in the morning and registered for the S.F.F. retreat. Lectures and workshops were scheduled for every day, led by a stellar group of New Age leaders that included Patricia Sun, David Spangler, Walter Starcke, Joel Andrews, Robert Mitra, Carol W. Parrish, and LeRoy Zemke. I went outside and wandered around the broad lawns of the peaceful campus, curious about what lay in store for me this week.

In the afternoon, I attended the first class of my Reiki healing workshop, for which I had signed up from curiosity. Over the years I had read books about natural healers and had always wondered how their ability worked. The Reiki class seemed like a nonthreatening way to check out this phenomenon first-hand.

Usui Reiki turned out to be an ancient Zen Buddhist system of laying on of hands, which supposedly had come into existence 2500 years ago, had been lost, and then had been found again in modern times. Our instructor was Virginia Samdahl, the first Occidental to become an Usui Reiki Master, and after recounting the delightful story of how Usui Reiki had been re-discovered, she began teaching us how to heal.

*Tuesday*

Late in the morning, I had a reading from a woman psychic. I said nothing to her before she began, wanting to keep the reading as objective as possible. Much of what she told me about myself was vague and general, but a few of her impressions turned out to be very relevant.

"In this past year you have gone through a period of change, a spiritual gift of unfoldment that you have been experiencing. Do not hesitate to use this as it begins to open within you. As you have these [spiritual] experiences, you lack confidence in yourself to believe that 'this can be happening to me—I am really experiencing this and it's not a figment of my imagination.' There is truth to what you are experiencing. Please accept it as truth and share it with others as it comes forward." At that moment, I wasn't certain I knew what she was talking about, but I discovered her meaning very soon.

When I mentioned that I had come because of a deceased person, she said she was seeing a small child—a soul that had left the physical body at the age of about two or three. I told her that I didn't know such a child. "These souls can come in for the purpose of receiving help," she responded, "and it seems this is part of what you're supposed to work with. It apparently is your soul's choice to help these souls who have no one to help them—and you're always drawn to the person who doesn't have anyone. This is why these souls come into your vibration for this purpose."

She asked who I wanted to contact, and I replied that my youngest son had died in January. She then correctly described a few of David's characteristics, including the fact that he was the one in the family who would try to cheer me up when I was depressed. "He knew you better than anyone," she told me. "He gives me a feeling of, 'Don't worry—I haven't gone any place. I'm not so far away that you can't call me back.' Any time you feel a need to touch into his vibration, just mentally ask him, and you'll be able to. He says, 'I'm here for the taking,' bless his heart. He had a good sense of humor, didn't he?" I said yes. "He was a great inspiration for you. A smart young man—loving, gentle."

Early that morning I had attended a meditation class, and sometime after lunch I decided to practice meditation in my room. Thinking back to the spirit child of two or three, I decided to meditate on such a child, so I closed my eyes.

After a few minutes, I began to visualize a boy of about three, although I could not make out his features. I don't recall what I was thinking, but I know I was trying to help him—although I had no idea how. As I concentrated on the boy, the figure of David suddenly appeared, seemingly from a distance, walking into my field of inner vision from my right, on a diagonal from a northeasterly direction. David was dressed, as always, in cut-off shorts, canvas shoes with no socks, and a grubby T-shirt that hung outside his shorts.

David did not look in my direction but straight at the boy. He walked up to the child, took the boy's right hand in his left hand, and—leading the boy slowly but stead-ily—walked away from me, back toward where he had come from. I could see the figures of David and the boy recede in the distance, becoming smaller and smaller, until they faded from sight. Tears suddenly began to flow down my face.

This inner event had been totally unexpected. I had not been thinking of David before or during the meditation, nor had I thought of David in connection with the boy. David's appearance in my inner vision was a complete surprise to me. Recalling what Marian had said about David's work in spirit with young persons who had died traumatically, however, I had to conclude that I had made inner contact with David this afternoon. I never had this sort of experience again—at least not consciously.

*Wednesday*

After lunch I had my second reading, this time from a male psychic. It was quite entertaining and interesting, touching on broad aspects of my life. Although the subject of David never came up, I wasn't concerned, since by this time I had decided that I had been led to this retreat more for myself than for David, and what the psychic told me about myself helped to strengthen me inside.

*Thursday*

At noon I went to lunch in the cafeteria and joined an elderly man sitting at a long table by himself. We began to talk about the retreat as we ate, and he eventually asked me what workshop I was taking.

I told him it was Reiki and that the word "Reiki" was a Japanese word meaning "universal healing energy." I went on to describe what had been taking place in the workshop, including people reporting energy or heat in their hands or elsewhere (when other healers put their hands on them), and how I had observed one slender young woman's arms begin to vibrate up and down from a surge of healing energy during practice, while she kept insisting that she had no control over her arms. I told my lunch partner that I myself had felt nothing so far.

"Could I put my hands on your shoulders and see if you feel anything?" I asked.

"Sure," he replied.

I got up and stood behind him and placed my hands lightly on his shoulders and back. I stood there for three or four minutes, feeling nothing. The man remained totally silent and did not move. I finally asked, "Do you feel anything?"

"Certainly do," he said.

"What?"

"Energy," he shot back quickly.

I still found it hard to believe, but the evidence had been shoved under my nose. I thanked him for his help and went off to my Reiki workshop bemused. Thereafter, any time that I put my hands on someone for a few minutes, the person reported feeling either energy, heat, or vibrations.

*Friday*

I scrambled into my clothes when the alarm went off at 6:30 A.M. and hurried over to my meditation class. I sat down with my back to the wall, closed my eyes, and listened to the instructor's voice leading us. The process had become familiar by now, and I wondered what this morning would bring.

As I meditated with my eyes closed in the quiet room, I suddenly felt (physically) and saw (inside) what appeared to be a half-inch-wide strip of colorless transparent plastic film with block letters printed on it being pulled across my inner vision, from right to left. The strip moved slowly, one letter at a time, as if some sort of teletype was clicking and printing each letter. It read:

"DAVID WANTS TO TELL YOU—"

I thought, "Oh, no, I'm dreaming up another conversation with David, but I don't believe that they're valid." So I tried to dismiss the image. The plastic strip came to a jerky stop when I thought this but didn't disappear (the letters already there remained on the screen of my inner vision), then began to click again anyway, without any control over it by me:

"—THAT HE LOVES YOU. HE SAYS HELLO."

I contemplated this message for a moment, then decided to pursue the thought, instead of trying to dismiss it. I mentally asked, "Who are you?" I expected no answer, feeling that a lack of response would invalidate the words I had just seen. The answer came anyway as the film strip began to move again:

"WE ARE YOUR—"

I thought, "I will anticipate what word will come next, which will prove that I am controlling this event. The next word will be 'GUIDES.'" It wasn't:

"—MASTERS."

"Hmm," I thought, then, "Will you communicate with me again?"

The film strip jerked into motion once more, inching across my inner screen:

"YES. WHEN YOU MEDITATE."

That was the end of the transmission. The film strip disappeared. Although this never happened to me again—probably because I didn't meditate much formally on my own, over the years when I would begin to ponder something, thoughts would sometimes come into my mind, seemingly from nowhere, giving me guidance and insight.

*Saturday*

I went to the retreat bookstore to pick up some lecture tapes which I had ordered and found that they had not arrived. Shrugging off my annoyance, I decided that I was not meant to get them yet and went downstairs to have lunch. As I was getting food in the cafeteria line, a young woman named Alicia from my Reiki workshop invited me to eat with her.

When I sat down opposite her, I noticed someone to my right, and when I glanced over I saw that it was Maria Illo, a guitarist who had performed several times during the retreat. We began to talk, and she asked me why I had come there. I told her a little about David and his journals, and she was very interested in what I said. I did not mention David's name, however, just that he was my son.

Suddenly, very intensely, Maria asked, "What's his name?"

"David," I replied.

"I knew it!" she almost shouted back.

"Why?" I wondered with surprise.

Maria then told me that she had written a novel some time ago, and not only had the central character been named David but his personality also sounded very similar to my son's.

"Yes," Maria concluded, "the book is about David and his friend Michael."

I almost choked on my food when Maria said that, and a moment later I told her about the David-Michael connection. Maria seemed stunned by my account. After lunch we traded addresses, and she promised to let me know the next time she would be in North Carolina. I then decided to return to the bookstore to see if my tapes were there.

Earlier in the week I had spoken with LeRoy Zemke, and he had said that he wanted to meditate on whether or not he should give me a reading about David. I had not seen Zemke since then, although I had programmed my mind with the thought that I would meet him at an appropriate time. Walking up the stairs to the bookstore, I wondered if there was any chance I would be able to find him now, since the retreat had just ended at noon. As I passed by a sofa near the entrance of the bookstore, I glanced at two people seated there. One of them was LeRoy Zemke.

A few minutes later I was able to talk with him. He told me he had meditated on my request and had received the impression that I should first get an astrological reading, after which he would be willing to do a psychic reading about David. I was disappointed, as Edna had told me that

Zemke was very good, but I thanked him for taking the time to meditate, and he then left. I went into the bookstore to inquire about my tapes once more, but they still hadn't arrived, so I couldn't leave for home.

Standing in the bookstore, trying to decide what to do next, I noticed a tall, well-built man with a square jaw and gray at his temples, who was talking with two young women. I had seen him several times during the retreat, and something had been tugging at my mind about him. When he walked out of the bookstore, a thought suddenly came to me, and I went over to the two women and asked if the man had ever been an actor. One of the women said he had been.

I ran downstairs and caught up with the man in the lobby of the building and told him that I thought I knew him. He looked at me inquisitively but with no recognition. I said I believed he was the leading man for a summer stock company in Massachusetts when I was an apprentice actor there twenty-two years earlier. I was right—it was Doug Wilson.

"You've got a terrific memory," Doug told me. "I hardly even remember that I worked in theater."

We spoke for a few minutes about our summer at the Red Barn Theatre, and when I inquired about his present occupation he told me that for a number of years he had been the business manager for a metaphysical center in St. Petersburg, Florida. I asked who headed up the organization. "LeRoy Zemke," he answered.

I tried not to gape at this almost bizarre coincidence. When I finished my conversation with him, I returned to the bookstore. Ten minutes later my tapes arrived.

I went back to the lobby of the building and got into a short line at the check-out desk. While waiting for my turn, I began a conversation with an individual standing in line before me and mentioned how odd coincidences had been occurring to me lately. A man behind the desk, an S.F.F. volunteer, hearing our conversation, laughed.

"That's not coincidence. That's synchronicity [a word coined by Carl Jung, I later learned]. There *is* no such thing as coincidence. Those events are just part of a pattern that you're meant to experience."

Although I had been aware of this concept for many years, I now saw that it was fact. Our lives *are* patterned, just as I had myself said at the Duke service, and I was in the middle of a precise and detailed example of this phenomenon. Suddenly I began to see the pattern of the past six months: how I had been directed from one person to another, from one group or organization to another; how the right books conveniently had come into my hands; how the right ideas had suddenly popped into my head. It all fit neatly—very precisely stitched into a much broader tapestry of events, the scope of which was to become greater and greater with each passing year.

I checked out and drove home to Raleigh, feeling very high from the vibrations which had been generated at the retreat. Veronica later said I had acted as if I were drunk on Saturday and Sunday. To me, it felt like I had been plugged into a different part of the universe that week.

A month after the S.F.F. retreat, I received a note from Maria Illo, in response to some of David's writing that I had sent her:

> Just received your ms. Most exciting! The David-Michael reflection continues to astound! I have been

invited to Black Mountain, N.C. The woman who invited me is connected with Jim Goure—you might like to come there at that time (October 20). I feel this would be enjoyable for you & *some more connections.*

I burst into laughter at the synchronicity. I had not told Maria that others had referred me to Jim Goure.

A few days later, Edna called to invite me to Black Mountain for the same event. She said I should meet Jim Goure. Someone apparently wanted me to visit Black Mountain.

I had lunch with Preston in Durham, and we talked for four hours. She told me she feels David with her all the time. A few days later I mentioned this to Krista, who was now attending Duke, and she said David is also with her all the time. I began to wonder how many others David was watching over, recalling that Marian had said he was a master.

Five days before the Black Mountain retreat, I attended a picnic organized by Marian's group in Umstead Park, where David had sometimes run. The first thing Marian said to me when I saw her was that she had "met David walking on the astral path last night." They had been on a very white beach, with David nearer the water, and David had "just towered over" her. "He was skinny, wasn't he? I can't remember what we talked about, but I knew you'd be here today," she told me.

The first song sung that afternoon was "Michael Row the Boat Ashore," and then Marian lectured the large group at length on St. Michael and the masters. She told us that St. Michael equals truth, that a master in spirit can individually guide as many as 100,000 people on Earth, and that not personality but the *essence* of a person is what is important. David's essence was love, I thought to myself then. I also remembered a speaker at the S.F.F. retreat stating that the second-born child was love and Preston saying, "David was a love essence."

I drove up to Black Mountain with Edna for the three-day retreat led by Jim Goure, and the weekend produced further synchronicity. On Friday, I ran into Alicia, who had led me to Maria Illo at the S.F.F. retreat, and a few minutes later I talked to Maria herself. Then, on Saturday afternoon I was startled to hear Jim Goure speak of the Tree of Life and the New Jerusalem, two symbols which had been very important to David and which I had been trying to understand.

Sometime on Saturday I was introduced to Jim Goure by Edna, and when she told him about David's death, Jim asked if he might give me healing. I said yes, and he then took my hands, closed his eyes, and seemed to meditate for a few minutes. After he finished, he gave me instructions for a seven-step healing prayer he had developed and said I should use this for both myself and Veronica. As he rose to go, he said, "I've been waiting for you for a long time—welcome back," then walked away from me.

I was surprised by this unusual statement from someone I had just met, and Edna—who knew Goure well—said she had never heard him say such a thing before. I didn't know what he meant then and still don't, and there was a part of me at Black Mountain that didn't want to know.

The vibrations at this retreat were as high as they had been in Greensboro, and I felt very peaceful. I often walked through the woods immediately outside the Blue Ridge Assembly or sat with my back against a tree, meditating or writing in my journal. It soon became clear that I had been brought here to continue my inner healing process.

At one point during the retreat, some of us formed a meditation circle, standing and holding the hands of the person on either side of us. When the meditation ended, the young woman on my right said, "Wow, there sure was a lot of energy in your hand." I told her that was probably Reiki energy from the initiation I had received in Greensboro. On the drive back home, I became conscious of what felt like a band of energy around the top of my head. When I mentioned this to the man who was driving, he said that my crown chakra[19] had begun to open. I spent the rest of the drive home wondering what this weekend had been about.

✦ ✦ ✦

From my journal:

> Saw Edna for an hour, let her read *The Answer* [a story, adapted from one section of *The Wilderness*—that David had written for a high school English class]. She told me she couldn't believe David had written that—especially the dreams—at age sixteen. But she says I have something more important to do than publish David's writing . . .
>
> . . . I am basically calm now—not desperate about anything lately. Only get sad sometimes thinking of

David when young (8, 9, 10), when I see children. Many Davids died in Baja . . .

. . . Hadn't worked on David's journals for a while, but now type two pages: suddenly David comes in loud and clear and brilliant, sharply etched. It is a shock, as if he were standing beside me, talking. . . .

Re: the above entry—I believe that when I get a vivid image of David while I am transcribing his journals, he is actually *with* me. (And a voice in me says, "Right on!") So, if I'm more motivated while preparing David's writing, I'm actually getting help from him.

. . . David was at the point where both the light and dark flowers in his soul had begun to open their petals. As he wrote: "The dark shines in the dark." There is such a brilliance to the darkness . . .

As I was typing a page of David's journal one day, the following thought suddenly dropped into my head: "As love in the soul is beautiful, so too is pain in the soul beautiful—a dark beauty. Don't ever forget that." Did David send this thought, I wonder . . .

It is impossible to record all the little bits of synchronicity that I stumble across—people would say I'm just reading meaning into nothing. I might be, sometimes, but—for example—when I had been most interested in the idea of masters and angels, both Marian and Jim Goure lectured on these topics. Just coincidence? I don't think so.

Although I still wasn't fully aware of it, my inner path had begun to lead me through some very unusual terrain.

# 8

# dreams and symbols

The case against Outward Bound hung in limbo. Lawyers in North Carolina, Pennsylvania, Ohio, and California were checking out various problems and options. I found the whole thing frustrating. While this legal merry-go-round kept spinning, Outward Bound just hid behind its stone wall. I decided to hold a press conference. I wrote up a ten-page summary of my research into David's death and Outward Bound's safety record and gave or sent a copy to local news organizations, wire services, TV networks, and national magazines. Only a small number of reporters showed up, however, producing only minor coverage in Raleigh.

I was perplexed, until a local reporter told me that all the news-gathering organizations were afraid of being sued themselves if they printed any of my charges. The reporter said no one would touch the story until a suit had actually been filed in some court, after which there would be no legal risk to the media. So, although at least thirteen people had died on Outward Bound courses, I couldn't get the story out. Feeling blocked, I turned back to the inner search.

I suddenly became aware of dreams, to which I'd never paid much attention because I had almost never understood those that I had been able to recall. Nor did I have the patience to write down my dreams on a regular basis, for the ones that I did remember were often very long and complicated. However, I had a number of dreams about David after he died, and I was able to record parts of a few in my journal:

> I dreamed about David but can't remember the content of the dream. I do remember that at the end of it I hugged him and told him I loved him very much and always would. I kissed him on the cheek. My impression of our communication was of thought transference, rather than of speech.
>
> . . .
>
> [In a second dream,] I believe I was at another level. There were several persons around me, but I don't recall seeing them. I was sitting and David was standing in front of me as I kept repeating, over and over, "David and I are one." Then I saw a new poem of David's, which he was showing to me. I was suddenly filled with sadness and burst into tears. I felt several solicitous hands touch my back and I awoke to find that I was indeed crying, but—with my eyes closed—still hearing and seeing myself repeat, "David and I are one."
>
> . . .
>
> I dreamt of David once more, but as usual can't remember what. I think that we (and others) were again discussing something. David was sitting to my left, and I decided to touch his back. I placed my hand on his back—he was wearing a navy-blue sweater—and his back felt completely solid and fleshy. This impression pleasantly surprised me.

These dreams were later analyzed by Marcia Emery, Ph.D.,[20] who wrote that my first dream represented closure, plus the beginning of meaningful communication with David through my dreams, while the second dream indicated my unity with David and that David would be a guide or communicator for me in dreams and/or meditations. Although the most impressive feature of the third dream was David's solidity, Dr. Emery noted that the dark blue of David's sweater—a sweater he never had in life—is closely related to the color indigo, which symbolizes the intuitive realm and again suggested to her that David would be my spiritual guide.

I know I had other dreams with David, when we would be talking, but I never could bring back what we had discussed. The dreams, nevertheless, felt very real and very significant to me. Based on these dreams, I believe everyone has the opportunity in dreams to communicate with and get guidance from loved ones who have moved into other dimensions.

When I began to read David's journals, I discovered he had kept one journal for his dreams and had carefully studied their meanings. I was very much struck by some of these dreams, which often fell into specific categories.

One group of dreams, most of them recorded in his last two years, seemed to have been concerned with David's coming transition, although his journals don't show if he realized what the dreams meant. He had one at age sixteen in which he had died and didn't know what to do—"sorta being a ghost," he wrote. Then there was a constellation of extremely unusual and prophetic dreams—one major element of which was death—set down in *The Wilderness*. Some of the phrases David used in detailing these dreams were: "I am still living, and I should not be . . . trees weeping . . . there is no life left . . . someone beside me was . . . trying to let me see . . . he was crying, too, and I felt it tear my heart. . ." Significantly, the person sitting beside David was his own mirror image, whose "brown, wet hair glistened in the morning light," perhaps as if he had just come from the sea.

At about the same time in David's life, he dreamt of hearing about a boy—himself, he wrote—who was lost, and he saw a newspaper picture of the boy staring off into space. David then set off for home through a tunnel in which there were people "who were homo" going the opposite way. David *was* lost, of course, and a picture of him like the one he described—showing him staring off into space—*was* printed in our local paper during the search. Tunnels are typically reported in near-death experiences, and the people going the opposite way, then, were individuals going to be born—probably those who David would later help from spirit. "Home" might well have represented God for David. He also wrote about telephoning his family, dialing 919 (the Raleigh area code), and finally managing to get through after some difficulty. This action could be interpreted as David's successful post-death communications with me and others.

Shortly before David left for Duke, he dreamt of climbing a rope ladder and getting encouragement from above, finally having to squeeze through a small hole in a ceiling to get into an attic. To do so, he had to first drop two notebooks to the ground. The attic can be interpreted as the next life, and the two notebooks could be the two journals he had with him in Baja. Since David's journals were found, I had to recall that David also wrote, ". . . when I begin to think about people finding my journal . . ."

In a very emotional dream, David observed himself with Preston, whom he described as saying, "What if

David died?" He also reported that he was waking up depressed in the mornings, which could have been the result of learning about his transition in the dream state, something Marian had mentioned to me in a reading. Yet, significantly, while waiting for the start of his ride to California, David fell asleep and had a dream which he later described as "A happy dream, full of hope. A happy dream." This could mean that David had subconsciously come to terms with his approaching transition.

David's dreams also touched on past lives. At age seventeen he wrote of dreaming he had previously experienced two lives as a sailor. There also were the dreams of having lived at the time of Jesus and of having either known or seen Jesus. The short section in *The Wilderness* about a man walking and praying in the desert again could be a past-life remembrance, possibly again during Biblical times.

There was a dream which may be both reincarnational and prophetic. In it, David saw himself in a "quite long" race with a girl and ten or twenty other people. They ran up a hill, and both the hill and the girl suddenly seemed familiar to David, "from another race." David's crew in Baja numbered nine, plus the second crew of ten. Brenda could have been the girl whom David had known in another life. The race could have been the spiritual journey that these people—whom David had known in other lives—were attempting once more.

Another type of dreaming, described by Edgar Cayce and written about by David, was the phenomenon of spiritual teaching in dreams. "I'm learning so much in my dreams. I do feel that I can learn even while I don't remember them," David wrote. However, David did remember a few dreams which obviously were instructional.

The first showed David hugging a boy in a lake, which he interpreted as an attempt to spiritualize his homosexual impulses. The dream may also have been telling him that his yearning for boys had a spiritual basis, as Marian had said, and if he had understood this it could have helped him to accept his sexual orientation. Another dream having to do with self-acceptance was one in which David accepted a boy who was always clowning around in school and whom David hadn't liked before. This dream appears to refer to David's own tendency to clown and to be displeased with that quality in himself, then coming to terms with this in the sleep state.

David had many dreams which appeared to deal with his homosexual concerns, but I finally realized that—as many writers have pointed out—often all of the figures in a dream represent different parts of the dreamer's own psyche. Thus, David's dreams about boys may well have been an attempt to bring into reality his own view of masculinity: physical, athletic, fond of nature, determined, involved, active, but also gentle, kind, thoughtful, loving, cooperative, sensitive, and spiritual—an emerging paradigm for male identity in the New Age. This was highlighted by a dream in which Preston told David that he had "so much more love in you," which would have encouraged him to continue to be loving, and when David embraced a boy in a dream, he was, in fact, embracing his own self.

There also were unusual, sometimes symbolic, sometimes mystical dreams. One, at age seventeen, concerned angels protecting David and giving him strength, which he wrote was "almost real." This dream occurred just a day or two before he wrote, "God definitely cushioned me . . . by giving me a dream in which I was accepted at Harvard."

Since David had not been accepted there, Harvard—the top spot in higher education—could have been the dream symbol of heaven for David, meaning he had been accepted there. Then came the many dreams recorded in *The Wilderness*, all of which clearly are mystical in nature.

For a long time I couldn't figure out most of these dreams, but "little by little, bit by bit," my understanding of my dreams and David's finally dawned. I had to learn the language of dreams, which was symbols.

✦ ✦ ✦

Despite all my education, I knew nothing about symbols, but everywhere I looked in David's life, journals, poems, and stories, I saw symbol after symbol. I felt ignorant not understanding any of them. I finally mentioned this to my A.R.E. study group, and a couple of weeks later one of the women in my group gave me a small A.R.E. book about symbols. That was my launch pad for investigating symbols, and I soon headed back to the library to find additional information.

The first thing I wondered about were the meanings of David's names. I discovered that "David" meant "beloved of God." "Albert," David's middle name, meant "nobility of spirit" and "bright." And when David was young, Veronica had teasingly nicknamed him "Sasha," which turned out to mean "helper of men." I mused over "Schwimmer" and decided it connoted someone active, physical, in water—and water, symbolically, equates to spirit, which equates to God. David's names certainly seemed to fit.

I also wondered—as had David—at the recurrence of certain names, especially Steve and Debbie, in David's life. When I asked Marian about this, she said, "These are particular states of consciousness, which were of a vibration he had to tune in to—that he was being drawn into. The name that an individual takes is chosen before he's even conceived. When he first decides he's coming back to Earth, he knows what his astrological sign will be, he knows what numerological vibration he's going to use, and he knows the name that he will carry. It's his tool box."

Marian's impressions were backed up by Edgar Cayce: "Was one named . . . by chance? No! . . . The name is the sum total of what the soul-entity in all of its vibratory forces has borne toward the Creative Force itself. . . . All [names] have not only the attunement of a vibration, but of color, harmony, and all those relative relationships as one to another."[21]

Although I found this information interesting, I wasn't prepared for what I discovered in *Man Crowned King* by Robert Krajenke, a book which deals with the times of the first two Jewish Kings, Saul and David. Krajenke's discussion of King David is based mostly on Edgar Cayce readings, and—eerily—a lot of what he wrote sounded like my David:

> The significance of [King] David's name is measured by its meaning. All who are named David share in its vibrations. . . . "One especially endowed with gifts from higher forces."
>
> As a model for man, and as one that was to set an ideal, King David was . . . a well-rounded personality, versatile and gifted. And yet . . . he was an example of humility. . . .
>
> One of David's greatest attributes was his ability to celebrate. When he was sorrowful, he prayed; but when he was joyful, he danced and sang and played, giving praise and thanksgiving for the glories of God.

Throughout his life he remained keenly aware of Nature. He was attuned to the beauties in all forms and walks of life. He was able to see God manifesting in everything! . . . As a shepherd David treated his sheep tenderly, with loving care. So God said, "He understands how to pasture sheep; therefore he shall become shepherd of my flock, Israel."

There were many times David was not able to conquer desire. . . . He was tempted in many ways and succumbed often. . . . When he was in error, David acknowledged it and blamed no one else for his shortcomings. . . .

[Cayce said,] "Study as to why David is called 'a man after God's heart.' Not that he was free from fault, but that his purposes, his hopes, his fears were continually submitted to God."[22]

These many characteristics of King David—especially the one described in the last paragraph—were all reflected throughout David's journals, to such an extent that I could only marvel. "Israel" made my mind leap back to a passage in David's journals, entered when he was sixteen:

I've never written about my search, my Israel. I'm trying to find out—well, I've found some. I have faith enough to know there is a God, that he loves me, and that I'm trying to reach perfection through reincarnation—but I don't have enough faith in me that I'll make it. God, there is so much to learn.

I had even more to learn than David . . .

✦ ✦ ✦

On the cover of David's Duke journal he had made an unusual drawing. When I opened my first book of symbols, I found each part of the drawing defined. The circle represents higher planes, as well as the superconscious mind. The circle divided and the yin-yang symbol (the number 2) express the combination of masculine and feminine attributes, the idea of balance, and androgyny. The triangle (3), with its point up, represents light and the urge to escape toward the origin; the triangle, point down, symbolizes water, and man's lower nature. The cross (4) shows the descent of spirit into matter, and also the way out—the raising of spirit above matter. The five-pointed star (5), known as the Star of the Magi, was used by magicians as a seal to prevent the entrance of evil spirits.

The six-pointed star (6), or Solomon's Seal, also known as the Shield of David, is the star of universal love: love that has gone from passionate to compassionate. Six is a number of the Christ force in nature, representing balance, intuition, harmony and beauty—the urge to perfection. The sixth principle in man is the soul principle, which can't rest until it finds its spiritual home. Seven (7) is said to be the most sacred of all numbers, representing perfect order, god and nature (3+4) combined in man. The symbol of seven is the Shield of David with a dot in its center—the dot representing the "mystic center."

A number of the words on the cover had been worn out by David carrying the journal with him all the time. The remaining words in the circle read: PEACE, ONE WORLD, THINK, ON EARTH, PEACE GOODWILL TO MAN . . . CONFUSION AND WEARINESS BUT ALL I FIND IS A . . . DOOR LEADING TO ANOTHER DOOR AH GOD SOMETIMES I WISH . . . WHISPERING I HEAR NOTHING IS FORGOTTEN . . . NOTHING AT ALL

*The Cover of David's Duke Journal*

WILL IT GOD WILL THE CIRCLE BE UNBROKEN
... I DO NOT KNOW MY SOUL TOO WELL ... SAY
AMEN. In the upper-right corner are the words: God Bless
us all, and please, Lord, save me and him. Amen.

I noticed there are twelve small triangles in the drawing, and found that the number twelve symbolizes cosmic
order, spiritual perfection and completion.[23] I doubted that
David knew the meaning of most of these symbols on a
conscious level, but I was certain he did know on the
intuitive level, which was why he had chosen to place this
unusual design on the cover of his journal. The design
represented David's spiritual path.

Then I recalled the way for working out the number
for any name or series of numbers. The numbers are added
together and are reduced to a figure from one to nine, or
to the master numbers: 11, 22, and 33—which may not
be reduced any further. The letters of the alphabet are
numbered as below:

1 2 3 4 5 6 7 8 9
A B C D E F G H I
J K L M N O P Q R
S T U V W X Y Z

Out of curiosity, I sat down to figure out some numbers
and discovered a few surprising correlations:

BIRTH DATES:
David        1/27/1959 = 34 = 7
Veronica     7/07/1937 = 34 = 7
My mother    8/11/1905 = 34 = 7

NAMES:
David Albert Schwimmer    92 = 11
Krista Ann Schwimmer      83 = 11
Eric Schwimmer            74 = 11

My book of symbols told me that 11 symbolizes a new and more advanced cycle of manifestation, emerging from the wisdom learned in the previous cycle. Eleven therefore can be seen as the number for reincarnation, in consciousness if not in body. Also, on the physical plane, 11 is the symbol of mastery, as 22 is on the mental plane, and 33 is on the spiritual plane.[24] Not only were my mother's day of birth 11 and Krista's day of birth 22, but when I checked I found that the name "David" equals 22, as does "Albert," and that Eric's birth number is 33. Although I still didn't understand the full import of all these numbers, I felt their presence was significant.

More than names and numbers, though, were several very major symbols in David's life, which he had lived and written about: trees, mountains, earth, water, and the New Jerusalem. In late March Debbie's mother had come by to tell us she had contributed money in David's name to plant two trees in Israel. At the time I didn't notice the symbolism of that gift, but later—thinking of Israel, a growing tree, nature, and David's novel *The Wilderness*--I decided to look up "tree" and found:

> For the return of oneness . . . it is necessary to blend . . . the positive and negative aspects, the perfect union of the male and female. This is symbolized by . . . a tree with a serpent twined around it . . . or the spiral evolution of the soul through following One God. . . . The tree, with its roots underground and its branches rising to the sky, symbolizes an upward trend; in this way it is similar

. . . to climbing the upward path [in consciousness] and climbing a ladder or stairway.[25]

Another book added:

> The world is seen as a cosmic tree; its starry leaves . . . hold the records of past and future, of destiny; victory over death, immortality; those that shed their leaves "die in order to live." . . .
>
> The "Tree of Life" often has a life-giving fountain at its foot; an ancient tree . . . may stand for the growth and development of psychic life: prophetic trees . . .[26]

These definitions vividly reminded me of David's writing. I thought of a children's book he wrote at the age of twelve, "The Chronicles of Aur-Bon," which included a tree, a fountain, and a white castle in one of its images. A castle, I discovered, is a symbol of the transcendent soul and the heavenly Jerusalem.[27]

Earth represents the material plane, is the "far country" of the prodigal son, or man's conscious mind. Water is the beginning and end of all things on Earth, immersion in water signifying death on one hand and rebirth on the other—rebirth of the spiritual man. A mountain is the realm of meditation, mysticism, wisdom, the contact between heaven and Earth, the place of revelation, and the entrance to the other world.

The significance of the last symbol was handed to me when I ordered the Edgar Cayce book that interpreted the Book of The Revelation.[28] Revelation 3:7 includes the phrase "he that hath the key of David." The entranced Cayce said that "he" is the Overself, "the individualized portion of God." The "tree of life" (2:7, 22:2) is the flow of subtle energy for supply, healing, and growth, which the soul furnishes through a perfectly synchronized endocrine system. "The morning star" (2:28) Cayce identified as the original state of illumination, which would eventually be returned to each person, permitting everyone to be a "complete master of his environment."

Speaking of 21:4—"for the former things are passed away"—Cayce noted that "a new heaven" meant a new, perfected state of consciousness in which man did not desire to sin. Thus, the New Jerusalem is not a place, but a state of cosmic consciousness, an experience of the soul. The New Jerusalem is a symbolic, holy place in the souls of those individuals who have put away earthly desires and have now "become the New Jerusalem, the undertakings, the new desires."

Also quite interesting was the meaning of 3:13, which Cayce explained as, "The man who has overcome on this [material] level, the Overself says, will be in possession of his entire soul record of all his experiences in the earth and in possession of [the] new consciousness (New Jerusalem) which will make it unnecessary for him to reincarnate any more. He will now be in complete God consciousness."

Summing up this Cayce material, the implication appeared to be that any man or woman acting in complete super-consciousness would be as a god. That has been the goal of mystics through the ages, and the story of their seeking—"Israel" meaning "seeker." This is the explanation of the state of Christhood—the archetype of the spiritually evolved and spiritually conscious person—about which Jesus stated:

Ye are gods. [John 10:34]

. . .

I say unto you, he that believeth in me, the works
that I do shall he do also; and greater works than these
shall he do. [John 14:12]

. . .

If ye have faith as a grain of mustard seed . . . nothing
shall be impossible to you. [Matthew 17:20]

After reading the meanings of all the symbols which
had permeated David's life, I felt convinced that David's
higher self had deliberately and clearly used these symbols
to communicate with David—and now with me. I had
been given a crash course in mystical symbolism.

# 9

# spiritual credentials

Christmas was approaching, and I was certain we all dreaded its arrival. I found it impossible to believe that we could be joyous without David's physical presence beside us to celebrate the season. I knew he was around in spirit, but my emotional self refused to be consoled by that belief. To compound the problem, my income was less than half that of the previous year. I simply wasn't able to sell life insurance the way I had the year before. Veronica said it didn't really matter. The worst had already happened, she told me; nothing could be worse.

Someone in my A.R.E. group had invited me to attend a candlelight service to be held a few days before Christmas at Unity Church. The service was healing, and at the end everyone was given a candle to light. Attached to each candle was a blessing. Mine was Luke 2:40: "And the child grew and became strong, filled with wisdom; and the favor of God was upon him." I decided that this passage referred to my spiritual birth this year and that it had originated from David, since David had several times quoted from Luke in his journals and since a major character in David's novel—one of David's alter egos—had been named Luke. On December 24, to honor David, I went to Christmas mass at St. Michael's. The gospel reading was from Luke.

I reluctantly began to acknowledge that something was happening in my life. For some reason, David's death was opening spiritual doors for me, as my meditative visions of open entranceways had shown me. I was continually being presented with opportunities to become more aware, to acquire more knowledge about the nature of existence in and out of the flesh. However, I resisted the process because I had started to walk this path for David, not for myself. I pushed aside the thought that the path was mine.

I hadn't embarked on a spiritual quest when David had died. I didn't even know what a spiritual quest *was*. I thought of a spiritual quest as a trek to India or Tibet, not as a journey through states of being which would be provided for me right here in the U.S. Nor did I care about myself. My ego had crashed into the fact of David's death with such violence that I hardly seemed to exist any more. I wanted nothing for myself.

Yet my spiritual journey had begun, if unknowingly, when I had joined the national A.R.E. and my local Search For God group. I had known about the A.R.E. for twenty years but had never become a part of it. Looking back, though, I can see that if I hadn't joined the Raleigh group in 1978, I wouldn't have known about Marian and might never have met her. Furthermore, my group was ultimately very important to me—first in helping me to get re-structured inside myself after David's death, then in giving me a solid spiritual grounding for all that I would experience in the next ten years. Marian's meetings served the same purpose.

Still, if I had known what path I was being led to follow, I probably would have rebelled. I distrusted religion, since it was man-made, and I looked with suspicion at the concepts of faith and spirituality, since these seemed completely insubstantial and therefore unbelievable. But I couldn't dismiss as lightly direct personal spiritual experiences or verifiable information from psychics—and I had a pragmatic streak in me: if it works, use it.

Going to psychics worked. Most of the information they gave me was either factually correct or at least made good sense. Sometimes different psychics even gave identical information. Areas they repeatedly brought up about me were writing, teaching, and psychic abilities. Howard Granger had told me I would publish David's writing but would write something additional beside it—a different viewpoint altogether. That different viewpoint, of course, turned out to be this book. Douglas Johnson had noted that I had psychic and writing abilities.

Marian had some things to say about me as well. At a personal reading with her on March 11, she began by saying that the primary purpose of her readings was to give people their "spiritual credentials," and this is what she would do. I had no idea what she was talking about, but I was game for whatever she had to tell me. Marian began by looking at the palms of my hands, then exclaimed, "Good God, how psychic are you?" I told her not at all as far as I knew. "Well, your hands look like mine," she responded. "They're like the road maps of time. You have a lot of psychic ability, intuition. You're clairsentient—you just *know*. All of the answers you searched for so hard to find from other people—you already knew these within yourself.

"Tremendous sensitivity, a great deal of feeling. You've been in female embodiment a good many lifetimes, so much of your sensitivity comes from that. You've got healing abilities—many marks of healing. Look at the Saint Andrew's Cross! Not only do you have a Saint

Andrew's Cross, you have it *double*. You'd make a fantastic healer! You've also got a great deal of mysticism—a very large mystic cross on your hand. As you move toward your fifties, you're going to find yourself opening up very much on a mystical level—and very much into healing.

"They're good hands—good strong hands, but the hands of a very sensitive person. A lot of guidance. I get good feelings about where you're coming from. There's a lot of spiritual protection on your hands. I noticed that over and over. Your life line is reinforced. You're being saved for something very special, because there's too much protection on your hands for this to be chance. You're stubborn—God, you're hard-headed."

I laughed and told her that was quite true. She asked if I had done any writing before. Not for publication, I answered. "But you do have the ability to write. That's in your hand. I very strongly feel that you're meant to make this experience count for something, to help others. And this is not just of your own doing—David is the one who wants his journals published."

As Marian released my hands, I asked her about the decision to sue Outward Bound. She said I was being used as an instrument to put a stop to something, that the suit would be successful, and that it would save the lives of others. "You are going to find support from an unexpected quarter in this," she noted. Events later proved her right about these impressions. Then she presented me with my "spiritual credentials."

"You are an extremely old soul," she began, "one who has been a teacher in many, many lifetimes and also in many, many times between embodiments and on other planes of existence." Marian said that in past lives I had been a dancer and composer—music had been important;

also painting; acting, the theater; that I had been involved in all of the arts. Marian had no way of knowing about my theater background, nor that I had studied the violin when I was young. And I don't know how many times since then I have met people who have looked me in the eye and said, "Oh, you're a teacher, aren't you?"

"Basically, you are mystical," she continued. "You came onto the Earth plane this lifetime for two different reasons: to finish up as much of your karma as you could and at the same time to move into a cosmic mission of healing, of counseling, of teaching, and of giving guidance to others through your own experience." This impression proved to be stunningly accurate, and totally unforeseen by me. "There will be a purification within your own soul, which will ultimately lead to a tremendous spiritual awakening, and you will in turn begin to speak and share this with others.

"You will write a book, and out of it will come a great deal of revealing of things that you have never revealed before. Things that will have a lot of mystical qualities to them. I see a manuscript and feel it will be well-received. I don't feel this will be David's writing." Marian saw that in the book there would be photographs. Although I had no photographs then, I later received some from David's Baja crew, a few of which are in this book. The cover photograph—of the Sea of Cortez—was one of those sent to me. At that time, however, I had no plans whatever to write this book.

"Most of your karma in this lifetime is of a subtle nature, not so much of the heavy karma that involves other people, but dealing with you as an individual. You're very close to completing what you contracted to do karmically in this lifetime. Basically, you're on a cash-and-carry basis as far as karma is concerned. If you step out of line, if you deliberately do something to hurt somebody, you can expect retribution to be very swift and very sure. But as long as you're not motivated by a desire to cause harm or humiliation, a lot of your actions are now above the law of karma, so that you're coming very much under the law of grace." I was tickled by Marian's "cash-and-carry-karma," and that still amuses me. But despite the humor, she was right, for if I stepped out of line even a little, I was immediately hit with some minor karma.

"You are also going to find yourself being led more and more into service, and you will be finding yourself turning more away from the mundane world and much more into writing and into dealing with people. I see another major move coming in the next seven years, and it will take you near a large body of water." All this also proved to be extremely accurate.

"You are on the fifth ray, and the fifth ray is the green ray of balance, of healing, of mind, of service to humanity. Here we find the peacemakers, the harmonizers, the healers, the teachers, the communicators of ideas, the actors, the writers, the musicians—because all of this is a form of healing and balance. Invariably, the fifth ray person must choose an occupation or an avocation where he can be involved in service to other people. That's where your fifth ray pattern takes you." Marian didn't know that I began as an actor in college and have acted periodically ever since.

"The aura around you has primarily blues, and a turquoise—which is an unusual color in an aura. It shows that you are under the protection of an Atlantean master. It also shows a great deal of healing energy, and from your fingertips there is a blue-green energy, which indicates that the healing ability is being activated. I did not notice that the first time I saw you. You have somehow tapped into another level of consciousness." Years later, in past-life regressions, I saw myself in Atlantis in four different lives. The blue-green energy she saw from my hands must have been Reiki.

Marian went on to tell me that my inner master teacher is a man named Joseph. In the post-Civil War period —when I was in a male embodiment—he had been a former slave, one who chose to stay with me after the war. He was quite an elderly man by the time he came into my life then, but he taught me a great deal about forgiveness, about love, and about tolerance.

"He is one that went clear back to the time of Atlantis with you, when you had been a student of his there in a healing temple," Marian said. "You had been very resentful of the authority trip he had put on you at that time, and so you had turned away from his wisdom. When it finally came time for you to come into contact with him again, he came in a form that was alien to you—because he came of the black race and had absolutely nothing that was of worldly goods. Yet he still brought the same wisdom that he had before and again laid them before you. But this time you were able to listen to him and not judge by what *appeared* to be, but to hear what really *was*. He really is a very wise man. He is not an ascended master—he has one more lifetime on Earth. He's a step ahead of you on the path, but he is still very much a spiritual brother." Much later, during a past-life regression, I recalled that past life with Joseph.

Marian then went on to discuss another of my inner teachers. "Your psychic development is coming under the guidance of Cassandra, who was probably the greatest psychic that we have any record of. She was a priestess in the Temple of Jupiter, in ancient Greece, approximately 2,400 years ago. You were then functioning as a prophetess, as an oracle, very much under holy vows in the Temple of Jupiter—and in that lifetime David was with you there, both of you in female embodiment. Cassandra teaches you mind over matter. She brings you the ability to create, to use your own mind to be able to open up your own psychic centers. She is helping you to become more aware of your powers—not to look outside yourself but within." Later, another psychic also told me I had been in Greece, and two of my friends—in regressions—saw me in Greece with them. When David was eleven, he read *I Capture The Castle,* a children's book whose central character, Cassandra, kept journals. She was David's inspiration for starting his own journals.

Marian now mentioned another of my past lives. "You were involved with David during the period of the Inquisition, when you were being accused of heresy—at that time you had been manifesting a great deal of your psychic ability. You two came from the same town in Spain, so you were in the same vibration. But I very definitely see you being put to death at that time for what you believed in. And you've been trying to find something to believe in ever since. Ever since the time of the Inquisitions, you have been fearful of making a total commitment to any one thing." That certainly fit, I told Marian, especially my feelings about organized religion, and she went on to say, "Because all too vivid in your memory is your time on the rack—when you begged to die." No wonder I was distrustful of religion and authority!

Finally, when I showed Marian a long list of current and past friends, including her, she responded: "All of us go back to a time in Atlantis, where we had been much involved in temple life. Each one of us has strayed very far away from the spiritual path. Each one of us here—and that includes me—at some point or another moved away from the truth as it was given to us in the beginning—we misused our psychic power then. Each one of us has returned now to put things into balance once more. Each one here is in a position of trying to awaken again their own creative abilities to bring back the old Atlantean powers, but to use them in a constructive way—on a personal level, as well as on a planetary level—for balance and healing. Because spirit *is* like water, seeking always its own level—those who are at the same level of consciousness do come very much into relationship with you.

"So, all these were Atlanteans, and all were Hebrews in bondage in the 450 years before Moses led his people out of bondage. All of them were also involved in the Negro—the black-white—situation, at a time of bondage, with the exception of David. Also, every one of them has a very singular vibration—an *intense* desire to be free. And there isn't a person on this list who takes orders very well from anyone else. That's the truth!"

I just roared with laughter at Marian's last comment, since it certainly applied to me, and she laughed as well. Marian's only other impression about my past lives was to mention in passing that my son Eric and I had been priests together in Atlantis. Later, in 1981, she told Krista that she, David, and I had been Essene scribes, recorders of wisdom, all males, before the time of Jesus, and that was why all three of us had come to be writers in this life.

"You've got yourself together, and I'm awfully glad," Marian concluded. I replied that my energy was better. "You feel David's energy very closely—because he's very much with you, because your work is beginning with him, and you know it."

Did I know it? I wasn't sure. All I was certain of then was that I wanted the world to know David and to walk with me on the extraordinary path which had been laid out before me.

# 10

## noreen

One morning the mail brought me an invitation to participate in a research project at the Psychical Research Foundation with an ESP sensitive from Virginia named Noreen Renier. Noreen would be trying to communicate with discarnates, the attempt to take place on a Sunday.

It snowed heavily that day, however, and the session was cancelled. The next afternoon I was called and told the meeting had been rescheduled for that evening. I had doubts about going, since there still was a great deal of snow on the roads and I had no chains for my tires, but I finally decided to take a chance and drove to Durham. When I arrived, I found the other participants already seated on pillows on the carpeted floor of the PRF meditation center. The only person there whom I had ever seen before was a PRF staffer I once met briefly.

A Ph.D. clinical psychologist from the University of Virginia Medical School who would conduct the informal experiment introduced Noreen, an attractive dark-haired woman with a light build, seemingly in her upper twenties in age. The psychologist, a man, explained that while Noreen was in trance two spirit personalities—identified as "Singh," an oriental woman, and "Robert," background unknown—might speak through Noreen.

After these preliminaries had been completed, the PRF staffer asked several people, including me, to place personal objects in envelopes. I hadn't expected to be involved, but I took an envelope and put my wallet into it. The PRF staffer then gave all of the envelopes to Noreen, who closed her eyes and quickly picked an envelope at random. It turned out to be mine. Noreen requested the first name of whoever owned the envelope's contents, and I told her.

Noreen spoke briefly about me, my family and my job, but although what she said was correct it did not interest me very much; however, I said nothing. Noreen then asked the psychologist to put her into a trance state, but as he began the induction, Noreen's trance personality Singh abruptly interrupted him, saying, "Words not necessary. Singh come speak to gentleman. Be most happy to continue in line man more interested in." My attention sharpened when I realized Singh had correctly perceived that I'd been bored by what Noreen had told me so far. I also was fascinated by this exotic personality. Thinking of David, I replied, "The past year."

Singh said, "Year you speak, '78? Correct?"

"Yes."

"Lost . . . feel lost person around gentleman. Understand?"

"Yes." I certainly did. Singh had apparently picked up David. I was very struck by her use of the word "lost" rather than "dead," since that had been the key word in both my mother's and my premonitions, and since David had been lost at sea.

Singh continued, "Name, please."

"David."

"Much love . . . David."

Tears came to my eyes. I had not said who David was—he could have been anyone, yet Singh had conveyed the only thing David could give me now: his love, which he had offered so freely to everyone while he was alive.

There was a long pause, and then Noreen came out of trance. She asked if David was dead and—when I said he was—whether I wanted to communicate with him. If I can, I replied. "Oh, dear, yes, you can, yes, you can," Noreen responded vivaciously, taking a deep breath. "I feel a young person is around you—the face more long than wide or fat. I feel this person has eyes that are full of trust and love. Hair is thick and high. Interest was wide. Would these be characteristics of David?" I told Noreen they were.

She asked if there was anything I wanted to know about David. Her question caught me off guard, and I could only think to ask her for the exact time of David's death. Noreen panted three times in a shallow manner, then in a low voice said, "Can't . . . can't *breathe* . . . throat, chest . . . can't breathe . . . oh . . . can't breathe."

Noreen began to cry. She seemed to be experiencing David's body at the moment of his death in the Sea of Cortez, but she finally told me she was unable to pick up the date or time that David had died, since she was not good at numbers. Then Robert spoke through Noreen but could only contribute that David's death had been an accident and that David had a brother. Noreen came out of trance again, asking why her chest was hurting, and I told her David had probably drowned, at sea.

The psychologist now asked for more information about David's last moments. "There is a lot of disbelief that this is happening," Noreen responded. "I don't feel that much fear at the end, because I feel he was a happy-go-lucky person—it sounds ridiculous, but I don't feel a lot of fear at all." Noreen now attempted to communicate directly with David, "David, David, David—talk to me."

Suddenly she exclaimed, "Good heavens—the man [David] is telling me a *poem*. I feel like it might be significant to David or something you know about David. Does that make any sense?" I told her it did. "The poem has the word 'leaf' or 'leave' in it. Maybe the title of the poem—'leaf' or 'leave.'"

This was extremely meaningful. No one in the world except me could have known what this referred to, since I had told no one yet. When mulling over what the title of David's book should be, I had thought of his journal and its pages. The fact that pages are *leaves* reminded me of how often David had written of trees and leaves—sometimes in poetry, sometimes in prose—and what a nice quibble it was to think of the leaves of a tree and the leaves of the journal. Then the title of David's book had suddenly dropped into my head, *DAVID: leaves from the journal of a soul*. I also had to remember the dream in which David had shown me a new poem.

"He used to shock people, tease people," Noreen went on. "David was very casual about his attitude. He says, if he said he was handsome, I'd think he would be lying. *He's* telling me that, *I'm* not saying that: I don't knock anyone's looks. . . . He's saying you weren't at all good at taking kidding. I just don't think you were that good of a sport, sir."

This issue was probably the main bone of contention between David and me, as far as I was concerned. David never seemed to know when to stop kidding me, and he would occasionally anger me, since I was sensitive to criticism and at times took his kidding as criticism, especially when David was young. "What else would you say about him, David?" Noreen asked. "'Not bad shape for an old man,' he says." Typically, David just couldn't resist a final wisecrack. With that Noreen ended her reading.

I was totally convinced that David had communicated with me through Noreen, and the most impressive aspect of the session was David's humor. I felt it was *the* critical evidence establishing David's survival. The following months and years strengthened my belief in this, for David's humor continually cropped up in situations concerning him—with family, friends, psychics. David seemed to speak through this humor, telling us, "What is my most *obvious,* immediately recognizable outer trait? Poking fun. Teasing. Prodding you. Who else but me, David, would crack a joke at a time like this? No father would make jokes about his recently deceased son, nor would a close friend. No psychic would dare joke with a bereaved parent. I'm the one making the jokes, as I always did! So you know that this is me, David, telling you—I'm O.K.!"

Even Veronica, as severely wounded as she was, couldn't escape David's irrepressible humor. A couple of weeks after the search had ended, she was trying to answer letters of sympathy and was having a very difficult time of it. She became completely mired in attempting to compose a note to the local Harvard alumni representative who had interviewed David for his application to Harvard, which, of course, had not accepted David.

"I don't know what to write," Veronica said. "Do you know what I feel like writing?"

"No, what?" I answered.

"Harvard's loss is Heaven's gain."

I immediately felt this was David speaking through Veronica, since—it must be kept in mind—she was in no joking mood then and for long afterwards. From where would this humor originate but David?—David trying to lighten his mother's dark mood.

Nor did David ever let up with his humor. Several years later, when I happened to think of David being lost, I heard his voice clearly in my head, saying: "Lost? Who's lost? *I'm* not lost—*you* are! Lost? Ridiculous!" Another time, when I thought, "Oh, David, will I ever get over your death?" David's immediate response was, "No, you won't. You're a hopeless romantic." Although I was sitting in a crowded commuter train at the time, I burst out laughing.

I was certain that David was using humor as the prime method for establishing his continuing existence; to me it was the most significant proof of his survival.

✦ ✦ ✦

Eight weeks after my meeting with Noreen, she returned to Durham, continuing her research, and I had a private session with her at the PRF center. When I told her I wanted additional information about David, she said she hadn't prepared herself to do trance work that day, didn't know if she would do well, but agreed to try.

Since three psychics had mentioned David's head, I asked Noreen if there had been any pressure in his head. "David—let me go into your head," Noreen whispered, closing her eyes. There was a pause, then, "Oh, my head hurts me—oh, my head, my head." The tone of Noreen's voice strongly indicated that she felt considerable pain, and she touched the left side of her head with her left hand, just where Douglas Johnson had touched his head, but she couldn't explain the cause of the pain.

I told Noreen that David had been aboard a boat out on the water and asked her what had happened to him after he was separated from his companions. "I feel a strong breeze coming up," Noreen replied. "The water doesn't seem to be that warm. I feel a chill coming around me. A lot of choppiness around me in the water."

"O.K., David, what happened?" Noreen continued softly, then paused for a few moments. "God, it seems like it was just—whoosh—under, just fell, just under." Her voice now came in a whisper. "Where am I going? Oh, God, there goes my head again . . . I feel like he drowned . . . the boat was capsized. It was severely damaged." When I later transcribed Marian's first reading, I was impressed by the similarity of her words to Noreen's: ". . . it was like—whoosh—and then that was it . . . something going under . . . capsized."

I had brought with me a mystical drawing David had made sometime in his last year.[29] I was convinced that this drawing was designed as a post-death communication from David, but I couldn't understand the meaning of its symbols. I asked Noreen to open her eyes and handed her the drawing. She studied it and then commented, "Bars . . . ah, look: they're crooked, or broken, or damaged. It's part of *him* that was damaged—there's some damage in him . . ." Marian had told me that she felt David had had a heart condition, but although David had noted a problem in his running a few months before he went to Baja, a routine physical examination he took for Outward Bound did not reveal anything wrong. It did show that David had a heart murmur, but I was told that was common with long-distance runners. Still, I also had to think of the heart as a symbol.

"David was straddling this fence, this life—whatever this was—trying to balance himself, till he came to this area." Noreen pointed to the bent part of the fence. "I feel another state of *being* here." Based on Noreen's impressions, I decided that the fence was his life, separating the physical and spiritual planes, with the bottom horizontal bar representing the body, the middle bar the mind, and the top bar the soul. When I asked about the ball, she said David told her, "It's part of my childhood—it's part of my past." So then the left side of the fence had to be David's childhood, and if each space in the fence from left to right represented two years of David's life, then the bent rods enclosed his eighteenth year: damage or death.

Noreen next spoke about the symbol that looked like an odd tree, which she said was the Tree of Life. I asked her what the small boxes represented, and she said these were states of consciousness—"different *spaces* of *reality*—different planes, or different ways to tune in. I can't believe he was as young as he was, because he seems to have a great deal of wisdom and insight, and if people talked to David, I don't think they would understand half the time what he was talking about unless they were really super highly evolved."

The "tree" also reminded me of the Menorah, and months later I found the following:

> The spiritual significance of Hanukkah lies in the Feast of Lights. . . . A special candle, the shammes, is lit [first], to be used to light the other candles. It is said that this shammes is endowed with special meaning, as the flame creates another flame without losing its brightness. This is representative of man giving of his love to his fellow man without losing anything of himself.[30]

I felt that David's life was like a shammes, lighting up others, who in turn would light many more.

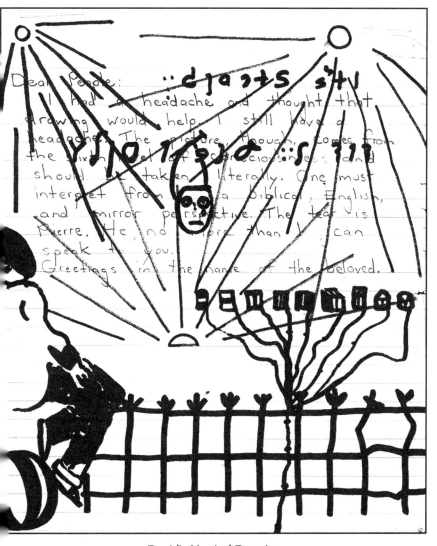

*David's Mystical Drawing*

I questioned Noreen about the three suns in the drawing, and she responded, "Oh, the father, son, and holy ghost—or you can call them body, mind, and soul. The way he's got them is really beautiful, too—like a triangle." Veronica and I both instinctively felt that it is a rising sun toward the bottom of the drawing—body and mind ascendant, the soul rising. Violet Shelley wrote, "The rising sun is the symbol of the rising of man's consciousness, and 'facing the east' represents man's desire to accomplish this."[31] Note that the body of the figure in the drawing is facing right, which would be east if the drawing were a map.

The most perplexing symbol in the drawing was what seemed to be a mask hung on a nail, with a tear dropping from its left eye. Since David had always clowned around and thought of himself as a sort of clown in high school, I felt this was the mask of a clown. And since he had *hung up* the mask which he had worn in this life, this symbol seemed to be prophesying his death: the dying clown. David had written in his journal:

> I had been to a mime workshop. Walking around in "whiteface" yesterday, I found myself hiding behind my face, yet not really there: Pierre was there with hunched shoulders and an unhappy mouth and a single tear of Joyce . . . yet . . . I was not there, David was. Yet Pierre still, too, with David, and all my other tears and smiles.

In May of 1977 David had created some fictional alternative personalities—Alice, Martha, and Pierre—which David had termed "members of my mind" and about which he had periodically written in his journal. When I asked Noreen about these, she said Alice represented David's sensuality/sexuality, Martha symbolized domesticity, and Pierre "was more or less his philosopher, or his intellect."

I now focused on the tear running down the face of the mask, telling Noreen that David had called it "the single tear of Joyce," which he had connected with a tear in his heart and with Pierre. "A tear," Noreen told herself. "Ah, Pierre, why are you? . . . the tear . . . I feel he's saying we're both pretty dumb, because it's very evidential, if either one of us has done any reading—" I burst out laughing at this: it certainly sounded like David "—we should be able to figure out what the hell the *tear* is." I laughed again and told Noreen it didn't matter, as I thought I probably could find the meaning of the tear later. I felt that David's caustic comments were a deliberate prod to get me to research the origin of the tear.

Noticing the word "headache" in the drawing, Noreen asked why David had had headaches. I said I didn't know. "Where I picked up the headache was on the left side," Noreen replied, again indicating the left side of her head. "When I first started meditating I got tremendous headaches. But the pressure [in David's head]—it was just terrible pain." Remembering Howard Granger, I repeated the word "pressure." "Pressure, yes—just shooting out," Noreen responded.

She asked if David had read the Bible a lot. I said yes and that recently I'd felt he had been trying to get me to read it. "He's bringing you a lot of awareness," Noreen replied. "I don't know how much you believe in reincarnation, but I think he was here for a purpose, and you might have a lot to do with the purpose, because through you—in your change, in your attitude, in your openness, or your perceptions being changed—I feel you're going to open up a lot of other people. I don't know what you're writing about, but—whether they believe or not—it's just to show them, to say, 'Look, this is what *I* found out.' I feel like you're going to help a lot of people."

Several years later I happened to read *Raymond*, by Sir Oliver Lodge, whose son Raymond died in World War I. What the medium, Mrs. Leonard, told Lodge expanded Noreen's last comment for me, and I began to understand why I would write this book:

> [This is] something which is only symbolic: . . . a cross falling back on you, dark and heavy looking, but as it falls it gets twisted around and the other side seems all light, and the light is shining all over you . . . a beautiful light. The cross is a means of shedding real light. . . .
>
> Your son is the cross of light, and he is going to be a light that will help you; he is going to help, too, to prove the truth to the world. You know, but others, they do so want to know.[32]

Noreen told me that David had been "*extremely* psychic, but it was almost a psychic awareness too fast, too soon, too strong." She added, "I feel that David couldn't turn it off—didn't know how to go back and forth, like I do." When I mentioned that Marian had said that David could see through to people's souls, Noreen replied, "Oh, yes. This is how I feel most psychics do readings, because the soul has all the information." That explained David's mystical writings, as well as his ability to understand people, I thought.

I handed Noreen a copy of David's journal cover and she tuned in to it for a few moments, then said, "David, I feel, had been on this Earth plane before. He has to have been to be so highly evolved. At eighteen no child could be this evolved. He came here for a purpose—he's accomplished his purpose." I wanted to learn what that purpose was. "I know it's through *you*," Noreen responded, "because you're a different man today from the man I saw that first night. The man I see today is changing right in front of me—the man tomorrow will be different. Ah, David, you're doing a pretty good job on your father, I'll tell you that. Oh, dear, this is so beautiful, just so beautiful."

I asked Noreen what kind of work David was doing on the other side. "Everyone says the standard thing, but I feel something different about David. I feel like David, although he's passed on, has got a lot of energy on that side too and is still working his little butt off. Although he was not attached to this plane while on Earth, David *is* still very much attached to *this* plane, though he is not here, and is now doing things to create or make things happen here. I don't know how to really explain this."

I told Noreen I understood what she was saying. David, loosely attached to the Earth plane while here, had been involved and very interested in other planes while he was alive. Now, he has reversed this pattern: although on another plane, he has not abandoned the Earth plane but has taken a keen interest in making certain things happen here on Earth—through spirit—that he could not cause to happen while he was in flesh. David was still straddling the fence.

When I mentioned Veronica, Noreen observed, "There's a flower I see him giving her. It's not a lavish flower—it looks like a simple flower—I think it's lavender or purple—a little bit of yellow in the center. I want to give it to her." That didn't mean anything to me, so I asked for the time of David's death again. Noreen finally got the number nine, which she said might mean 9:00. I also questioned her about David's solo in Baja, since I still felt David had had some sort of mystical experience then.

Noreen seemed to slip spontaneously into trance and began to whisper, as David, "Ah, father, to share with you the *light*, the brightness of the light that was revealed to me—the voices that I heard—" Noreen paused. "I'm so sorry—I'm blocking him out. It's my ego. David, please work hard with me. I feel incompetent with you, David—you've got so much wisdom . . . ah, but he says, Wisdom is sometimes a fallacy, because it's *all around*. It's *awareness* that's more needed than wisdom. That's pretty neat! Oh, I *like* your son—oh, I think he's so marvelous!"

The reading ended. During the session I had the feeling that David was more mature now, which shouldn't have surprised me since we continue inner growth after death; nevertheless, it was unexpected. Noreen and I both got very high during our meeting, since tremendous energy was present, and Noreen was obviously quite excited by David's personality and by the material coming through her. She afterwards told me that it had been a wonderful experience for her, and she even gave me a hug as I left. I later wondered if I had gotten the hug from her, from David, or from the both of them.

For the next few days I felt miffed by David's comment that I should know what the single tear of Joyce meant, so when Saturday arrived I went to the university library again. I rummaged through the section devoted to James Joyce, certain that I would find the answer in *Portrait of the Artist as a Young Man*. I discovered a book that catalogued the location of every word in *Portrait* and looked up "tear."

Then I pulled a copy of *Portrait* from a nearby shelf, opened the book to the page indicated, and read:

> The second pain . . . in hell is the pain of conscience. . . . Conscience will say: You had time and opportunity to repent and you would not. . . . The Ruler of the universe entreated you, a creature of clay, to love Him Who made you and to keep His law. No. You would not. And now, though you were to flood all hell with your tears if you could still weep, all that sea of repentance would not gain for you what *a single tear of true repentance* [italics are mine] shed during your mortal life would have gained for you. You implore now a moment of earthly life wherein to repent: in vain. That time is gone: gone forever.
>
> Be not afraid . . . repent. . . . He calls you to Him. . . . Come to Him. . . . Now is the acceptable time. Now is the hour.[33]

David had read *Portrait,* whose principal character is Stephen Daedalus, sometime in high school, and he was greatly influenced by it. I also remembered that David had written "Daedalus Schwimmer" above the return address of a letter he had sent us from Duke, and I recalled that the wings of the original Daedalus had not melted as he flew over the sea.

As for the purple and yellow flower that Noreen had seen David giving Veronica, I mentioned this to her, but she said she had no idea what it meant, so I put Noreen's impression out of my conscious mind, since the image seemed to simply be a message of love from David to his mother.

When I came home from work the following Wednesday, however, Veronica said, "Did you see the flower in the front yard?" I had briefly noticed, in the middle of the yard, a single open flower with a tall stem and three buds on it, which had apparently opened that day. "It is purple, with yellow in its center," Veronica continued.

I went outside and looked at the flower. It was the only flower blooming in our yard—a purple iris with a yellow center. There were three sets of three petals: the outer petals were purple, the next three were lavender, and the innermost three were yellow. I remembered that Noreen had mentioned all three colors. When I returned to the house, Veronica said, "It's not a simple flower, though—it's a bearded iris."

Feeling tired, I went upstairs and lay down. As I rested in a drowsy state, the day's date—April 25—popped into my head. Why, I wondered. I felt an impulse to add the numbers of the day together: two plus five. Seven is the number of both David's and Veronica's birthdays. Add in the month, another thought came to me. Four and seven are eleven, the number for David's full name.

Since there were nine petals in the flower, I later looked up the number nine in the book of symbols and found that nine is often considered the number of the initiate, the end of the numerical series before the return to unity $(9+1=10)$, the symbol for matter which cannot be destroyed. For the Hebrews, nine was a symbol of truth, a bringing of things to an end in preparation for a new manifestation. And it was at the ninth hour that Jesus was said to have breathed His last upon the cross.[34] I also remembered Noreen saying that David had died at 9:00.

I puzzled over Noreen's comments that David's purpose for coming to Earth had to do with me. And Marian had said I would be one of David's channels. Neither of these statements made much sense to me. But if they were accurate, what was David up to? I didn't know—and he wasn't saying. He just kept grinning in my mind like the Cheshire Cat.

# more evidence

My conversation with Preston had impressed me so much that I was anxious to speak with David's other close friends as well. Doing so was important to me for several reasons. To begin with, I felt that meeting them and hearing about their experiences with David would somehow bring me closer to him. Also, I wondered if any of them had had a premonition of his death—or if David had told any of a premonition. Finally, I wanted to find out whether they had felt David's presence or had been hearing David's voice in their minds.

I contacted Alice first, not only because she and David had been good friends in Raleigh, but also because exactly one year before David's death Alice had sent a letter to wish David a happy eighteenth birthday, writing, "May you begin a year of living," which seemed like an unconscious premonition to me. Her Christmas card the following year certainly was, whether she later realized it or not. Both her envelope and card to David showed a white dove in flight—traditionally a symbol of the soul—and on the card Alice had written:

> David –
> Merry Christmas. Have a happy
> New Year, too . . . survive!

Alice was away at college now and came to meet me at my office during one of her school breaks. After we chatted for a few minutes, I asked her if she had had any impression of David's presence. She said she hadn't. When I mentioned what Marian had told me about David's past life at the time of the establishment of the Jewish kings, an odd look crossed Alice's face.

"Do you know what topic I chose for my religion term paper last spring?" she asked.

"What?"

"The founding of the kings of Israel."

We spoke a little longer, and then Alice left. Afterwards I realized I hadn't asked her why she had sent David the precognitive Christmas card, but I decided it didn't matter, because by now I had decided that everyone close to a person knows subconsciously—long before the fact—when the person will make the transition to the next life. Still, where had Alice gotten the idea for her paper? I finally concluded that David hadn't failed to contact Alice at all. He had simply touched her through her writing. David was using different ways to reach everyone, his method for each depending on the person.

I then called Brian, and we met one morning at my house. Brian again commented on how much David had influenced his running, saying, "It really helped to have somebody just always making me go faster and work harder up the hills—I'd never run so hard up the hills before." Brian also talked about how David had convinced their two track coaches to change their philosophies of training, one coach even acknowledging David's influence during a meeting of the entire team.

Brian told me he couldn't really remember what had happened after David was lost, but that in a way he did sort of recall something like Preston's experience of David's presence. "It wasn't near that *strong* [as for Preston], I'm sure, but . . . I might just have been thinking about David for some reason, and all of a sudden—it does bring back some . . ." Brian's voice trailed off, and he just stared into space.

I next had a long conversation with Debbie at her Raleigh apartment near N.C. State University. I asked what sorts of things David had discussed with her in high school. Her answer surprised me a little, although by now it shouldn't have. "We spent a lot of time talking about David's philosophy of life and religion—reincarnation," Debbie told me. "He was very, very much an advocate of everyone struggling for perfection—that everyone can improve himself, and that you learn something from each person you meet. So, with every relationship you're learning and growing."

I asked if David had mentioned any premonitions to her, and Debbie said it wasn't so much premonitions as, again, philosophy. Shortly before his last Christmas, David had told her about his planned trip, and she had said to him, "David, you're crazy—you're going to kill yourself," to which David had replied, "You're right, I am, but the trip is something I really want to do. I'll never be happy with myself unless I do it. It's something I *need* to do for myself." David told her he realized he was taking his life in his hands, that he might never see her again, but that he felt like he wouldn't be able to exist with himself if he didn't go on this trip—explore himself and find out what he wanted to do with his life.

I mentioned that David had seemed to sense he would die young, writing a will at the age of twelve, for example. "That's David," Debbie laughed. "I can remember in high school he always used to joke about how he'd die before me, but he would also tell me very seriously, 'I am going to die first, Debbie. I might be in really great shape, but that doesn't mean I couldn't be in an accident or something.' And he said, 'I've come to grips with death. I really think that when I die it will be very peaceful. I'm not going to enjoy it, but I'm going to accept it very well.'

"He had this whole philosophy of how natural death was, and how it didn't bother him at all. I remember him saying that death was just like birth and just as beautiful as birth—how he had no gripes about it and how he wasn't scared at all. So perhaps he *did* know something." Debbie also told me that she had gone to the Outer Banks with David in October of 1976 for a couple of days, and David had hardly spoken to her the whole time. He just stared at the ocean for hours.

Debbie was much clearer about sensing David than Brian had been. In response to my question, she said, "There are times when I'm doing something, and it's kind of like—if David were here, he'd be saying that I really shouldn't react this way, or something like that, and I feel this *presence* standing over me, guiding me . . ."

I asked if—when she perceived David around her—this was just a feeling, a thought without words, or if she ever seemed to actually hear David's voice saying something to her, in her mind. "It's a fine line," Debbie responded, "between me thinking about David and hearing his voice. Lots of times when I'll be thinking about him, I'll hear him say something. I'm not sure if that's just memories or if it's something he is saying to me. But there definitely are times when I can tell he's saying something like, 'Now, Debbie, you know it's dumb to act that way. You really should do *this.*' That's very, very strong at times."

As on Earth, David seemed to have fun while doing his work.

I had obtained copies of David's correspondence from his friends Alice, Dale, and Fig, and I decided to write all three to thank them for sending me their letters. As I composed what I meant to be only short notes, I had the strangest impression that David was writing *with me*, especially the letter to Fig. I felt extremely whimsical as I wrote to her, which was very odd, since I knew nothing about Fig and couldn't recall even having met her. But David had been (was still) whimsical. Below is part of that letter:

> Dear Fig,
> I started to write, "Dear Michelle" [Fig is Michelle's nickname, of course], and David's voice popped into my mind and said, *"Don't* call her 'Michelle,' her name is *Fig!"* That was some time ago. Now he says to "say I said hello and that I love her." Does all this sound quite mad? Perhaps, but vintage David, nevertheless. He had, as someone wrote a year ago, a habit of popping up unasked—most recently in many people's minds. Yours too, I expect. So if you perhaps have thought during the past year that you have an over-active imagination or that you are slightly demented, don't worry—you are in good company.
> I feel as if this letter is being written by David. I try to push him out, but he says, "Hey, hey, not so rough on your buddies," and proceeds to sit down cross-legged in the middle of my mind. Typical. Now he's just grinning at me. It is a few minutes after midnight, and perhaps I am mad. It has been a strange year, and many strange things have happened.

During this experience, I was aware of the same sort of joyous energy which I had experienced in Greensboro, at Black Mountain, and during my sessions with most psychics. I also felt great inner pressure to address the letter "Fig," rather than "Michelle," although I was very reluctant to do so.

On another night I had the one-time experience of suddenly becoming aware of something which I can only characterize as a complex of energies floating in the space behind my right shoulder while I was typing at my desk. The feeling that something was in back of me was so strong that I finally looked over my right shoulder, trying to see if there actually was anything there. I saw nothing, but I did feel something.

The last of David's friends I wanted to see was Cindy, another of his companions on Project WILD. I most wanted to ask her about the Christmas card she had designed, drawn, and sent to David for his last Christmas. The card showed a flock of sheep low in the left foreground, a shepherd's stick lying in the bottom right-hand corner, the ascendant Christ star in the sky, but no shepherd present. For me, Cindy and David's other friends were his flock, and he was their shepherd. Now he was no longer in the physical picture, only his spirit—the Christ star—shining down on his sheep.

Over the past fifteen months I also had wondered if David had invented the complex design he had drawn on the back cover of his journal or if he had found this somewhere, but I decided I'd never discover the origin of that design. David, however, had his own plans for me. Cindy and I had arranged to meet at the Duke chapel at 2:00, but I arrived early, so I wandered around the campus a little. I noticed the Divinity School where David had taken some classes and walked into the building. In the lobby, straight ahead of me on the far wall, was a large wooden prototype of the design on David's journal cover. David was apparently leading me around now.

I returned to the chapel to find Cindy waiting for me, and we sat on the chapel steps. We spoke casually for a few minutes, and she told me she was majoring in religion and art. When I asked her what had been in her mind when she drew David's card, she was silent for a few moments, then said, "I don't . . . I . . . it was weird, about David's card. I usually take a long time to do people's Christmas cards and don't worry about it if they get there after Christmas, but I wanted to get *David's* done really *fast*. And I'm not sure . . . I mean . . . I've thought about that."

For the next forty-five minutes Cindy shared a very personal picture of how David had impressed her. Afterwards, however, I discovered that my tape recorder had broken down, playing back only garbled sounds, and the only thing I could recall from our conversation was Cindy saying that when she had met David she had felt at once he would be someone she would know for all of her life—a statement Preston also had made.

I wrote to Cindy about the malfunctioning recorder, and she sent me a few entries from her May Project WILD journal, plus some of her recollections of David and thoughts she had written down after she learned that David was lost. It was all very touching:

> We hiked through the most beautiful mountains up to Pilot Mountain. We couldn't decide whether to climb it or not. . . . Dave Schwimmer wanted to go over it, though, and somehow convinced us all.
>
> . . .

David was so hilarious today. He's a riot: "There *is* sex after death—you just can't feel anything." Barb, David and Linda sing *constantly*. All I can do is laugh. I *love* it.

. . .

In this crew are lots of very sensitive people. David Schwimmer was interviewed last night, and we think so much alike it's scary. I feel very close to him. . . . He's deep, too, a writer inside—sensitive and vulnerable.

. . .

During the fall semester I saw David often between classes. He always had on a pair of blue shorts and a T-shirt with holes. He always gave me a hug when I saw him. He asked me to dance with him in the 24-hour dance marathon that Wilson House was having, but I had to do something else.

. . .

After David was lost, I dreamed about him twice. One dream he was just in, the other he was active and talking to me, but I'm not sure about what.

Cindy wrote the following after she heard what had happened to David:

'David always went over mountains.' That is what Preston said. It is true. David does always go over mountains. Like Pilot Mountain in May—and it was beautiful. So is David. And now I may never see him again. He's lost. But David did live—why him? He's so special. Special in the very way he left.

Crying does no good any more. My weakness engulfs me. I cry for David, I cry for no one to play with, I cry for the new way things are. That life is . . . I want to do everything right now—for *David* . . .

Oh God, why? Why? Please God, help me to be strong and good. Help me give every ounce of me until it is all given out, and then let me give more . . . and if David is alive, God, please let him get back okay. Love him, God. Love us, too. We miss him, God.

One of David's special people, who would help bring healing to the planet, I was certain. And, after speaking with these friends of David, I had no doubt at all that David had been and continued to be with every one of them.

# 12

## transition

The case had been shuttled from one lawyer to another for almost a year. Eventually it was decided that the only state where the suit could be tried was New Mexico, and, after some effort by our Raleigh trial attorney, someone willing to try the case had been found in Santa Fe. Preliminary legal work had dragged on for several months, but finally on Friday, September 14, 1979, a two-million-dollar wrongful death suit was filed against Outward Bound on behalf of the parents of David and Tim in Santa Fe U.S. District Court. Due to health considerations, Mrs. Herman, a widow, had withdrawn from the suit, although I was told she had received a financial settlement from Outward Bound.

In order to force changes in Outward Bound's program, I had been trying over the past twelve months to obtain national publicity for our charge that Outward Bound had been negligent in David's death, but I had had no success.

After the filing of the suit, however, I received prompt responses to my telegrams. The first to break the story was *The New York Times,* and its article about David, Brenda, Tim, and Sonya Ross immediately drew the interest of others in the national press. *Newsweek* soon published a full-page article, which was quickly followed by a very lengthy feature story printed by *The Washington Post* and syndicated to 300 newspapers. Reporter Megan Rosenfeld began her story with a single sentence: "Everyone said that he was special." We were interviewed by other newspapers and magazines, National Public Radio, Connecticut PBS-TV, and local TV and radio stations.

CBS-TV also taped us for a segment on Charles Kurault's *Sunday Morning*. Shortly after the taping, I recalled a dream David had at the age of eighteen. Halfway through the dream, David asked what time it was, and a man answered, "9:30—you must have been traveling at least half an hour." Then, David wrote, a van from the "General Broadcasting Company" arrived; two middle-aged men got out, one of whom "entered the house to interview the inside man's wife for a tragedy." This sequence closely paralleled the actual CBS visit—although CBS producer Mel Lavine and reporter Jerry Landay had a car, not a van. David, of course, had most likely died around 9:00.

Jerry Landay concluded his story on *Sunday Morning* with the final lines of David's poem "Meditation":

Winter and summer, the tree grows inward.
The temple of myself again comes free,
And I flow with the stream:
A wanderer found in the midst of the sea.

When our law suit became public knowledge, the parents of another young man from Raleigh who also had died at sea invited us to their home one evening. While discussing the experiences of the two families, Veronica told the boy's mother that she sometimes thought she heard David saying, "Momma," as he had when he was alive. David had finally broken through to Veronica.

✦ ✦ ✦

One of the really strange examples of synchronicity was the way books would find their way into my hands and then open at appropriate places, the lines of print themselves seeming to pull my eyes toward them at times.

Earlier that fall, as I was dusting the books in our library, I saw one small, old, leather-bound volume, *Longfellow Birthday Book*, which Veronica had once bought but I had never looked into. I opened it. On each page were two dates, two printed quotations by Longfellow, and two spaces for names to be entered. I flipped to January 27, David's birth date, and found David's name, in his handwriting, below the date. I read:

Ah, how skillful grows the hand
That obeyeth Love's command
It is the heart, and not the brain
That to the highest doth attain;
And he who followeth Love's behest
Far exceedeth all the rest.

The poem not only characterized David accurately but also was a message for me, I later realized. Under February 14, my birthday, David had written my name. The lines beneath that:

Life is real! Life is earnest!
And the grave is not its goal;
"Dust thou art, to dust returnest,"
Was not spoken of the soul.

The two selections could not have been more appropriate. David had written our names—and those of Veronica, Eric, and Krista—in that book in 1974 or 1975. David had been preparing us for his death for many years.

David—and it has to be remembered that he was a very literary person—really put this method of interdimensional communication into high gear near Christmas. When I came home on the evening of December 18, Veronica handed me David's copy of Browning's *Sonnets from the Portuguese*, saying I should look at these poems since David had loved them. I casually flipped to the first page of poetry and read, underlined by someone,

> So weeping, now a mystic shape did move
> Behind me. And a voice said . . .
>     "Guess now who holds thee!"—
>     "Death," I said.
> But there the silver answer rang,
>     "Not Death, but Love."

This was David's Christmas present for me.

The next morning I found a small *Book of Common Prayer*, which Veronica had been reading the previous night, open to number 77 of the Psalms of David, the last two paragraphs underlined:

> Thy way is in the sea and Thy path in the great waters, and Thy footsteps are not known.
> Thou leadest Thy people like a flock, by the hand of Moses and Aaron.

The following day I went into Krista's room to make some phone calls and sat down at her desk. I glanced idly at the books before me and noticed three volumes by Kahlil Gibran: *The Prophet* was in the center, with *Sand and Foam* on one side and *A Tear and a Smile* on the other.

I pulled out *The Prophet*; inside was a bookplate with David's name written on it. The bookplate—blue, white and pale yellow—showed two slim boats at the right, heading into an enormous sea wave at the left, with a mountain in the background—a scene which greatly resembled the events in Baja.

FROM THE LIBRARY OF
David Schwimmer

Two of David's other books also had something to tell me. As I was thumbing through David's Bible one day, I noticed an inked asterisk beside the end of Ezekiel 1:1: ". . . the heavens were opened, and I saw visions of God." Nowhere else in his Bible had David made any mark or notation. Then Veronica told me I should read Leon Uris' *Mila 18*, since she said David had been very much drawn to the book. In David's copy of the novel, I found—underlined and starred by David—a quotation by Thomas

Paine: "The world is my country, all mankind are my brethren . . . to do good is my religion."

I later ran across other synchronistic passages in books, but the last one was the most extraordinary. Veronica handed me a mystery novel one day and pointed to a paragraph:

> David was a splendid person; everybody loved him. There were those qualities about David that are found, somehow, only in those who die young, those who seem to be sent directly from Heaven for a short while to light up the world. Only for a short time. Those people get killed in wars . . . if they grow up and don't get drowned. . . . David was the sort of person whom knowing for a small part of one's life makes all the rest of life worth living.[35]

The character David died, of course.

Years later, I noticed another pattern connected to these books. Almost every one in which I found such passages had somehow come to me through Veronica. So she apparently also was part of this hidden dance of life and death.

✦ ✦ ✦

From my journal:

> There are tensions and uncertainties in me now. My self-confidence seems to have weakened. First, I wondered about all this publicity: was I being unreal, over-reacting? I don't think so, yet I feel vulnerable. Then I feel vulnerable about David's book and my psychic research. David wrote that fear is contrary to faith. I agree, so I am fluttering along the edge of a spiritual crisis.

What is wrong? I have been living too much on inner levels, and the outer world becomes alarming. I must get everything done and leave Raleigh. I can't escape myself, but I'd rather meet myself on more friendly ground.

. . .

I feel I have weathered the storms. Am I better than two years ago? A tiny bit, I think. I am far more calm and reasonable than before—not ideal, but improved. I certainly *try* (not nearly enough, a voice inside says) to be more *aware* of people, more *sensitive* to their problems.

. . .

Sitting by the fire, watching Duke basketball on TV, I looked into the fire and suddenly lost myself. The strangest feeling—as if I weren't myself anymore, as if one door had opened and another had closed.

The second anniversary of David's death had come, and I felt I was at a crossroads. I hated selling life insurance and could see no future for myself in Raleigh. I had come only to help my father, but his business was on firm footing now, so he didn't need me any more. Eric and Kris were on their own—Kris was doing well at Duke and Eric was getting straight A's at N.C. State. Veronica appeared to be living inside herself, and our marriage was moribund. Our lawyers were clearing up the issue of whether American or Mexican law would apply to our law suit, and I was still editing David's journals. So I had to see where I was now and what I should do with my life. I had made it an article of faith never to look back at the past, only to the future, but I saw no future now, so I had to look back first.

✦ ✦ ✦

I was born in Hódmezövásárhely, Hungary, moved to Budapest when I was four, but remember almost nothing of that time. The only significant thing I recall from my first ten years is being hit and knocked unconscious by a truck in New York City at the age of nine. Clear memories surface in my mind only from about my eleventh year, when we were living in Chicago.

My father, János, which name he changed to John when we came to the U.S., was a lifelong businessman, who seemed unable to develop any interests outside of his work and family. He had no hobbies, no close friends, and the only things he seemed to like were playing bridge and going on vacations to the mountains or the sea. He was physically slight and to me seemed very shy, pushing himself to be outgoing and forceful. He tried to act as a paterfamilias but didn't know how to carry that off.

In Hungary, he had done extraordinarily well buying and selling goose down and feathers for bedding, and his decision to flee Hungary in 1939—on an impulse, leaving everything behind—most likely had kept us from the Nazi gas chambers. In the U.S. he had many business struggles but at the end of his life was able to succeed again, manufacturing bed pillows. However, having been torn from his roots, he never was able—or maybe willing—to really become integrated into U.S. society.

He appeared incapable of revealing emotion, except anger, which he often expressed in an explosive way, flying into seemingly unprovoked rages that were frightening. He wasn't physically abusive, but his words could be as cutting as a blade, making those he attacked feel inadequate, and he used his tongue to wound family, friends, business associates, employees, even waiters. The only times I remember seeing him show other feelings were when he was in his forties, after he learned that his mother, and later his youngest brother, Feri, had died in Hungary. I have to credit him with being a fighter and survivor, though. He never gave up.

My father's behavior was probably just one part of a family pattern, for he once mentioned that as a child he had sometimes been beaten by his father, who had been a compulsive gambler with a drinking problem. Unconsciously, my father mirrored his father's pattern, never drinking but exhibiting behavior associated with alcoholism, and at times making very risky gambles in business ventures and suffering heavy losses.

Perhaps he was just disappointed with life, for in a rare moment of self-revelation he confided that he had wanted to be a doctor but instead had had to enter the family business when he was sixteen because his father's drinking and gambling were ruining the firm. So my father was a basically unhappy man, who repeatedly gave the same sad performance. Paradoxically, he could be quite charming in company when he wished to be.

My mother, born Margit (Marguerite) Roth, was a vivacious, cultured, and talented woman, simultaneously sensitive and strong-willed, who allowed my father to dominate her. When I was older and he made her frantic, I sometimes would ask why she didn't divorce him. She'd always say, "I still love him," which I had trouble understanding, especially as she claimed he had stopped her from pursuing careers as a pianist and tennis player, activities at which she excelled. Yet once, in tears, she cried out to me that all she had ever wanted was to have a lot of children. She taught me to play tennis, encouraged me to read, and took me to plays and concerts as I was growing up.

She had always tended to be somewhat high-strung, and as the years passed she became as difficult as my father to relate to. After she passed fifty, she seemed to progressively give up on life, first abandoning tennis and later her piano playing and pupils, saying my father didn't want her to work. As she grew older, she became quite depressed and seemed rudderless and lonely in her later years. I felt sympathy for her, but she seemed so set on feeling hopeless that I found it very hard to be around her for long. I sometimes speculated that she might be suffering from survivor's guilt, having lost her parents, her brother, and both her sisters by the time she was forty-eight. I never was able to understand her, or my father.

Nor can I remember my parents ever saying they loved me. Maybe they did when I was young, but I have no recollection of it. This is not to say they didn't care about me, but my family's code of silence prevented such words from being spoken. The only way my father seemed able to show me affection was to give me money, but even this was usually offered in controlling ways.

My sister Kathie, four years older than I, eventually couldn't endure my parents' behavior any longer. She left the country in her mid-twenties, married an Englishman, and after one visit home refused ever to come back to the U.S. Needless to say, I grew up reflecting my parents' patterns, becoming a fiery, and sometimes charming, co-dependent. Later, one of my acting instructors, a woman, once turned to me and said, "George, you can be so charming when you want to. Why don't you want to?" I had no idea why, then. Although I was quite intelligent and perceptive, I found grammar school and high school incredibly dull, and, being subtly rebellious, avoided doing much work, although I managed better than a B average. I was delighted to finally escape to college.

I became an indifferent English major at Washington and Jefferson College (then an all-male school), more interested in playing pickup basketball at the gym than in studying many required—and uninspired—courses, which often put me to sleep. In my sophomore year I considered being a writer but could think of nothing I wanted to put on paper as fiction. My life and my parents' lives seemed insignificant to me, I found the fifties mind-numbing, and I refused to be part of the beat generation. I decided I just wasn't cut out to be a writer. Later that year, however, I discovered the school's theater group, and over the next five semesters performed four major roles, directed one play, and did a lot of backstage work. I also was elected to the student council, where I invariably was the lone dissenting voice.

More important were my relationships with two of my teachers. The first, Dr. David H. Newhall, my philosophy professor, was the most brilliant, balanced, rational, and compassionate person I have ever met. Then in his mid-thirties, he was the complete antithesis of my father. He became my spiritual mentor, not only teaching me Western philosophy, formal logic, semantics and ethics for three years, but also demonstrating what he taught with his life, which included raising three children. He was the most significant part of my college education, as well as my tennis coach, while his wife Gerry had me to dinner and listened to me moan about my academic crises. They were Quakers and, without saying a word, illustrated daily how life should be lived. My father was a fighter, Dave and Gerry were peacemakers. My son David was named after Dave.

My second mentor was Dr. Edwin M. Moseley, then also in his thirties, from whom I took two excellent courses in the novel. Edwin was a gentle, kind, soft-spoken Southerner and a great listener, who gave sensible, mildly-worded advice and fed me one-eyed Egyptians (a piece of bread fried with an egg in its scooped out center). It was Edwin who nudged me away from my misguided notion of doing graduate work in English and instead steered me toward theater training.

An additional influence on me in college was Albert Schoepf, another student, who was one year behind me in school. I disliked Al on sight and avoided him whenever I could. Al was somewhat Bohemian—too much for me to deal with at first. One day I saw him in our badly-lit dorm lobby trying to take still photographs without using a flash or tripod. Annoyed by this ineptitude, I went to my room, got my tripod and handed it to Al without a word, much to his astonishment.

The next fall we became close friends, talking endlessly, sharing secrets, and shooting off to Pittsburgh in his car to savor food, wine, and jazz in tiny restaurants and bars. I had not dated to that time, being quite shy then, and Al dragged me off to a women's college in Pittsburgh and got me dates. When the drama club produced *Mr. Roberts* in my senior year, he played Ensign Pulver, while I portrayed Mr. Roberts.

Dave, Gerry, Edwin, and Al became my surrogate family in my last three college years. I kept in touch with all of them, and sometimes visited them, long after I had graduated. They showed me a very different side of life and of people than my parents had.

However, even they and my philosophy courses hadn't resolved my spiritual dilemma, although they had laid the groundwork for what was to come. When I was twenty-eight I bought a copy of *There Is A River*, a biography of Edgar Cayce by Thomas Sugrue. Cayce, a photographer with little formal education who died in 1945, could place himself into an altered state of consciousness and then provide accurate medical diagnosis and suggested treatment which was often unorthodox but often also quite effective. In addition, Cayce gave what he called "life readings," during which he spoke of the past lives of the people for whom he was reading and of the impact those past lives had on people's current lives.

The book blew me away. I finally had answers to many of my questions, especially the one about personal identity and survival. The book also allowed me to understand that we had a reason to be on Earth, often came back with souls we had known before, and—living more than one life—had the chance to grow in consciousness and make up for past mistakes and omissions. I particularly noted Cayce's trance statement that the original meaning of the word *sin* had been "error." A whole new vista opened up before me: I now believed that I—like everyone else—had the opportunity to develop myself as far as I was willing, in any aspect or dimension of my being—spiritual, emotional, mental, physical, psychological, social, vocational. What a gift from the universe! What a gift to learn this! What an effort by Cayce and his associates to reveal this gift!

As more books about Cayce were published, I bought every one I stumbled across, as well as books on other esoteric subjects such as near-death experiences, human energy fields, ghosts, natural healing, telepathy, the Seth material, and so on. I sometimes told Veronica and the children about some of what I had read, and David eventually was attracted to these books, mainly the ones about Cayce, which he read and commented on in his journals.

Then there was my outer life. After graduating from college, I spent twenty-one miserable months in the army, mainly at Ft. Benning, Georgia. During the next eighteen years, I got an M.F.A. in theater directing at Carnegie Tech, acted in summer stock, directed at the Texas theater, completed most of my Ph.D. in theater at Tulane University, directed and taught theater courses at two colleges, helped to start a professional resident theater at North Carolina State University, set up a college theater department and a summer theater in Michigan, taught acting and directed in Ireland for two years. But although I often got rave reviews, I was directing in theatrical backwaters, so my work was unknown elsewhere. I also had frequent financial crises, since none of my theater jobs paid much.

I met Veronica while I was at Carnegie Tech. I was sharing an apartment with Al, who was doing graduate work at the University of Pittsburgh after having completed an army stint in Germany. I remember my first glimpse of Veronica because it was unusual. I came home from class late one afternoon and opened the apartment door. The door swung inward to the right, hiding the living room, also to the right. Just as I walked past the far edge of the door, my head turned toward the living room, and from the corner of my right eye I noticed a young woman seated on a sofa, directly facing me. The moment I saw her, a brief flash of fine pale gold light seemed to leap from her head toward mine. Much later, I decided I had seen that flash psychically, that it was a greeting or sign of recognition between us. At the time, however, I shrugged this off as my imagination, and a minute later Al introduced her to me. She was from his home town. We married during the last year of my studies at Carnegie Tech.

As time went by, Veronica and I drifted apart. I guess it was unmet expectations on both sides and an almost total lack of either communication or emotional intimacy. One of my contributions was that I didn't really know how to love. My parents had never taught me to love, and I had never even heard of unconditional love, except in one of Dave Newhall's classes, where he had spoken of *agapé*. But I was unable to understand what that Greek word meant, then. I also had a lot of anger in me, like my father, which caused me to blow up or simmer at times.

Distance continued to grow between Veronica and me, and we both became more withdrawn. Our periodic financial problems took their toll on us, as well; neither of us really knew how to manage money. Our relationship became very sad and disturbing. I think we both were angry at how things had turned out. Neither Veronica nor I sought counseling—we each felt we could handle our personal problems by ourself. We couldn't, but wouldn't admit it.

I didn't *understand* anything of what was happening, and took Veronica's behavior to mean she was rejecting me. I don't know if she was in emotional hell, but I certainly was. After our return from Ireland, all of us felt quite depressed, but it hit Veronica the hardest. She seemed to pull inward more and more, until I felt there was no way I could reach her.

One night, perhaps a year after David's death, I came into the kitchen for a snack and found her with a glass of wine in her hand. She suddenly turned to me and said, "You'll have to leave me, I can't leave you," and then walked out of the kitchen. I was shocked. I had been thinking of divorce for a couple of years, but Veronica had never indicated in any way that she wanted to end our marriage. But I couldn't see how divorce was possible. We had no money, I was just making enough to get by, and Veronica had almost no job experiences and no college degree, and even seemed fearful of getting a job. How would she support herself, if we were divorced? It seemed like an insoluble problem for both of us.

✦ ✦ ✦

So, what would I do now? As I read David's journals, I saw how he always had made a real effort to reach the goals to which he'd been drawn. I looked into myself again. I found I still had a yearning to direct theater, especially in New York City. I felt I wanted to give theater one more shot, and that if I didn't go to New York I'd hate myself for the rest of my life. Then I thought of David once more. If he were in my shoes, what would he do? No contest, I decided; he'd head for The Big Apple. I told Veronica I was going to sell the house and go to New York. She agreed and said she would go with me. I was surprised by her response but thought that perhaps this was an opportunity for her as well. I got a bank loan and resumed fixing up and painting our house. I had a goal again—I was in motion. It felt good.

# 13

# david's life plan

Before David's death, I'd had little respect for astrology, since what I'd read about it had seemed like hokum to me. I'd found books on astrology to be stultifying in their technicality, never giving any instructions on how to interpret the charts. So I ignored astrology, even though I remembered that the entranced Edgar Cayce had said that the stars and planets created conditions in time and personality that everyone had to deal with.

Consequently, when LeRoy Zemke told me to get an astrological reading about David, I brushed aside the suggestion. But, as always, I wasn't in control of the cosmic scenario in which I was involved, and at one of Marian's meetings in Raleigh I was introduced to an astrologer, Steve Forrest. After speaking with Steve on a few occasions, I told him about David's death, and Steve said he'd like to do an astrological reading about David.

I put aside this offer for several months but finally decided I had little to lose except some time, so I made an appointment with Steve and met him at his apartment in Chapel Hill. Steve is a gentle, quiet, sensitive man, and one reason I had decided to get this reading was that I felt I could trust him. After Steve had made me comfortable in his living room, he handed me David's astrological chart and proceeded to talk, virtually nonstop, for two hours. The quotations that follow are excerpts from a very lengthy transcript. To conserve space, I have omitted most of Steve's mention or definition of the various symbols in David's chart.

Steve was very clear about the significance and influence of every person's astrological signs. "An astrological chart represents a range of possibilities—a spectrum of opportunities—that is made available to a person at the time of his birth," he said. "You can respond to your chart in a very selfish way, a very automatic way, but through the urge to grow and to explore what you have within yourself you can begin to make a much more sensitive response to the birth chart, to react in a more thoughtful way, a more principled way—eventually in a selfless or even in a spiritual way.

"Initially, with the Aquarian sun, David came into this world to experience a very intense, very packed-in process of individuation—personality—the freedom to express the self. Aquarius is the sign under which the ego is perfected—ego as the necessary tool we must have to exist in this world and to gather the Earth's lessons.

"David, like everyone else, was born into a world that told him what to do, what to be. After a while—as soon as you reach something like the age of reason—you're ushered into a room full of *masks*, and people say, 'Here, try on any of these masks; you can be anything you want: you can be the banker, the actor, the insurance salesman, whatever—it's a wonderful world.' What happened, however, was that David walked into that room, trustingly as we all do, started trying on masks . . . and none of them fit. As long as he lived, even if he had lived a normal, average length of life, he still would never have found a

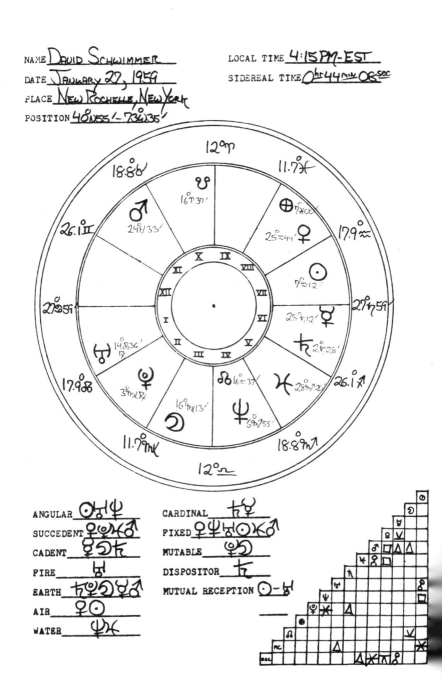

NAME David Schwimmer
DATE January 27, 1959
PLACE New Rochelle, New York
POSITION 40N55' - 73W35'

LOCAL TIME 4:15 PM - EST
SIDEREAL TIME 0hr 44min 06sec

12°♏

18.8°♉          11.7°♓

☊ 16°♈30'
♂ 24°♉33'

⊕ 7°♓00'

26.1°♊          ♀ 25°♒44'          17.9°♒

25°♒44'

X  IX
XI        VIII
XII        VII
I        VI
II  V
III  IV

⊙ 7°♒12'

27°♊59'          ☿ 25°♑12'          27°♐59'

♅ 14°♒36' ℞

♄ 2°♑26'

17.9°♋          ♇ 3°♍℞          ☋ 16°♎37'    ♃ 28°♓13'    26.1°♐

16°♍13'    ☽          ♆ 3°♐55'

11.7°♍          18.8°♐

12°♎

ANGULAR ⊙♄♆
SUCCEDENT ♀☊☿♃♂
CADENT ☿☽♄
FIRE ♅
EARTH ♄♇☽♂♀♃
AIR ♀⊙
WATER ♆♓

CARDINAL ♄☿
FIXED ♀♆♅⊙☊♂
MUTABLE ♇☽
DISPOSITOR ♄
MUTUAL RECEPTION ⊙-♅

202 • the search for david

<u>KEY TO THE SYMBOLISM</u>

**SIGNS:**

| | | | | | |
|---|---|---|---|---|---|
| Aries | ♈ | Leo | ♌ | Saggitarius | ♐ |
| Taurus | ♉ | Virgo | ♍ | Capricorn | ♑ |
| Gemini | ♊ | Libra | ♎ | Aquarius | ♒ |
| Cancer | ♋ | Scorpio | ♏ | Pisces | ♓ |

**PLANETS:**

| | | | |
|---|---|---|---|
| Sun | ☉ | Jupiter | ♃ |
| Moon | ☽ | Saturn | ♄ |
| Mercury | ☿ | Uranus | ♅ |
| Venus | ♀ | Neptune | ♆ |
| Mars | ♂ | Pluto | ♇ |

**POINTS:**

| | |
|---|---|
| North Node of the Moon | ☊ |
| South Node of the Moon | ☋ |
| Part of Fortune | ⊕ |

**ASPECTS:**

| | | | | | | |
|---|---|---|---|---|---|---|
| Conjunction | (0°) | ☌ | Semisextile | (30°) | | ⊻ |
| Sextile | (60°) | ⚹ | Semisquare | (45°) | | ∠ |
| Square | (90°) | □ | Sesquiquadrate | (135°) | | ⚼ |
| Trine | (120°) | △ | Quincunx | (150°) | | ⊼ |
| Opposition | (180°) | ☍ | | | | |

STEVE FORREST

CHAPEL HILL
NORTH CAROLINA

mask. For David came into a world where he was a free spirit in a world of automatons, or slaves. He had an intense need to achieve individuality—to achieve and create his own freedom."

I was very much struck by Steve's discussion of masks, not only because of the mask in David's drawing, but also because David had written a short essay for his application to Duke University, entitled "An Unseen Mask," which dealt with this concept of "masking":

> A country moans about lack of brotherhood, lack of caring, lack of love. One can't love unless one understands, and very few try to understand the people they meet every day. They take the surface values as the real person and never want to look beneath. They very likely can't. It's very hard to see another if one does not practice first on oneself.
>
> I admit I'm the same. I didn't try to peek behind the mask I had glued onto myself. I didn't consciously know I had attached it. Maybe I tried to tell myself through puzzling, confusing dreams, but the consciousness was blocked. I see what the dreams said now, though. They said that I did not know myself . . .

Steve went on: "We find a person who by nature and by destiny was meant to walk a very different path than what others had walked before. That old thing we used to see on all the college dormitory walls in the late 1960s about 'I hear a different drummer.' David *did* hear a different drummer, he *was* marching to a different drummer, and this march would have carried him further and further away from the mainstream of his culture, the older he got. He was already doing that a lot, even in his teenage years."

Some of Steve's impressions were quite eerie in their accuracy, and this was one of them, for in David's application to Duke he also had written:

> I suppose I would describe myself as Christian-by-belief, talkative, hard-thinking and semi-hard-working, and above all, as Thoreau beautifully wrote, definitely "marching to the beat of [my] own drum." At least *I* think I am marching to my own beat, whether others do or not, and really, that is what counts—just so I know where I am marching to.

"This is not a misanthropic hermit kind of image," Steve noted. "It is simply a person who—in being true to himself—is being called false by the world. The world is saying that he is somehow doing things that are illegitimate. It's as though there is circle of safety that society has formed, and within that circle are all the masks—all the legitimate and accepted masks and all definitions of sanity. And the way that life on the planet evolves is that that circle grows, gradually, to include more and more diversity.

"We see that what David was doing in the course of his life was simply taking a few steps outside of that circle, and the people who loved him, first seeing him go in that direction, said, 'Be careful—there's quicksand out there, there are dragons out there.' But he went out and stood there, and looked healthy, looked happy. And people were watching him—everybody saw him doing this. Now, the older he got, the more he was doing it. And what we find is that some of those people who were watching him were saying, 'Well, maybe he's right—it looks safe enough.'

"The point really is, though," Steve emphasized, "that *everybody* was *watching*. Everybody could see that, 'There he is, standing outside the sacred circle. He's standing on solid ground.' And even if those people were all scared to do it themselves, the place within them that wasn't scared could see that and become that much braver. And *that* was the great gift he was giving the world and a big part of his cosmic mission within the world: it was simply the willingness to *embody alternative views of reality*, alternative styles of living, alternative value systems, alternative perceptions. Now, all of this is his cosmic work, and it's impossible, really, to describe it too strongly—it's so powerful within him."

This way of approaching life was well exemplified in David's last semester at Duke. Preston told me, "David knew Hebrew cold but didn't get a high grade because he didn't do the homework. I know he got an A on his final. I know he got an A on his quiz average, and it was a graduate religion course. He just didn't turn in his homework—he just felt, 'I had no need.' Then David said, 'Well, I'm not upset for *me*. I know [the material] and that's what I went in there to get. But I am really upset for the professor, because he had to give me the grade he gave me.' And I thought 'Oh, wow, David, you're going to teach me so much before you're finished.'"

"The second and the most subtle of all the enemies Aquarius faces," Steve continued, "is that David was given an incredible clarity of vision in looking at the society around him and judging it. The only way out of that is to evolve beyond the normal and traditionally assumed prejudices and descriptions of the world by which the whole society operates. Specifically, the assumption that we are all individual egos in competition with each other. He *had* to get beyond that, because David's true destiny in the world was to be a revolutionary. I'm not speaking of throwing Molotov cocktails, but I am talking about a person who in his freedom was exploring a new way of living, a new way of thinking, a new lifestyle. And *demonstrating* that to the world with his own body and his own life. In this sense he was a revolutionary.

"But David needed to realize that despite his intense individuality he was one cell in a much larger organism—the total body of life on the Earth, composed of billions and billions of individual cells, each with the illusion of its separateness, but each an integral part of the whole. David was one of the cells within that great organism which was undergoing mutation, which was an experimental laboratory for a new world, a new life.

"Now, when a cell mutates within the human body, the body is inclined to reject the cell. David faced exactly the same pressures, and here we see that he served a necessary evolutionary role in relationship to his society—to the rest of life on the planet. But it was a role that brought him a great deal of pressure—the pressure of conformity.

"We find here a personality that radiated power, charisma, energy into the world, but underlying that was much more the quality of insecurity—a hunger to prove himself, somehow, a hunger to reach his limits. What we find here is that David was attempting to learn the art of *unconditional self-love*—to accept the self. This kind of easy self-acceptance did not come easily for him."

Steve then focused on the difference between the length and the vibrancy of a person's life: "There was a need to prove his competence, to himself—often in very unorthodox ways, because of the basic Aquarian force. Even in the relatively short number of years that he was alive, David lived the experience of a long lifetime, just because of the hunger for life, the intensity with which he was living."

DelRene—who had known David for less than three weeks and who was a student nurse—wrote, "Dave had a full life—one much fuller than a lot of kids his age, and even more so than some people who die when they are sixty years old." David himself, on December 8, 1977, had written to us, "If I can't follow my own heart, what can I follow? You see, I'm not interested in longevity, but in life, and living, and dreaming."

Steve added, "Even though David was just a teenager at the time of his death, in this chart we see very clearly that he was already thirty or forty years old in terms of his *experience*. This was a chart that packed in an awful lot of life." I told Steve that David had written in his journal, "Why do I feel so *old* in this young body?" I also found, in David's novel, *The Wilderness:* "He stared at the eyes in the mirror. They were the eyes of a tired man who was tired of pretending that he was still young." And during her second reading for me, Noreen had impulsively blurted out, "So young—this child was so *old!*"

Steve now began to discuss the second greatest force which had propelled David through life: his capacity to love and be loved. "We find David's evolution was bound up with his ability to dissolve whatever walls stood between him and other people. We find a friendly personality here, a quality of warmth, an outgoing nature—at least, once he had initially begun to trust someone. One arch virtue that David had, one thing that was just handed to him on a silver platter, was the ability to put himself in another person's shoes. He had more than sympathy—he had empathy: the ability to feel another person's suffering, the ability to feel another person's joy.

"The contradiction between love and freedom was a great pain within his life. Many, many times he *knew* he had to do things that threatened people who loved him, that upset them, that put pressure on them, and yet he knew he had to do them anyway. And this was the source of *tremendous* travail—and psychological pressure—for him, because he would see what he was doing to other people when he was being himself. David was very, very sensitive to that, because again and again and again he knew he had to do the unexpected, the unpredictable, the extreme, and he also knew how—very often—he was really dragging people through the wringer by doing that. And this was a real internal pressure, a real paradox within him."

Of course, David did just that in his decision to take the Outward Bound kayaking course, upsetting quite a few people in the process. He also made us nervous by doing things like backpacking alone in some North Carolina mountains during his last winter—during which trek he experienced an unanticipated overnight snowfall that could have been deadly for him.

"All his life we find a sense of his being touched very deeply by other people. Even though he was a very free-spirited kind of person, his evolution was virtually always catalyzed by the effect of some impressive and powerful other person who came into his life—or someone he granted power to: this could be a girlfriend who touched him deeply, a teacher who touched him deeply. Certainly you and your wife touched him deeply. And David is a person of incredible loyalty, incredible sensibility—all the time.

"But David had come into the world to turn himself inside out. He had come to learn how to love—to learn to experience true intimacy and true tenderness between himself and other people—how to *let* himself be *touched,* how to reveal himself, how to accept dependency upon other people and interdependency with other people. He came to enter into relationships such as he'd never been in before—relationships based upon a spirit of equality.

"One of the great transformations of his life, and one of the most difficult things that he was facing in the course of his life, was that in the karmic past his *identity*, his sense of security, was always built up and supported by everybody patting him on the back and saying, 'We know just who you are: you're the governor, you're the king, you're the boss.' David experienced positions of considerable power and influence in other lives, so he never really had to deal very much with the natural insecurities of the human ego, because all of reality around him was a conspiracy to make him feel good about himself.

"In this life he had come to do a very difficult thing, and that was to break that dependency upon having a mask to wear within the world. He had come in to identify himself with his inner life, rather than with his outer life, and that was the fundamental transition that he came into the world to accomplish. It was the opening up, much, much more, of a capacity to experience love with other people. He was making peace with the insecurities, making himself get to the place where he could share those with others and say, 'We are *all* just simply vulnerable consciousnesses facing a mystery together.'

"David at times was a counselor, a helper, a healer with words. There was something gentle and soothing about his speech, but there was also an honesty as well. Simply the *sound* of his voice—something about the quality of love that he focused on people when he was speaking to them—had a healing impact. We find a tremendous capacity in him initially—but one that had to grow for him to find his true strength—to nurture, to heal, to protect, to mother people, to mother the weakness within them, which is a strange image to use for a male incarnation but an accurate one: this mother energy is available to everyone."

Steve then explained the hidden agenda beneath David being sexually attracted to some people. "With Jupiter in Scorpio in the fifth house, we see here a feeling that very likely led to some problems within his life—problems that can make us smile a little bit—in the area of falling in love. His problem was that he was in love with an awful lot of people at once. He had a hard time narrowing down. The Jupiter in the fifth gave him the capacity to fall in love, and he had that in spades. So what we see here is that while he derived a great deal of pleasure and insight from the process of falling in love, he had a hard time keeping it under control.

"He had a great store of love within him, but the sexual and universal love were *crossed*: they were operating together. So he could fall in love with a lot of people, and his body's neuro-circuits would interpret it as sexual love. I'm not banalizing this just for the physical—but the *bonding* energies, the male and female kinds of energies. This would lead him to be in love with a lot of different people at one time.

"Weaving all of this together, we can really see his guardian spirits in action. They've left us a little note here, in terms of the trick that they played on him. When he, or they, or all of them together were planning his incarnation, planning his chart, I can hear them saying, 'Well, we have a person whose fundamental task is individuality and freedom.' But they also see that he needs to find that freedom in the most difficult of ways, and that's in the context of a loving and open sort of life—a life that will allow itself to be touched by other people and allow that great pressure toward the lack of freedom to come into his life and to maintain his freedom under those very difficult circumstances.

"So they probably said, 'What we find here is a person who's got a dangerous amount of self-sufficiency, so what we need to do is turn up the volume on his mating drives slightly, so that he will feel a compulsion to get *close* to people. We'll let this come to him in the form of sexual energies, but many times what will really be going on will be a touching of souls, a touching of spirits with other people.'"

Again a direct hit by Steve. David was capable of being in love at one time with, let's say, two girls and a boy. He greatly enjoyed being in love, although he often did not follow up on his feelings in any overt way, for—as he noted in his journals—sex was not a big thing for him, but love was. For me, Steve's analysis of David's sexuality showed the really ingenious ways that a person's life can be designed prior to birth.

"David's ultimate goal in life was the development of courage. We find that in order to fulfill the destiny that I've described in this chart he simply *had to be* a courageous person, because he was going to draw an awful lot of fire to himself—to draw an awful lot of pressure to himself to be something other than what he really is, that he really was. Every breath he took, every decision that he made, *had* to be based on *bravery*. The path of least resistance was a path of self-destruction for him. He was not born to go with the flow: the flow would have carried him away from himself. He was here learning how to swim upstream; he'd meet resistance with courage.

"And here we find that hunger for adventure that characterizes his life. What he really needed was the existential courage to live his own life. But one of the ways of developing that is to face physical peril, things that are frightening in much more mundane ways. He had to prove himself in the face of difficulty. This compulsion grew stronger and stronger throughout his life—every day he woke up a little bit more adventurous, and this would have increased all through his life, even if he had lived to be seventy or eighty years old."

However, David's spiritual quest had ultimately been focused inward in his life, Steve told me. "The Cancer ascendant indicates a very, very powerful imagination within him and suggests that a capacity to visualize was at the cutting edge of his inward evolution. We find that he was very much needing to learn how to work with *energies*, symbols, colors, and with *light* within the consciousness, rather than with ideas, rather than with concepts. And this is the basic evolutionary stuff of Cancer, the working of the inward images that are generated by the imagination, providing pre-verbal imagination." I was once again struck by the intuitive thrust of Steve's reading, because David's last term paper in high school—a beautiful piece of writing—had as its topic the subject of light in the Bible.

"David was opening up in many ways, in terms of psychic centers and spiritual centers of consciousness—the sense of 'I have an *inner* world.' He had experiences within the course of his life of an inexplicable nature, experiences that could be accounted for only through the assumption of linkages between the conscious mind and higher levels of reality. Direct experiences of the invisible worlds and transcendent potentials of the mind, although not commonplace for him, had probably occurred enough so that he was beginning to have a belief in the idea that the description of the world that we're taught simply does not account for experience and reality completely.

"There was, in general, a strong inclination inwardly toward mystical thought, mystical kinds of awareness. So what we find is a very vivid inner life, a life full of the sense of the presence of God, the presence of the infinite. And yet an extremely difficult time *translating* that state of awareness out to the surface. He had a personality that didn't seem to have *space* for that kind of awareness—that didn't seem to make sense of that kind of awareness, and yet he *had* that awareness within himself. It tended to be always buried: the hidden self. Yet there was a reserve of spiritual strength within him, that other people wouldn't even be aware of, wouldn't even suspect. But in times of crisis, it was there.

"What David needed in order to bring himself together to a focus was a spiritual perspective upon life. He needed some sense of the ultimate need to investigate consciousness, the ultimate need to explore the limits of awareness. He benefited tremendously from meditation. This was something very much of a help to him, very good for him. And I would think that he probably did considerable work in that regard, but I think he probably did it in private.

"David was moving into the inner worlds very rapidly. He had come into this planet to make a great leap in terms of the inward dimensions of spirituality, in terms of the psychic qualities of unfoldment, the visionary dimensions of spirituality. The other half of spirituality is the ability to take the love that we're given and give it back to the world in some concrete way, some outward way—something you've given: self-forgetfulness rather than self-remembering.

"The moon in the third house suggests that there was ability within David as a writer, and that this is something that was developing within him and would have developed considerably further in the course of a long life. There was a sense of the need to express himself verbally, but his practice for this was writing to himself,[36] and the need to keep a journal, perhaps to write poetry—to record his feelings and to develop the discipline of expressing his feelings in language.

"The whole motivation of the life, though, of the karmic evolutionary life, was to flow *inward*, a flow that would have carried him deeper and deeper into himself, and further and further away from the world of what people thought and expected of him—a world that would have taught him more and more about the strength that is inherent in the process of yielding, of bending, of flowing. He had learned the strength of conviction, the strength of determination, the strength of will [in earlier lives]. He had now come into the world to learn the strength of bending, of loving, of being receptive, of relaxing, of accepting, of feeling. And this was the *purpose* of this life. We can only assume that he had fulfilled it to the extent he could with this [personality] tool."

As noted earlier, the image of death had been an integral part of David's life, and Steve showed me how that had fit into David's life script. "The Part of Fortune in the eighth house speaks very clearly that he needed to make peace with death. And he knew that, as long as he lived, he had to somehow recognize that time was running out. Not that he had—through this symbol, at any rate—any clairvoyant perception of the time he was going to die—he may have had that, but I don't see it in this symbol—but what we are seeing is that his life had to be permeated with the spirit of living at the edge, living right at the edge of the abyss. This is the only way he could have the intensity of spirit that he needed, in order to fulfill his destiny. So, this is one of the things that drew him into programs like Outward Bound. He needed to actually be physically near that edge a lot of time; he needed death to be close to him, in order to give him the kick in the pants that he required to live with the vibrancy and intensity that he had come into the world to experience.

"With Aquarian Venus in the eighth house, *David had very little fear of death*. Death came to him in the guise of Venus, and I'm not speaking here of his actual death. I'm speaking of the *image* of death—death as a sort of cosmic presence that had come to him ever since he was young, and this was getting him familiar with it. What we find here is that death wore the mask of Venus for him. Death as a symbol of peaceful transition for him, death as a *calming*, death as a release of tension. Because of this, we find little real fear of death within him. Perhaps a fear of dying, a fear of pain, as in all human beings, but the idea of death itself was not a threat to him. I *don't* see a death wish here, but I do see a sense of being at peace with death.

"Despite the seemingly extreme and violent qualities of David's death, it was accompanied within him by a spirit of peace, a peaceful succumbing, and a death that he actually enjoyed. That's a kind of hard idea to swallow, but that's what [Aquarian Venus in the eighth house] says: a feeling of peace would have come into David's consciousness in the face of his death."

Steve then touched on a very unusual aspect of David's transition: "What we're seeing here is that there was a guardian teacher who drew very close to David during the time of his death, a guardian teacher who stood, I'm almost tempted to say, as a mother to him, but a better word would be a lover, in that sense of equality, that sense of partnership. This would not be at all inharmonious with the idea of mystical, visionary, transcendent experiences at the time of death: the Aquarian Venus very much suggests that. But an aura of protection that surrounded him at that time."

These mystical concepts greatly eased my anguished thoughts that David had died alone in the Sea of Cortez and had suffered during his transition. I also realized that the physical symptoms that Noreen and Mr. Johnson had experienced and described belonged to David's body and that by the time these had come into being, David had already left his body. Understanding that David had been spiritually protected as he died and that he was able to quickly slip out of his body before it actually drowned, I was able to release my feeling that David's manner of death had been unfair. I still grieved that David was gone, but now I at least knew that David had been helped with his rebirth into spirit.

When I asked Steve about the length of David's life, he said that the time of death can't be predicted by astrology, but—knowing about life plans—I pursued this question of life span. Steve replied that this aspect of existence moves beyond astrology and into the whole philosophy of spiritual evolution—of karma, basically. "The assumption is that the soul will use a chart to gather a certain kind of experience and when it has done that, there is no point in having that tool any more. Very often a soul, through rapid evolution, can live very intensely in a short time, while in another situation a theme that has been nearly finished in a previous life needs just a little bit of wrapping up."

Steve noted that the level of soul development was not reflected in a chart either, that a chart is just the vehicle into which the soul enters, and that there is no way to look at a chart and say anything at all about a person's level of spiritual unfoldment or psychological integrity. In the chart the problems a person is facing can be seen, but not the response that he's making. Free will, therefore, is very much a part of our journey through life.

I said to Steve, "So psychology and theology will have to reconsider certain areas of life, because the things you've discussed we now make value judgments about, but from what you've said, it's often not necessarily a question of a value judgment at all."

Steve responded, "No, not at all."

"It's a question of what you *need*."

"Yes," Steve answered.

I was extremely impressed by this reading, for several reasons. First, although I had mentioned a few things about David's death to Steve, I had not spoken of David's life to him. Nevertheless, Steve had told me things about David that no one except me knew, since I was the only person who had read David's journals up to that point. Steve's reading—and I *do* feel it was a psychic reading, in which Steve used David's astrological chart in the same manner as other sensitives use photographs or objects belonging to individuals—was stunningly accurate and insightful, encapsulating or expanding on what I had learned about the inner David.

I was also floored by the depth and breadth of Steve's analysis of David's chart. I was especially struck by the meticulous way that a soul and its advisors plan and create an individual's personality traits, drives, and mission for a given existence. I had expected to hear some broad generalities; instead, I was shown the spiritual configuration which had molded David's identity and life.[37]

This tour de force by Steve was very important to me, for what it showed was that man is not just a physical body, that life is not simply a series of random events and encounters, but that a soul has a plan or destiny which it *chooses*—with guidance from spiritual mentors—even before it incarnates. Irene Hughes had said we are co-creators with God, and I am certain that this is what Jesus meant when he said, "Ye are gods." With our minds, bodies, and spirits, we help the creative force to bring into being this world and the universe. "Mind is the builder," Edgar Cayce had said. Chance does not rule our world.

Over the next ten years, I discovered parts of my life plan and was able to see the broad outlines of the road I had laid out before myself. I often didn't know what was behind the next bend in the road, but I had great faith that the road I followed was mine, that I was traveling in the right direction, and that guidance was always there for me.

# 14

# the father is the mission

Curiosity can be addictive. While doing the research for my doctoral dissertation, I often would discover a thread of information going off somewhere, and I would doggedly follow that thread to see whether it would take me to a dead end or to the promised land of significant fact. My biggest find then came from a small footnote in an obscure article, which led me to a treasure-trove of critically important material. The psychic research I was doing now was exactly the same. I had to follow every thread I noticed because I never knew where it might lead me—but I needed help to do that. Since I felt I hadn't reached the ends of some threads, I returned to Marian and Noreen.

When I made another appointment with Marian, it was first scheduled for the eleventh of the month, then was changed to the twelfth. I did go to her meeting on the evening of the eleventh, though, spoke with her, and gave her some of David's writing to read. Weeks later, I noticed that all of my other personal meetings with her had been on the eleventh of each month: February 11, March 11, June 11, February 11, and March 11. In addition, my session with Douglas Johnson had been on July 11. When Krista decided to get a reading from Marian in 1981, it was held on April 11. To me this said that one of David's signatures from spirit was eleven, his name number.

For this meeting with Marian, I had written down a list of questions for her, the first one having to do with publishing David's writing. Marian told me, "I feel that David is going to work through you, because you are one of the channels that he established. I get very strong feelings that your book *is* going to be published, and not only David's writing but your own writings—your own growth experience through all of this and through the suffering and through the pain, and the wisdom that will finally emerge from it. By the way, Betty and I are both amazed at the light around you these days—how you have changed in this last year, an incredible change. You shine in a light of your own right now."

I really hadn't been aware of any change in myself, yet in the years after David's death a Raleigh therapist friend of mine whom I visited periodically always would comment that every time I came to see her I was a different person.

In an earlier reading, Marian had mentioned something about David's perception of reality, and I questioned her about this. "At times David was very much caught up into the illusion of outer appearances, but there also was a part of the soul that *knew*. Often he saw *beyond,* and didn't see things as they appear to be but saw more of what really was. He didn't always understand what he saw, and so there was a tremendous sorrow and pain on his soul sometimes—partly for himself, because he didn't completely understand, and partly because there was an intuitive knowing: 'This is not *real.*'

"He looked for a world that was better than what was at hand, and he tried very much to penetrate the veil that would let him be able to see through the illusion. There were times when he had very clear vision, when he would get a glimpse of reality. Then the mist would seem to close down, and he would again be seeing with these all-too-human eyes. But the soul, the spirit that was within, was very much aware and had been aware—I would say probably since about his thirteenth year—that there was so much more than what actually meets the eye.

"David came to establish knowledge of what our cultural problems are all about, so that he would be able to work in a creative way, trying to alleviate some of the needless, senseless suffering that we have. After he had gotten into college or into a place where he was spending time alone, I feel he was beginning to get a few bits and pieces but lacked the education or *awareness* to be able to put it into words. And that comes across in his writing, too. There was a soul which was crying for something that he didn't have the words to describe. But David was a *prophet*—"

I remembered David's Duke English paper, "The Prophet Paul," an analysis of D.H. Lawrence's short story, "The Rocking-Horse Winner," whose main character is Paul, a name with which David had identified personally. One segment of the paper particularly struck me:

Paul becomes a prophet whose life becomes his message . . .

If a prophet turns the hearts of the people, he can depart, for a prophet's success destroys him. He has come into a country where he knows he will not be honored, to a people who he knows cannot hear what he will say. Yet the power of his words is so great that sometimes the people do regret and do turn and listen to him. If this happens, the prophet becomes only a man, or, rather, the men become life to the prophet and do not need his sight for their eyes. This new sight for the people does not come easily, yet the prophet holds this hope always in front of himself: a hope that someday the people will cast him off, able to see God clearly themselves . . .

I feel that David was a prophet whose life was his message, which his journals record.

Marian continued: "David was under the sign of Aquarius, and Aquarians are definitely the prophets of the Zodiac. They're always ahead of their time. No one understands an Aquarian—they don't even understand themselves. They live on more than one plane at a time. David was puzzled by his human self. He was puzzled by many things." I asked Marian what she meant by saying David was a prophet. "David knew he was going to die. He saw beyond today. He had always known that he would not be on Earth long, and he has written it somewhere."

One place where David recorded prophetic impressions about his death was in a story about the mythical Hope. David began two versions of Hope's adventures, the first written when he was twelve and the second when he was eighteen. Both versions note that water is fatal to Hope, and Hope actually does die in water in the first version. Yet David wrote (in the first version) that although Hope died, "the truth is that there is always hope," and (in the second version) that "Hope dies, but a second life comes."

When I re-read David's journals and poetry, I found a substantial number of references to death in them, far more than I would have expected from a teenager. Yet these references did not seem to come from depression, but from David's simple acceptance of "life's other door," as Edgar Cayce had called it. David being subconsciously aware of his death opened a broad new vista in my thinking, for if one knows when one is to die, then there really are no "accidents" or "coincidences" in life.

I kept feeling that David had had a mystical experience on solo, so I asked Marian. "When you said that," she responded, "I had such a flash of him in a lifetime back a few hundred years, when he was a young Indian boy—maybe eleven, twelve years old, tied to a tree—where he was sent out to have the vision that would give him his path through life. I feel like the solo that David was out on in this lifetime was almost a re-living of the Indian experience of trying to find the inner self. I do feel something happened on his solo—I don't know what it was, but I feel he penetrated the veil at that time. I think he saw some things, but I can't say what. I only know that finally—the vision he didn't get as the Indian boy, he did get this time. With this vision he completed something on the Earth plane."

Marian seemed most effective when given people's photographs, which she used to tune in to each person's vibrations. So I had brought with me pictures of my family, plus a couple taken in Baja by one of David's crewmates. I handed Marian pictures of my mother and Krista.

Marian told me that my mother had been David's mother in more than one lifetime and that she was "probably in contact with David on the astral plane." That would explain my mother's experiences with David since his death, I thought. Marian's impressions of Krista were equally unusual. "Here is another—she is also from the angelic force, very much connected with David—very close ties with David. It's incredible that they weren't twins. She is what we call a guardian spirit. She volunteered to come to Earth at this time."

I was really struck by Marian's comment that David and Krista had almost been twins, because when Veronica was pregnant with David she had told me that her doctor had heard two heartbeats early in the pregnancy. Krista probably changed her mind about being born a twin and withdrew, but she *was* very close to David. As a small child—born seventeen months after David—she followed David around like a puppy, and, right up to David's death, she followed in his footsteps in many ways. She took David's death very hard, and I don't know how she could have dealt with it if she had been born David's twin.

Since David had been identified as the best Latin student in North Carolina in 1975, I suspected he had had a Roman life, and I asked about that. "He had several Roman incarnations," Marian noted. "As a matter of fact, you knew him in Rome. He lived during the time of the Caesars and experienced almost a trinity action under the Romans."

In a Greek life David had been a Roman slave, then had the opposite experience of being in a very high position in Rome. "He later had a third Roman life—sometime after the crucifixion," Marian recounted, "when the early church was first being established—at a time of great mortal danger for him, because he was a follower of Caesar and was switching gears from seeing Caesar as God to beginning to follow the one God."

Marian then looked at the photograph of the Baja sunrise on the cover of this book and said, "That's beautiful." I responded, "What a place to die. If you're going to pick a place—" and Marian cut in, "I was just going to say the same thing: what a place to die! What a fantastic place to die! Sort of like going up on the mountain to make your ascension."

She asked how many people had lost their lives in the storm. I told her three and then handed her the picture of David, Brenda, and Tim that DelRene had taken. "I find this picture very interesting," Marian observed, "because the auric energy around them is already separating. What I'm feeling over David's head is an auric force, and there is a cord [probably what is called the silver cord] which should be very, very strong but is merely like a thin tendril—it's almost as if it *is* separated. Around her is tremendous darkness, as though it has already begun, and here [around Tim] I see no life-force at all. This was definitely in order—it was the right time."

*Crew and instructors share moments around a campfire. Clockwise from bottom center of photo: Elmo, Catherine, DelRene, BeeBee, David, Tim, Jana, and Larry.*

I handed her another picture from Baja. It showed several of David's crew and two instructors around a fire, David in the center of the picture behind the fire (facing the camera), Tim to his left and BeeBee to his right. David seemed to dominate the picture. "This picture intrigues me particularly," Marian told me, "because I feel like many of the individuals in this photograph have sat around a similar fire—in a similar group—just trying to stay alive, in a time when they were escaping from some great danger—when there was some kind of carnage or pillaging. I feel that the town which they had come from was in Asia, Asia Minor. They lived in Afghanistan when the hordes of Genghis Khan came down across Afghanistan, raiding and raping, pillaging and murdering. They are a group that escaped into the desert and were just people trying to stay alive. It's very interesting that, literally, this was what they were doing again in this lifetime. I feel that this definitely was group karma that brought these people together."

*David in Baja.*

I said, "You mentioned that David had incarnated during the times of Buddha, Abraham, Moses and Aaron,

Jesus, and in ancient Greece. Do you want to give any further details about these?"

Marian replied, "No. The only thing I would say is that every time—as near as I am able to see—every time that a Christ spirit has come forth on the Earth, every time that there has been a change in the mass consciousness, where it's like a release of more *energy*—a release of more truth to humanity, he—and many like him—have made an appearance, have somehow played a part in that particular release of energy."

From Marian's insights, along with the Cayce material, I now began to perceive and understand that all of our lives have a spiritual subtext and that the real drama taking place in our lives is usually hidden from our consciousness. These dramas are far more fascinating than what we seem to be experiencing in our daily lives. A few years later I was given many opportunities to explore how these hidden scenarios operate, both in my own life and in the lives of others.

Noreen was back in Virginia, so I wrote to her, requesting her impressions about several things, including the events in Baja. Noreen took my letter to a class in psychic development that she was teaching and a few weeks later sent me the transcript of what had come through her. She had had some difficulty going into trance but had finally managed to do so. Her first words then were, "Oh, to escape . . . Let me tell you what I'm feeling. I'm floating. I'm flying up into the air." She apparently was again inside David, experiencing what Marian had described in her first reading.

Then she murmured, "There are some mountains below."

I thought this was an odd response, considering that all I had ever visualized of the Baja area was the Sea of Cortez and a few cliffs. However, I later found the following: "Punta Púlpito is a bold headland about 470 feet high . . . at the outer end of a peninsula which projects about half a mile from the general line of the coast. . . . Detached rocks extend about one cable [720 feet] off the point. A remarkable triple peak rises to an elevation of 1,640 feet, about 3¾ miles southwestward of the point."[38]

As Noreen continued her reading, a dog barking outside pulled her out of trance, but she tried to go under again. "I want to contact David. David, speak to me." She tried to clear her throat. "David is not ready to talk right now. My head hurts. David is here. I'm going to speak." She kept clearing her throat. "I can't. Just ask questions, and I will filter it through from David." David apparently still was unable to directly control a medium's organs of speech.

The conductor asked Noreen for the name of David's boat. "I don't see a name . . . it's more red in color." He inquired about the boat's size. "Two. Two . . . small, it's light." He then requested that Noreen describe the circumstances of the accident. "The sea . . . I feel turbulence in the water. Not storm, but there are strong waves. Strong waves . . ."

Noreen again entered David's mind and began to speak as him: "A heavy sea. It's a little rough, but we can handle it. There's not going to be any trouble . . . low whitecaps. They're low, they are right around us. We're out, fairly far. There's a point, a point that is jutting out. It looks more like rock or stone." This was a good description of Punta Púlpito, which is simply a gigantic piece of rock. When the conductor asked if the point was to David's right or left, Noreen slipped out of David's mind and said, "I feel it to the right. Like he was trying to get to—there is a point there."

Noreen continued, "I felt that I could navigate into an area that wouldn't upset us, wouldn't upset the boat. Because the wind is coming in strong now—it's coming from behind us . . . I'm really not that efficient [at boating] as I pretend to be. The boat really is more in control than I am . . ." The conductor asked if David was by himself. "No, Brenda is here. She's in front of me . . . I keep telling her it's going to be all right. 'We're going to be all right, Brenda.'"

The conductor questioned how David had got into the sea. "The boat. By the boat," Noreen said softly. The conductor asked what happened then. "I know I'm not going to make it. I'm trying to hold. I'm not going to do it. There's more waves—"

Noreen began to cry. "I'm sorry. I'm sorry, I'm going to have to come out. Oh, my God. Oh, my God. I'm David. I'm reliving the whole damn thing . . . what are we doing this for? I'm sorry. I'm sure this is very important. What can I tell you that is significant?"

A few minutes later, Noreen picked up what appeared to be either a past-life personality of David or David's cosmic personality, and in the transcript below Noreen is speaking as this other consciousness.

Noreen: "There is a lot of love in this room. There are a lot of good vibrations, and I feel very happy, so I choose to make all of you feel very happy. The questions you are about to ask me, don't feel badly about them. Let's just try to make people happy with the answers."

Conductor: "I want to ask about David's writings."

N: "I wrote in another life, too. I used to be a Hebrew master. I taught the language. It was difficult with David's mind being as it was. He had trouble controlling the energy that I needed. David being a young person was hard, and his headaches came from my not being able to enter at the times I needed to. Is that clear?"

C: "What was David's mission in this life?"

N: "To bring awareness to the man who seeks so many answers to a simple truth."

C: . . . [Unintelligible.]

N: "The father is the mission, not the child."

C: "What can the father be told to aid in his growth?"

N: "The understanding of what is before him."

C: "What is this understanding?"

N: "The knowing of the past. The past holds the keys to the future, if applied to the right door."

C: "The keys?

N: "The keys are in the journal. In the two-third section of the journal, of the book, lies many answers which the right mind should perceive. The search only has to be within one's self."

C: "The father looks outside himself and doesn't see?"

N: "Your words speak with wisdom. It is clearly true."

C: "The father needs to re-read the journal?"

N: "The father will not return to the journal, but the right pages that will be in his writing will answer the questions he needs. The words will come from within himself. Time will come when many understand through those words."

I didn't understand. This part of Noreen's reading made no sense to me at all. For years, every time I read it over, I just shook my head in puzzlement. How could I be the mission? What was I supposed to learn? I read David's journals again. And again. I still didn't understand. Then how would others understand, when I couldn't?

# 15

# moving on

August of 1980 had come, and I knew it was time to leave Raleigh. My catalyst month has always been August, and I felt the house would sell quickly and bring a good price. I had almost finished restoring it, so I put it up for sale. Eric was nearly done with his studies at N.C. State and had decided to join the Peace Corps. Kris was still at Duke, doing well. Like David, she had become involved with Project WILD, and although this made me very nervous, I felt I couldn't interfere.

Preston and I had become friends. I sometimes phoned her and a few times came to Durham and had breakfast or lunch with her. In late August, Preston, Susan, and Brian were in Raleigh to give depositions for the trial, and I had lunch with Susan and dinner with Preston. The depositions painted a brilliant picture of David, but I was most affected by Preston's last comments:

> David came in [before he left for Baja] and said, "I don't think I will ever see you again, but I love you."
>
> To this day, I have never met anyone who has made so many people happy. If there is one image I have of him it's of one big smile, and he often told me that his goal each day was to be happy, but it took a lot of work and it wasn't easy. He really expended a lot of energy on

people. His gift to us was trying to make us happy, which in turn was his gift to himself.

He is always with me. He has never really died. I've run over these thoughts many times since he died. I was really crushed when he died. It took me a long time to get over it. But then I started carrying with me the values of what he had been. I felt like if he was going to die, he would die in his own way. If he was going to die, he needed to be free. He was a free spirit.

I had attended all three depositions, and when they were finished, Preston spoke with the attorney representing Outward Bound. She later told me he had said that many changes had been made in the Outward Bound program as a result of David's, Brenda's and Tim's deaths.

Before leaving North Carolina I got a reading from Don Hudson in Charlotte. Don correctly pinpointed things in my life and background and also accurately described David and some of his characteristics. Although he didn't produce any new information about how David had died, he did pick up on David's premonition: "David went on this adventure knowing he wasn't coming back. You can tell that by some of his writings. O.K.? Yet he went anyway, knowing, deep inside, that he wouldn't come back."

When I asked about David's spiritual development, Don told me: "David's religion was only within him. He could care less about the dogma of all the other religions. He felt very strongly in his own beliefs in God—and man. He *was* a spiritual man, but not as a Baptist or Methodist or anything. It was *within* him: the God within, and that was very strong. However, he didn't try to pressure it on anyone else, but neither did he allow other people to pressure him—because he had his *own* way of thinking." No doubt about that, I thought to myself.

David's journals had revealed that the tensions in his life during the months before his transition were causing him to search through every part of his mind, and when I asked Don about this, he said, "David went through some trying times within himself during that year. But there again, he was only trying to find David—and he found him. He was getting it together there, at the end. He was his own individual.

"David had a mind on him that wouldn't quit, a terrific mind on him. He had many interests, but most of all he had interest in the *mind*. But not psychology—much stronger than psychology—the mind itself: what the mind can *do*. That was what he was trying to prove to himself: 'This is our universe, what can we do with it?' He was a very good young man. Very interesting."

The house sold for only a thousand dollars less than I had planned, escrow closed, and the movers picked up our furniture. I was finally ready to go. I shoved our enthusiastic dog Samantha and the very unenthusiastic Lord Peter the cat into our station wagon, and with Veronica beside me drove up to New York, arriving October 31. I had determined to live in Manhattan but had been able to afford only a small one-bedroom apartment on West 89th Street. When the movers unloaded all our furniture and boxes, there was almost no room to walk around, but after I built floor-to-ceiling bookshelves in the living room and set up my desk, things became somewhat reasonable, if snug. I didn't care. I was in New York and was about to produce and direct a play.

From my journal:

> November 12. I feel a little crazy tonight. What am I *doing* here? The world has been so unreal since David died. Up to then it seemed firm—at times depressing, hard, apparently unyielding, but *real*. Now . . . it's as if someone has cut all the taut strings in me, and I am insanely running around inside myself trying to tie them back together—but there's not enough to tie! So I must build a new web in this vast cavern of myself to catch those bits of life which fly past me: catch them, hold them, inspect them, then devour them. Oh, the *echoes* in the cavern, now that all the cords have been cut.

I decided to try one last psychic for my research. On November 9, I wrote to the headquarters of Spiritual Frontiers Fellowship, which I had joined two years earlier, and asked if S.F.F. could recommend any psychics in my geographic area. S.F.F. replied that I should contact the New York City S.F.F. chairwoman or call the chairwoman of the central New Jersey area, Joyce Winner, who was herself psychic. There also was a psychic visiting New York City until November 27, I was told.

For some unfathomable reason I was very reluctant to call the visiting psychic, but when she left the city I phoned the New York S.F.F. chairwoman. She immediately replied that the person who could do what I wanted was Joyce Winner and that Joyce would be in town the following week. I decided I was supposed to see Joyce and scheduled an appointment with her. The only thing I ever mentioned to either woman was that I wanted the reading for a deceased person. I was determined to make this final session as objective as possible.

I met Joyce on December 3 at the upper westside apartment of the woman who had scheduled my reading. When I arrived, Joyce greeted me in the large foyer of the apartment and then we went into a spacious living room. When we were seated, she told me she couldn't guarantee what she would get, then asked for a key to "screen out things" around me. I gave her my house keys, and she held them briefly, then handed them back.

Like Douglas Johnson and Don Hudson, she inquired if I had three children, but I didn't know how to answer her. I *did* still have three children, but David was in spirit now, so I said, "Yes and no," evasively. "O.K., because I see three with you," Joyce replied. Three were born, I told her. She asked if this was who I wanted information about, and when I said yes, she questioned if my child was a girl. I told her no, and she then responded, "O.K. Artistic, though, and things like that. Very gentle kind of person."

Joyce sighed, "This doesn't seem to have been very long ago, but it's over a year, isn't it?" I replied it was more than two years. "But it feels so close to you—still too close, very difficult to deal with." I agreed. "You're still married, aren't you," Joyce next stated.

She asked if the name Marie or Maria mean anything to me in particular. I responded it didn't, but I had a mental lapse here, which I didn't realize until two days later, for Maria was my paternal grandmother's name. A few moments later Joyce wanted to know if the name John meant anything to me in particular. Surprised, I said it was my father's name. "He's still living, isn't he?" I told her he was. In retrospect, I decided that my father's name was given to Joyce to confirm that "Maria" was connected with "John."

Joyce now asked if I had brought a photograph of David, and I handed her one of him taken in Baja. I noticed that she didn't look at the picture and that she turned it face down in her hands. She held it throughout the entire reading, continually rubbing her fingertips over the photographic surface of the print.

Her first impression of David was that his was not a normal death, that it felt too traumatic, but that it wasn't murder either. She finally said it was an accident. "I feel despondency with your son, though, so he was working through a rather serious problem with himself at the time, wasn't he? And he seemed to have been doing well with it." Joyce had obviously picked up David's struggle with his sexual identity. "I don't see any real emotional problems with him, though," she added. "He was certainly what the psychologists would classify normal. Very bright. Very quick mind."

Suddenly Joyce said, "Was there water involved with this accident? Because I'm just seeing water *everywhere.*" I replied that there had been water. "He seems to have been alone at the time, though. There were other people around, but I'm just seeing him alone at the time."

"David . . . does that mean something to him?"

I was very shocked to hear Joyce say David's name. "That's his name," I managed to say.

Even Joyce seemed surprised: "David is his name? All right. Well, he's certainly very much with you . . .

"I'm being shown an empty coffin. They didn't find the body, did they?" I said they hadn't. "This part of it seems to have bothered your wife more . . . Is your wife Roman Catholic?" Yes, I said. "You're not." I told her I wasn't.

Joyce now started to laugh. "David was very modern in his phraseology, wasn't he? Do you know what he just said to me? 'Way to go, baby!'" Joyce laughed once more. "He's satisfied that I'm getting it through properly."

"A few weeks before you came here," Joyce continued, "you were getting pushings toward me, I'm told." She asked if I had noticed this. I told her I had. "When did you get my name, about a month ago?" I said yes. "O.K., that's what David is telling me. He's been—it's very interesting, because they can see us on the other side. They know who [which psychic] they can get through, and then they'll work, until they can get you here." That also explained my reluctance to see the other psychic that S.F.F. had recommended, I thought.

"The import of what your son is trying to bring through here is to assure your wife that he has a *better* body. He doesn't need the physical body." The problem, I told Joyce, was that since David's physical body had never been found, Veronica had been unwilling to admit that David was dead. "Yes. Well, she *must*," Joyce answered, then paused momentarily. "O.K. Some of these things I'm getting, I'll bring through just the way I get them: 'Dead is a matter of opinion.'" David's humor was back again. "It's not the same as we are here, of course, but listen to what they say in the funeral service of her church: existence absolutely continues, there's no question about it."

I observed to Joyce that no one really knew what had happened to David, but that he had been with other people and had become separated from them. "Oh, that's why I see him alone," Joyce commented. "David had been having some spiritual stirrings. He was helped, very much, so he wasn't really by himself. Yes, he was alone when it happened, but he had plenty of spiritual help there with him.

And he had had his total belief in God renewed, so he was O.K. spiritually—there was no problem at the time of his death. 'God isn't as fussy as the rest of us,' he says."

I recounted that Brenda had been in the kayak with David, that perhaps he had become separated from her too, and that her body had been found. Joyce interrupted to say, "They found the boat, though, didn't they?" It had been found, I replied. "The boat had a hole in it?" I told Joyce I didn't know, but that another psychic had said the same thing. I asked where she saw the hole. "Toward the front, but this may have been shown to me symbolically. What I feel happened is that they hit something submerged and then flipped."

Outward Bound disposed of all of the kayaks before our suit was filed, and no one testified on this point, so I never found out if the boat had been damaged or not. If it hadn't, it would seem to me that David and Brenda would have stayed in the kayak as they were taught to do and as BeeBee and David R. had. Later, in a sworn deposition given for the lawsuit, Catherine stated, "One of the things we were trained to do was to watch for the rocks, because the rocks down there are one of the major dangers. Sometimes they are just under the surface, and it is very easy to crash on the rocks." BeeBee testified similarly.

"There were several—quite a few kayaks, weren't there," Joyce went on. "They purposely went off in another direction—quite intentionally went off in another direction." Joyce obviously was picking up that David and Brenda had been paddling either after Jana or toward shore to get help from the instructors. "I'm seeing white, bubbly aspects of water now—hitting rocks."

Joyce's next observation was a shocker. "They were . . ." She paused and breathed deeply three times. ". . . his life jacket's gone. They *had* life jackets." I asked how David's jacket had come off. "It got caught on something. The girl's life jacket was still on her, wasn't it?" I replied it was. "All right. I'm seeing your son's life jacket gone." I asked Joyce whether he had removed his jacket for some reason or had it swept off him.

"It's like he . . . he got pushed along rocks and things, and it got [pulled] off." Joyce paused. "It was a good life jacket—Coast Guard approved, he says. He used it right: he says he knows how to use it. It got *pulled* off—not anything he did, not anything he did—that's very important for him. It was buckled properly, everything was done properly. There was no way he could have helped her. He was moved in another direction, and it was pulled off."

Joyce went on to emphasize that when the boat was found there had to have been damage to it. She paused again. "He wasn't that far out," she noted. Had David been caught by the undertow when they capsized, I asked Joyce. "No, he just—he was a strong swimmer, wasn't he? Good swimmer. He tried to find her. He couldn't. There just was no way he could. He says it's very disorienting.[39] He didn't know—it must have been—he must have been in the middle of a bad storm, because he couldn't see which direction to go."

Joyce went on to say that David had been quite aware of what was happening to him. When did he die, I asked. "From the feelings I get, it wasn't very long. It was—the boat was thrown, he hit something on the—" Was it rocks, I interrupted. "Yes. And flipped. And he also had been injured somehow." I asked her what part of his body. "It seems to be the head, but more the face than the head. Up in this part somewhere." Joyce touched the left side of her head, moving her fingers from the side of her skull down beside the temple to the left cheekbone—the same general area that Douglas Johnson and Noreen Renier had indicated.

Until now, I had never been able to understand why David had not survived, when six others had. Certainly he could swim better than many in his group, was stronger than most, was in better physical condition, had more training in physical and mental endurance than most. The flipped kayak and the blow to the head explained why David hadn't made it to shore.

Joyce paused again, listening inside. "'I did the best I could,' he says."

That brought up a great deal of emotion in me. Of course David had done his best in the storm—he had always tried to do his best. "I know that," I answered with feeling.

"He tried to *help* her—it was important for him to help her," Joyce went on, "but he *couldn't*." David didn't need to tell me that. There wasn't any doubt in my mind that he had been thinking more of Brenda than of himself. I knew who David was, and I was proud of him.

Joyce said, "And that seems to be his regret, if I can call it that—that he couldn't help her. He felt bad about that."

"He was very loyal to people," I responded.

"Yes. Extremely. . . . *He did try*."

I asked, "What happened to his body? Was it washed out to sea?"

"Yes . . . 'It's O.K.,' is what he's telling me, 'It's O.K.'"

"All right," I said.

"David is fine," Joyce concluded.

✦ ✦ ✦

The story of David's death in the Sea of Cortez was now clear to me. David and Brenda had tried to go after Jana, but the height of the waves had hidden her from their view almost at once. So David and Brenda had headed toward shore, trying to land on a small sandy beach on the south side of Punta Púlpito and get help from the instructors. As they were paddling toward what they hoped was safety, their kayak struck a submerged rock and flipped over from the impact and from the violent action of the off-shore waves.

David and Brenda were thrown into the water and were separated immediately by the waves, and the kayak quickly filled with water from the hole created by the impact. Although he wanted to help Brenda, he couldn't find her. The force of the waves flung David against a rock, and he received a blow to the left side of his head. His injury, the cold water, the loss of weight and diarrhea on the course, the fast on solo, and the trauma and exertion of the day's events threw David into shock. Dazed, disoriented, and weakened, he was pulled under the water by wave actions and by the tide, which was going out. He died almost instantly.

His body became lodged underwater in rocks when his life jacket snagged on something. The currents, waves, and tide of the Sea of Cortez pulled David's body from his trapped life jacket. His body was then carried to Carmen Island by off-shore currents, and his life jacket later worked free from the rocks and also floated to Carmen. When David's body was not found by searchers, another storm arose, and the sea that David loved so much carried his body away.

My search for what happened to the physical David was over.

# 16

## a new life

I decided to direct a play I had done very successfully in Raleigh years before, *A Song For All Saints*, by James Lineberger. I tracked down Jim, and he agreed to the production. Then I slowly and painstakingly started to find a theater and rehearsal space and to build up a production staff. Since I didn't have much money, the production would have to be done as an Equity Showcase, but I intended to use it to attract capital for a bigger production.

I worked very hard. I felt happy and more free than I had since coming back from Ireland. Veronica seemed unchanged. I had hoped she would be tempted by something in New York, but the city didn't appear to affect her. As always, I had no idea what was going on in her mind, and by now I had learned not to ask.

One night I came home from somewhere and found her seated at our circular Georgian table, in right profile to me, shoulders slumped, staring straight before her. As I looked at Veronica, I realized that she was sliding deeper and deeper into depression and that I was tacitly enabling her to do so. Right then I decided that I would not continue to be her accomplice in this slide and that we could no longer remain together. But, as always, I didn't know how we could separate. Nor, apparently, did she. We seemed trapped with each other.

More than a year had now passed since the suit had been filed against Outward Bound. A trial date had finally been scheduled in Santa Fe, but due to various circumstances, the case had to be settled out of court in March. After attorneys' fees and legal expenses of almost $40,000 each, each family received $60,000.

Our suit did result in positive changes, however: Outward Bound was required to turn over to us all information about what had happened in Baja (which to me clearly demonstrated Outward Bound's negligence); the kayaking course in Baja was permanently discontinued; Southwest Outward Bound's director resigned; the safety policies and instructor training of Outward Bound were greatly upgraded; Outward Bound adopted a policy of full disclosure to parents in the event of an accident. And in the three years following David's death I was able to find no fatalities in U.S. Outward Bound courses. I was also told that the entire outdoor industry had been very much aware of the case and was now generally more conscious of safety for its students.

✦ ✦ ✦

With Outward Bound behind me, I moved ahead with my production of *Saints*. Potential investor response wasn't very good, but I kept working. Then I heard that Virginia Samdahl would soon be in town, and so on May 13 I became a second-degree Usui Reiki healer. After the instruction and initiation were completed, I felt a great deal of heat in my right hand, and my hand continued to feel hot for the next twenty-four hours. A short time before, Lord Peter had come down with feline leukemia, which he must have contracted in Raleigh as he now was an apartment cat, and I began to give him Reiki. He seemed to respond.

In the spring, I received notice of a Spiritual Frontiers Fellowship retreat to be held in Elizabethtown, Pennsylvania. S.F.F. has several retreats a year in various parts of the East and Midwest, and I had been getting their brochures for over two years. This particular retreat was titled "Reflections of the Light." I could see no reason to attend it, as I noticed nothing special about the retreat, but for some reason I kept looking at the brochure, kept feeling the urge to go, for several weeks. I finally gave in and sent off my application, but I still didn't know why.

On Sunday, June 28, I arrived by train at Elizabethtown and registered for the retreat, which was being held on the campus of the local college. That evening I went to a lecture entitled "Let There Be Love, Light and Beauty," and the next day began the round of lectures, workshops, and meditations that S.F.F. always provides. Late Tuesday morning I went to get a one-hour reading from a trance medium, Ron Scolastico. Although Ron channeled a great deal of esoteric material about me, the main topic he kept circling back to was love.

"You seek a greater opening of the soul," he said, "and in this period of time you do prepare to draw your focus upon the heart portion. For it is this which has caused difficulty with self throughout this livingness, which has caused a great confusion. In this time you do prepare to take forth the challenge which would have self be responsible for a loved one, allow self to see the true purpose of the sharing of a soul. That it does strengthen the resolve to love, strengthen the trust within the heart.

"Therefore, you shall no longer hold self aloof, no longer attempt to hold self in protection. For you do recognize now that this causes painfulness, does cause self to withdraw, and does cause a blockage of all areas of your being. There is also a great restlessness within self, for you do attempt to move self into new relationships, into new sharings with one . . .

"More and more you shall draw those ones who shall challenge self in this area, but it shall not cause a painfulness. For you have released a fear here, you have become of greater trust, of greater strength. And this does inspire those who do come near, does help them to release their fear—help them to release their need to control, to manipulate. Therefore, for many, you shall be an influencing one, who shall bring a patience, who shall bring a love that shall help themselves to make the opening of the soul.

"For a three-month time, therefore, draw before you the vision of a loved one, one who does cause a warming of the heart, and for small moments of time see this one in perfection. Do not allow sadness to enter here, but know that it is a love that does exist beyond the circumstances of the Earth, that cannot be lost, that does extend beyond time, that is of the eternal portion. And in this knowledge you shall begin to train self to not fear the loss of love. You shall allow the feeling of love to exist in a certainty, in a beginning of knowing that it shall not part, it shall not be taken from self. For it is this blockage which does prevent self from entering deep into the eternal portion—fear that you shall be separated from the ones of loving, that you shall find a great eternal aloneness."

I left the reading in a daze, the tape of the session in my pocket. Ron had channeled a great deal of important information for me that I would return to for a long time, but he hadn't said where I would find a loved one to meditate on for the next three months. In any case, it was time for lunch. The body had its needs, too, so I went to the cafeteria.

As I was eating, a woman walked over to my table from the serving line. She looked about forty, with short dark blond hair, well-groomed, attractive, medium height, trim, wearing a conservative suit. She headed straight to the chair opposite me and said, "Mind if I join you while I eat my dessert?" I didn't mind, since I hadn't yet become acquainted with anyone at the retreat and I had begun to understand that these retreats were less about the lectures and workshops than about the people you met. I will call the woman Faith to protect her privacy and because faith is what she came to represent for me.

As we talked about the retreat, Faith asked why I had joined S.F.F. When I told her about David, she seemed almost stricken. I could sense her compassion flowing openly toward me, and she looked as if tears were about to come to her eyes. I talked about David for a few minutes more, then our lunch was over, and we walked together to the afternoon lecture. From then on we were inseparable, leaving each other only when we attended different workshops and when I went to the S.F.F. healing center to give Reiki every day for at least an hour.

Faith and I talked as if we had known each other all of our lives and were simply continuing an interrupted conversation. I was comfortable in her presence, as I never was with a stranger. As I started to know her, I sensed the same sort of light and energy that David and Preston emanated. She obviously was very spiritual, as well as knowledgeable about metaphysical matters. She was married, with half-grown children, but told me she felt her marriage was about to end. I told her about my present relationship with Veronica.

On Thursday night we talked until 2:00 A.M., then I walked back to her dormitory with her. She hugged me and said, "I love you," and went inside. Friday night we had a conversation that lasted until the next morning. After the first hour or two, we began to feel energies swirling around us. We finally decided that our personal energy fields were being connected for some reason.

I mentioned to Faith that I thought I had a blockage in my heart chakra, and she said she saw a black rectangle in my heart. So Saturday morning I asked her to try to heal the blockage. We went to my room, and I sat on a chair. She put her hands first on my head, then over my heart and on the back of my neck, channeling energy. After several minutes she said the rectangle had grown smaller, and she then instructed me to imagine sending unconditional love out through my heart chakra. When I had concentrated on this for a while, she told me to hold my hand before my heart, palm inward, and asked if I felt anything. I certainly did! I could feel a radiating warmth coming from my chest. It was quite extraordinary, but also felt very natural. At a later time she told me that the black rectangle now looked like two swinging doors.

When I told Faith that I wanted to see her after the retreat, she said I had misunderstood her saying she loved me, that she was speaking of spiritual love. I became frantic at the thought of losing her. Seeing my distress, she finally agreed to let me write to her in care of another retreat that she was attending the following week. We also decided to meditate on each other at 12:55 every afternoon, starting today, when I would be returning home.

On the train, I found a seat by myself and when the train had left the station closed my eyes and started to meditate on Faith. In a moment I had lost the world and was out of time. Then I began to feel Faith's love flowing gently through me. Suddenly a deep sadness rose from the depths of my heart, and I couldn't stop it. I turned toward the window and began to sob quietly. A second wave of sadness welled up in me but left as quickly as it had come. I felt at peace. Faith's love had freed something very old and terribly sad in me.

I had written nothing in my journal during that entire week. I couldn't believe it. Nothing at all. That quickly changed, though, when I got home and began to record my life again:

> The unreality of last week simply says to me that I am in another spiritual event like David's death. I've been tossed up to a higher plane again, for various reasons which I think I understand this time. But understanding doesn't make the trip any less unreal. I feel very shaky inside. I've set events into motion, and I can't tell where they're going.
>
> . . .
>
> Today I see the struggle between the soul and the ego emerge in high gear. I know which will win: soul, but I don't relish experiencing the struggle. I hope it will be short.
>
> . . .
>
> I have a feeling Veronica has begun to move on her own path, too. Oh, yes, Eric [in Honduras with the Peace Corps] called to say he is marrying a Honduran girl. Kris has decided to leave Duke and finish her studies at New York University. She's going to stay with us for a while. *Saints* is coming along—I have a theater and rehearsal space. Did I say things are changing?

I had become used to the synchronicity in my life, but meeting Faith only fifteen minutes after Ron Scolastico told me to meditate on someone I love seemed deliberately whimsical in its timing. In any case, as soon as I got home, I wrote Faith a letter that blazed with my love and sent it off by Express Mail. Within days, Faith responded. Now both of us were completely engulfed by the love that flowed through us and washed over us continually. I wrote to her every day, one continuous letter on a pad of lined paper, jotting down whatever came to me at any time, then mailing what I had written every couple of days. Eventually I sent her almost 300 pages.

This was not a garden variety romantic relationship. I was not just "in love." What I was experiencing was of a vibration—and I use the word deliberately—much higher, finer, more delicate than normal romantic love and passion. It wasn't psychological, it wasn't physical. Perhaps it was what people have called ecstasy. I don't know, but looking back I feel this love didn't came from either of us. We were just channels, sending this extraordinary love to each other, helping each other to open and keep open our heart centers. This love was so powerful that fourteen years later when I pulled out the file of my letters to and from Faith, the love energy from her letters snapped open the swinging doors in my heart once again.

Faith lived a hundred miles away, in another state, and was still ostensibly married, as I was, so our relationship for now existed only in letters, phone calls, and through our psychic faculties. I could feel her love—and even her presence—at times, as she could mine. We even were able to feel the love surge over telephone wires when we called each other. She often was able to sense my mood, and sometimes I could sense her emotions too, though we were far apart.

We met in the city around the middle of July, walked in Central Park, checked out the zoo, had dinner. We saw each other in town once again a few weeks later, had lunch somewhere, strolled in the park again, finally sat down on a bench, Faith to my right. As we were talking, I looked out across the park. Suddenly I felt Faith's spirit/energy field—I don't know what to call it—begin to enter the right side of my body, then it seemed to fill me. I turned and looked at her and said, "What are you doing?" She just grinned and replied, "Oh, you finally let me in, did you?" That's how close we got.

The situation with Veronica was a stark contrast. Tension just crackled in our apartment now, but as usual, I didn't know what to do. I finally decided that after my show was up and running, I would ask for a divorce. I felt our relationship had become quite damaging to both of us, and if we didn't separate, we would start walking down a very destructive road.

During the first week of August, Faith and her husband agreed that their marriage was over. Meanwhile, a weekend S.F.F. retreat was coming up on Staten Island; I decided to go and urged Faith to attend, too. She came, and that night we finally made love. The next morning she said she didn't want a physical relationship, didn't want any commitment, wanted no structure.

I was devastated and worked hard to change her mind. The crisis passed, but there remained tensions in our relationship. Living purely in spirit had ended, and our everyday egos and psychological tapes began to intrude. We kept fighting our way through our garbage, however, dumping huge loads of negativity and low self-esteem. We passionately supported each other's growth process and willingly accepted each other's negativity when it rose to the light. We were going through a spiritual cleansing which brought both joy and dismay. It wasn't easy, and it often created confusion and uncertainties.

Faith and I were both learning a great deal from our letters. We weren't just writing to each other, we were channeling insights, too. Once I wrote, "O.K., we work for our higher self first, but this can't be done in solitude. Also, let me put out a hypothesis for you: On July 3, we both feel we somehow merged and became joined. Are we not then a synthetic soul—positive and negative—learning how a soul *should* work? Is this not what a *real* marriage is all about? So, in the manner that we treat each other, are we not learning how to treat the rest of our soul? You practice on me what you then give your soul and practice on your soul what you then give to me. Think about that. It is really eerie how we tend to pick up each other's moods and thoughts. I know it ties in with you seeing us surrounded by one aura."

Later, I wrote, "You are right! We are meant to *improvise* our lives and relationships. People usually come into life with a structured relationship, which has been necessary in the past but which prevents much freedom. We have *done* that. *Now* we are being asked to improvise, as a new mode to experiment with, and then present to others the lessons learned in this improvisation. And we have been given no limits on this improvisation. Are we *ready* for this freedom? I see the audience sitting around us, waiting and smiling to see what we will show them. It is a very supportive audience, though.

"Commitment equals *attachment*, and so commitment becomes a fixed structure and a trap. Support and love is what we must offer instead—to everyone. I love you so, and our love keeps growing and changing and adding new dimensions. Like God, we are a force discovering itself in joy and amazement and exuberance. I surround you with light and send you a rain of love to help you grow."

I moved ahead with my production of *Saints*. I put out a casting notice and got almost a thousand actors' résumés. I interviewed about 200 actors and auditioned seventy, and, since I was so filled with love, the experience was extraordinary. I didn't see them just as actors but as people who had pain and despair and joy and exuberance. It was an event for me, and for the actors, too. I could sense it.

On the first Friday of September, Faith and I met in Central Park again. Saturday morning we had breakfast together, then went to Saint Patrick's Cathedral, the only church I have ever felt really good walking into. We sat down inside the cathedral, and I began to meditate. In my mind, I saw Faith on my right and put my right arm about her shoulders, then saw Veronica on my left and put my left arm around her shoulders. I was shown Veronica as a body of light, joyful and happy. I was told inside that I had not failed my mission with her, that it was all right to release her. I left the church at peace.

I cast *Saints* and began to rehearse the play. Jim had done an extremely fine re-write of *Saints*. A brutal play, it was a symphony of words filled with spiritual truths. I had some of the best actors I have ever directed, and my direction just flowed out of me, much of it channeled, I was certain. The last three weeks of our rehearsals were held in a large hall of an old church; the space and the vibrations were perfect. My scene designer, Robert Alan Harper, conceived and built a wonderful set. My other designers, my stage manager, our technical people, and our box-office staff were great. I thought we were all on our way. I was on top of the world.

Pride goeth before the fall, it is written, however. I remember when I was eighteen and working for my father one summer, a business associate of his turned to me and said, "All you Schwimmers are so damned proud." At the time I had no idea what he was talking about, but he must have been right, for hubris now caught up with me. I felt I had control of events, but I didn't.

On September 13, a Sunday, close to midnight, I was in our bedroom writing to Faith while Veronica was in the living room watching TV. I went to take a shower and, incredibly, left my letter sitting face up in the middle of my desk. While I was taking my shower, Veronica decided to balance our checkbook. At midnight. And she rarely bothered to balance our checkbook. The checkbook was on my desk. Veronica saw my letter to Faith, read it through, and confronted me. That was not how I wanted our marriage to end, but that's how it ended. I told Veronica I would leave the next day, but we finally agreed I would remain for a time.

When I went back to our bedroom I suddenly sensed—or perhaps heard—something snap, like a bubble bursting. Looking back, I believe that the energies that had joined Faith and me had separated from us at that moment. I instinctively knew that my relationship with Faith—as it had existed for the past two months—had ended that night, but I pushed the feeling out of my mind. I wasn't ready to have that love disappear.

I was both producing and directing *Saints*, an almost impossible task without a full-time staff, which I didn't have. I spent my mornings rushing around doing my producing work and rehearsed in the afternoons and evenings. There also had to be rehearsals and technical work on the weekends, so I was leaving the apartment around eight in the morning and returning close to midnight. But even the short time I was home each day was highly charged. I could feel the emotion the minute I walked in the door. Fortunately, Krista was staying with us, and Veronica was able to turn to her.

*A Song For All Saints* opened on October 1 in the Chernuchin Theater of The American Theater of Actors. Jim dedicated the production to David and wrote on my copy of the program, "I loved every minute." The production was a triumph—and a total disaster. My principal actors—Kevin Kelly, Ralph Wakefield, and Fran Barnes—gave outstanding performances. Kari Page, playing a smaller role, was incredible, and the rest of the cast supported them to the hilt. People who saw it left in a daze. Agents who came were stunned by the quality of the casting and of the performances. One theater professional told me the play had been brilliantly directed. The production glowed with spiritual light.

There was just one catch. No one in New York would review the show because it was an Equity Showcase, i.e., the actors worked unpaid. I had hired a publicist, but neither she nor the woman whom I had taken on as assistant producer to help me navigate the New York theater scene had told me we would be unable to get reviews, in fact had led me to believe we *would* be reviewed. No reviews meant *Saints* was unknown—was commercially invisible. The audiences grew smaller and smaller. The actors were in agony, and I couldn't blame them. But I was helpless. I had no funds for paid publicity, which was incredibly expensive in New York. To drive the last nail into the coffin, potential financial backers who read the script or saw the production were not interested. It was too serious, too radical. I had failed to understand that New York theater is primarily business, not art.

The slide downward continued. Faith and I began to drift apart. The main issue was that both of us really needed to become our own persons, by ourselves. I understood this at some levels, rejected it at others. Love still flowed between us, we still cared for each other, but inner and outer events had begun to overtake us. In retrospect, it is obvious that Faith and I were brought together to open each other's hearts, midwife each other into the realm of spirit, and help each other to separate from our spouses.

Veronica and I walked a razor's edge. Our situation had become intolerable for both of us. I packed a bag and moved to a YMCA.

The four-week run of *Saints* ended with everyone totally stunned, many of the actors angry with me. I had done the best I could, but it hadn't been enough, and I had no money left to go on elsewhere. I was in shock and didn't know what to do next. Closing any show, even a hit, is a trauma, but this was much worse. Here, an entire dream, an entire life that I had worked on for a year, had disintegrated. I started to shut down emotionally again. I couldn't process everything that had happened to me.

In the second week of November, Veronica flew to another part of the country to visit two of her sisters. I was alone. *Saints* was gone. Faith was distant. I had just myself. I didn't understand it then, but that was what this was all about. For the first time in my life, I belonged to no one else. I belonged only to myself.

✦ ✦ ✦

One night something inside me began to stir. I pulled out my pen and wrote:

> November 12. Such a strange day that I feel a need to put it down on paper right now. I'm in Grand Central Station—a vast cavern—on the floor of the main hall, eastern end, and I feel as if I'm standing on an empty plain. It is getting close to midnight.
>
> Lord, everything is running together somehow. This place always reminds me of Gail [a young woman I had dated many years before], trips in and out of the city from New Rochelle, and all the memories of what happened while in the city—(bells just chimed a quarter to twelve)—and meeting Faith downstairs and walking up . . .
>
> Now I'm on the western balcony of Grand Central, leaning on the marble railing, looking down at the main floor. I finally steeled myself to move my things out of the apartment and put them in storage today, hiring a man with a van. It was suddenly painful, since the reality of what was taking place took physical form. As I ate dinner at the restaurant I just let the pain exist, felt it, did not fight it. Not much of it surfaced, but it hurt.
>
> I thought, "Well, it is a *feeling*, let it go. You're opening the door to other future feelings." Yet it seems to have been a release also, for tonight I was able to love Veronica for the first time in years. Our scenario must be finished.
>
> And as I stood on the marble floor of Grand Central, I felt I had died. The psychics were right. The old George S. is dead, and I could view him with nostalgia and love, as if he were another person.
>
> I feel a river flowing through me tonight, filled with all the currents, eddies, sunlight, shadows, frothing white, slick jade-greens of a mountain river. It is gently bringing to the surface my emotions, letting me look at

them, and then just as gently flowing away with them. Beautiful. My spirit guides touch my aura lovingly. A tingle runs down my spine.

Two minutes to midnight, and I write on hastily. The day is almost over. What will the next day bring? Midnight! Now who will I turn into? Ten strokes left. Seven. Three. One. A new day—and I am reborn.

# 17

# channeling david's solo

After much searching, I found a tiny apartment on West Forty-Eighth Street, near Eighth Avenue, in an area called Hell's Kitchen—an appropriate name, in retrospect. The building was old and run-down, and the apartment was a wreck. I didn't care. It was in the heart of the theater district, subways were near, and the rent was only $275 a month. I spent the next two weeks putting a new floor in the kitchen, filling every crack in the apartment with spackle to keep the bugs out, painting every square inch (even inside the closets), putting down a rug in one room, and installing burglar bars on all of the windows.

Then I set up my desk and bookcases, put my books on the shelves, hung curtains made of sheets. I had discovered I had much less need for physical things now, so besides my desk and books I had brought only my typewriter, my papers, a chair, a small stool, and a mattress. But my place felt great. In the middle of a drug-infested neighborhood, I had created an oasis of peace.

Veronica, having decided to move to the region where her sisters lived, filed for an uncontested divorce. None of what was happening to me was easy. I didn't know how to go about parting from someone with whom I had lived for more than twenty years, and I also was concerned about what would happen to Veronica.

I still had an inner connection with Faith. One day, closing my eyes and tuning in to us, I saw a sort of gossamer web of energy: fine lines coming and going between us, a web that seemed woven or intertwined but not attached from one to the other. Rather, the lines went through each other, touching but not tied or knotted—with a constant flow energizing the lines. The image felt good to me. I still corresponded with Faith, too. Toward the beginning of December, I wrote:

> Oh, Lord, Faith, I feel sad. Veronica is in such pain, and—as always—I can't help her. Three nights ago she called, told me she had called you. I asked what you had said to her, and she just told me, "Faith is a sweet woman."
>
> I feel sad, I feel sad. She and I were messed up as children and clung to each other like children in the dark for all those years, both meaning well, both incapable of helping the other or himself/herself. It's so sad that we only seem to learn in pain. I asked her to have dinner with me on Friday, and she accepted. Oh, I hope she will be happy one day—I hope we all will be happy one day. I feel sad, sad. Oh, Lord.

Veronica left New York a week later. I went over to her apartment, packed up everything she and I had ever acquired together, and then watched as the movers drove away with all of it. Lord Peter and Samantha came to live with me.

I felt stripped. David was gone, Veronica was gone, Eric was in Honduras, my parents were in Raleigh, my return to theater had crashed, I had no job, no prospects, not a lot of money, I was in a strange town with strangers, no roots anywhere, and I realized Faith and I would never be more than friends. I wrote in my journal, "Jesus, I can't believe all that has happened to me. I feel like I've been caught up in a tornado and then sent off on the yellow brick road. My God! 'Well, you want to be cleansed and cleared, don't you?' Not with wire brushes, guides! Let's use washcloths and gentle soap from now on, O.K.? Lord!"

The transition was over. I was on my own. I didn't know what would happen to me and didn't care. I had survived this long, I'd keep surviving. In mid-January I wrote to Faith:

> Veronica called last night and was in a very good frame of mind, very friendly and relaxed. I feel I can let her go now, though with trepidation, like a mother bird with its young. I don't know where I'm headed and feel like a voyager embarking on a sailing ship.
>
> I can see it, and walk up the gangplank. The ship sets sail, the ocean lies in front of me, I watch the sun start to come over the horizon. The darkness lies behind me, yet it is a comforting, womb-like darkness, soft. I shiver a little as a wind of change blows over my back. The sails of my ship fill with the wind, blue-green water flows along the bow, and bubbles of white light dance along the surface where the sun touches them. Dawn rises before me, and I must go where my ship takes me.
>
> I send you my love and the light of the universe once again, companion voyager.

Faith and I kept in touch sporadically for another three years. I sometimes wrote to her, she sometimes wrote to me. Once in a while she called. We met a few times, in her hometown and in New York. She was on her path, I was on mine. I made a promise to myself, however, that I never would stop loving her, never would stop loving anyone ever again. One day in a subway store I saw an inexpensive semi-precious stone set in a necklace, and I bought it for her. At home, I put the stone against my heart and channeled love into it. I mailed the necklace to Faith, writing that if she ever again felt unloved she should put it on and she would always feel my love. The next time I met her, she said, "What did you do to that stone?" She could feel my love in the stone. She always will.

✦ ✦ ✦

As time and events passed, I began to sense I was being led somewhere. But who was leading me? About a month after David was lost, I had had a dream in which I saw David on a track, running a race. David was moving at a steady measured rate on the inside lane of the track, and I was running in this long race with him, in the lane next to David, one stride behind him. He was setting the pace, showing me the way. The dream made no sense to me then, but now I understood—it was David who was leading me!

But where was he leading me? Obviously in a different direction, since instead of running counterclockwise on the track, as was normal, we were running clockwise. What was he teaching me, then? The first lesson he taught was obvious: we don't die when our bodies do. There is no death—we are beings of light who can't be destroyed. But David had much more to teach me than just the lesson of survival.

As I pored over his journals, we seemed to grow much closer. I often felt he was with me as I worked on his book. Although I hadn't been able to tell him I loved him while he was alive—my dysfunctional legacy—I could now think, "I love you, David," and know he'd hear and understand. Interestingly, both Marian and Preston commented that David and I had become much closer than we had been in life. Through David's writing, I was attracted even more to his openness, his sensitivity, his spirituality, his capacity to love and be loved, his humanity.

However, I was being led not only inwardly, but also outwardly—to places and people and knowledge which I had only read about in books. First it was the psychics, next the A.R.E., then Spiritual Frontiers Fellowship with its many workshops in meditation, Reiki, and other transpersonal and transformational subjects and disciplines. Then a woman I'd met at the June 1981 S.F.F. conference dragged me off to a Unity service one Sunday in 1982, and I kept going there for two years.

Things sometimes crossed my path in peculiar ways. As I was walking down Eighth Avenue one day, a couple of blocks from my apartment house, a flyer taped to a light pole caught my eye. It was advertising a course in aura and chakra healing and balancing. In Hell's Kitchen? With the pushers and prostitutes? It turned out the training was held downtown, and I took the twelve-week course, taught by a woman named Devorah. It was a strange and almost unbelievable experience to find that there was such a thing as a human energy field and that I could actually sense it with my hands.

I was then drawn to a week-long intensive course in mediumship, which I found described in a very small article of a Spiritual Frontiers Fellowship newsletter. I had great inner resistance to taking the course and wondered at length—even after I had signed up for it—why I was doing so. I eventually went to North Carolina in June of 1982 to take the training, which was given by Patricia Hayes, a student and friend of the deceased medium

Arthur Ford. Here I learned how to receive accurate psychic impressions and how to do past-life regressions, being regressed three times myself. When I later began to do readings for friends and others, I discovered that—using the techniques I had learned from Pat Hayes—I was also able to psychically pick up the past lives of individuals.

Toward the end of her course, Pat conducted a seance with us, and David came through the entire group of students and instructors. They correctly described David's personality, his writing, his scholastic abilities, the fine quality of his mind, his love of the outdoors, comments about his book, and other—accurate—information. David also brought through the names of Debbie and Steve, and affirmed that he and I were continuing to get closer. As always, a lot of joy and love were present, and at one point David had everyone roaring with laughter.

A couple of months later I went to another S.F.F. conference, where a man conducted a past-life regression during a presentation, after which he mentioned that there was an organization called the Association for Past-Life Research and Therapy (APRT) in California. I obtained APRT's address and joined the organization. Over the next two and a half years I flew out to California periodically to take training in past-life therapy, eventually becoming the first graduate of APRT's new training program. I later was elected to the board of directors of APRT, also edited its quarterly newsletter for three years, and wrote a number of articles for the newsletter and for APRT's journal.

On January 14, 1985, I went to a one-evening seminar on psychic development given by Joyce Winner. As we meditated, I perceived my father falling to the floor, his body surrounded by golden light, and I got that he would die in three months. On January 25, Mother called to say that Father had fallen to the floor in their living room, had been unable to get up, and had been taken to a hospital. He was in and out of the hospital for the next two months, then went to a nursing home, and finally died a few days after a stroke, on April 20.

In September I attended a week-long training in consciousness expansion at The Monroe Institute in Virginia. Mornings, afternoons, and evenings, I and about two dozen other participants listened to Hemi-Sync® audio tapes developed by Robert Monroe, a former broadcast executive who had experienced out-of-body states and had written about them in *Journeys Out of the Body* and *Far Journeys*.

The Hemi-Sync tapes put everyone into various state-specific levels of consciousness, some of which were quite extraordinary. It is impossible to write about most of these, since there is no human vocabulary to describe and identify much of what was experienced. I had no doubt, however, that I was continually moved from one energy level to another, from one level of consciousness to another. The next year, I took the Institute's course in becoming an outreach trainer, and I afterwards conducted Hemi-Sync workshops in North Carolina and California.

Still living in New York City, I began to do past-life recall workshops for the general public, and also worked one-on-one privately. Later I began to train others to conduct past-life regressions and healing. I continued taking seminars about chakras, quartz crystals, and past-life recall, read a great deal about all of these subjects, and attended most of the APRT conferences, seminars, and training workshops.

I didn't know where all this was leading me, but each time that an opportunity arose to increase my knowledge, expand my consciousness, or be of service the best I knew how, I went ahead and took the next step on the path laid out before me. The biggest lesson for me through all this was to convince myself to believe in the information and the direction which my inner guidance was providing for me. I became aware that in order to keep moving ahead on my path I had to learn to banish fear and develop trust in the inner workings of the universe and of my own mind.

✦ ✦ ✦

By the end of 1985 I had become totally disillusioned with New York City and felt burned out, so I decided to move to California. It was the middle of 1986 before I finally arrived in Santa Barbara, but when I did I immediately fell in love with the city's seashore. It became obvious that I had been directed to Santa Barbara to receive healing from the area's wonderful vibrations, and I learned that Santa Barbara was fabled to have been on the eastern coast of the legendary lost continent of Lemuria. I set up a small practice in past-life therapy and transformational guidance, and I continued to edit David's book and to transcribe the psychic readings I had obtained.

I now had some time to reflect on what I had found in my search so far. To begin with, I was certain that synchronicity was a fact, that there was a purpose and pattern to my life. My clients' past-life regressions strongly reinforced this belief, but I still was unable to simply take for granted the more unexpected or odd instances of synchronicity that would surface in my life. It's not all that easy to accept the idea that unseen forces and consciousnesses are guiding one's life—although I did find that my spiritual guides had a very wry sense of humor.

Yet it was the very invisibility of these forces and patterns that kept driving me to uncover ever more information, tangible and intangible. In the past I had never been able to learn anything *specific* about the workings of spirit, and I was convinced that it was this lack of specific knowledge that prevented me from being able to really understand my life. Knowledge has always been power, and I was determined to empower myself—and everyone else I could reach. This drive was like that of the research scientist: *the need to know.* Although I had started out just to find out how David had died, I was now determined to bag much bigger game—an understanding of how spirit operates on this planet.

I had discovered at the S.F.F. Greensboro retreat—and afterwards, especially through my clients—that although there is an *apparent* surface agenda operating in every person's life, the *real* agenda in each life operates sub rosa. I wanted to be able to clearly demonstrate to myself and others that there is a spiritual pattern in each life, there is a purpose to each life, and if you hunt hard enough, you will find that pattern. Discovery of the pattern frees you and returns your inner personal power to you. Although I had learned the agenda of David's life from Marian, Noreen, Steve, and David's journals, I also wanted to know the spiritual agenda behind David's *death*.

By this time I had come to understand the spiritual principles that were in action in my life, and I often was able to see beneath the surface of personal events. But in mid-October of 1986, I still hadn't found out why David had died. I felt that something had happened on David's solo in Baja and that knowing what had taken place there would give me important insight. No psychic had been able to tell me anything specific about David's solo, and I was feeling a lot of frustration about this.

In the back of my mind, though, reverberated Marian's oft-stated dictum, "The guru trip is over—everyone has to be his own guru." That statement had been like a kick in the gut to me, because I had been looking forward to finding a guru for twenty years. Now Marian was telling me, Forget it, George! I can't say I was terribly pleased with the idea that I had to be my own guru.

Still, I did have more than four years of experience behind me as a trained channel, and I had led a couple of Monroe Institute outreach workshops in consciousness expansion. I decided to utilize my knowledge and try to pull aside the veil that hid whatever had occurred almost nine years earlier during David's solo. I had nothing to lose, and I remembered that Marian had said I was a channel in my own right.

Since it was around noon when I prepared to make this attempt, I pulled shut the curtains in my living room to block out some of the bright sunlight, then put an audio cassette tape of consciousness expansion signals designed by Robert Monroe in my stereo, sat down cross-legged facing away from the windows, and—feeling an impulse—clasped my hands (to close a circuit, I now believe), holding a microphone in them to record anything I might perceive.

I closed my eyes and went through the procedures I had been taught by Pat Hayes and Bob Monroe, eventually raising my consciousness to a level which Bob Monroe identified as no-time/no-space. In just a few minutes I was in a very deep trance state, although I was still completely conscious.

I began to visualize David before his fire and soon was perceiving figures standing on the other side of the fire, who began to communicate with David as he observed them. When I started to tape-record my impressions of this scene and all that followed, I became aware that I was speaking in a manner and in a voice that I felt was not my own. Although my consciousness was present and observing both the scene and the consciousness which was speaking, and although my vocal cords were making the sounds and I heard what my lips and tongue were saying, *I* was not the one giving this message. I was in a profoundly deep trance state, unaware of anything that my senses were perceiving except for my voice and the microphone in my hand.

I had *dual* consciousness, and what is reported below in italics is what I perceived or understood, as opposed to what was narrated onto the tape. This is what I recorded:

It is night. David is squatting by his fire, *[staring into it]*. He begins to have an impression of others on the far side of the fire. *[I had the perception of several figures, and I now feel there were five.]* There is one large robed figure *[in dark robes]*, male in appearance *[who seems to be quite tall and broad-shouldered under the robe]* in the center. He now takes the hood off *[and throws it back, so it lies on his shoulders and back]*. He has long *[and thick]* white hair and a long, thick white beard—*[almost stylized, like a painting, reaching to the center of his chest]*.

The other figures *[behind the fire]* are also hooded, and they now also take their hoods off their heads, so they can be seen. Several of them have non-humanoid features, which is to say features structured out of energy *[each of which is quite different, and the energy patterns in these keep fluctuating]*. The outlines of the "bodies" are such—it is simply a method of conveying a "presence" to David. They *have* no bodies. *[I could see no hands or feet on the figures.]*

They lift David out of his body. He is being held as if he were a child. *[I had the impression of these figures holding a baby, which I took to be David. But this image of a baby was only momentary and symbolic, I feel, and faded at once.]* He is lifted into The Light, and the entire review of his life—and in fact all of his lives—is made. This is a special dispensation, because of his advanced evolvement, that he be given this review before death, rather than afterwards, so that he may see where he is at this point in his evolution--*[normally one is not given this review except at death or near-death]*.

He is shown what he may accomplish through his death at this time *[if he so chooses]* within the karmic situation wherein he is presently involved. He is also shown other future possibilities of how his life would evolve, were he not to die in the sea. And he and his karmic council, for that is who they are, his guides, examine and discuss—in spirit, in thought *[telepathically]*—the various options and alternatives available to him.

He is given at this time a panorama of his soul evolution, and where this moment of Earth time fits in *[to his soul evolution]*. He is given the spiritual truths and the spiritual background which have brought him to this point, and told the spiritual laws that are in operation at this moment. And he is asked to choose—although a path already has been placed before him, and he *knows* what this path is: he has been given this in sleep and—to a certain extent—in waking consciousness. Nevertheless, he is asked, once again, in full consciousness now *[and to fulfill the laws of free will]*, to choose which path aids to the greatest advancement for his soul progress and the soul progress of those who he is closest to—*[At this point I suddenly began to sob and stopped recording. I continued to sob for a couple of minutes, and for the rest of this communication tears flowed down my face, for I understood that David was not just helping those in Baja but also was helping me and everyone who loved him.]*—and how he may best serve both himself and those whom he loves, and the planet itself, through his choice.

He sees clearly that the choice which he made [previously] at other levels is indeed the correct choice, and the one which he needs to follow. As always, as [was] indicated in the horoscope reading [for David], his choice is one which is distressing for him and tears at him inside, emotionally, for he knows that what he must do will cause great pain and anguish for those who love him. Yet he knows that this is the best course for soul-development of all who are important in his life, and all those who will—at a future time—read about his life.

*Understand* that he made this decision with *joy*, and although there was sadness in leaving the physical, yet he knew this was the proper moment for his ascension into the next life. His spiritual partner, Brenda, concurred in this decision which David made, and joined him in that decision.

He was given the blessings of the Masters, which was shown to him *[and to me]* as a *[brilliant]* cap of light *[shaped like a yarmulke, only slightly larger]*—*[I now saw David, kneeling, as a figure of light, the Masters as figures of light, and I saw the hands of light of one of the Masters place this cap of light on David's head, with other Masters in the background of the scene]*—and the purifying properties of the sea and his transition through the sea were explained to him, as was explained to him the purifying properties of the sea for the others of his crew, whether they lived or passed on.

He returned to his body with full consciousness of what he had experienced and with full knowledge of what was to take place. He went into his final mission with the courage he had always exhibited during this and other lives, and also with the knowledge that what would happen would ultimately be a group action and be of the utmost benefit to all those involved, purging many of karma accumulated over other lifetimes, allowing them to be born into a new consciousness—the consciousness of light and love. And so it was.

I now understood the events in Baja to be those of *atonement* (for errors in past lives) and of the purging of those portions of The Light which had been made dark (the polarity had been reversed) by those whom David was helping. The experience of this communication was deep and powerful, leaving me emotionally shaken.

# 18

# a ritual journey

I had repeatedly promised myself that I would someday visit Baja and view the scene where David had made his transition. I didn't know why the trip was important to me or what I might discover, but I felt a need to experience this region that had been so critical for David. The urge to go became stronger when I went to California, and in November of 1987 I decided to make the trip after the Christmas weekend—I felt it was time to see Punta Púlpito and the Sea of Cortez.

I began the drive south to Loreto on Monday, December 28, taking along my tape recorder and journal to chronicle my experiences. I arrived on Wednesday and found the weather brilliant, the area very peaceful. After registering at my hotel, I called a charter service to rent a boat. None was available for the next day, so I made a reservation for Friday. Then I went out to the sandy shore that bordered the Sea of Cortez. Calm, shimmering water stretched before me for miles, and I could sense the attraction that the sea had had for David.

I couldn't gauge my emotions—they seemed to be on hold. I realized that in ten days it would be ten years that David had arrived in Loreto, but I decided to stay in the present and not think about the past or the future. Only God knew what this was all about, why I was here.

On Friday, around 5:30 A.M., the owner of the charter boat service, a Mexican national named Pete, arrived in a van at my hotel to pick me up. Pete spoke English, but we were silent as he drove south through the last dark minutes of the night over a narrow, winding road.

We arrived at a sizable marina about twenty minutes later and stopped at the edge of a concrete dock, but there was no boat in sight. Pete attempted to reach his captain by radio, without success. After another thirty minutes or so, a small cabin cruiser finally appeared. When the vessel docked, Pete spoke to the captain in Spanish, then told me that the boat was ready and that the mate would catch me some bait for fishing. I said I wasn't interested in fishing, that I wanted to go to Punta Púlpito.

Pete just looked at me in an odd way and asked, "Punta Púlpito?"

I said, "Yes."

Pete began to hem and haw, saying that Punta Púlpito was quite a ways up the coast. I repeated that I wanted to go to Punta Púlpito, and Pete then went over to the captain and began talking to him once more. When Pete returned, he again started to say that Punta Púlpito was too far away.

At that point I said emotionally, "Look, my son died there, and I'm going."

Pete just stared at me in the first faint light of dawn and finally almost whispered, "Kayaks?"

I said, "Yes."

"Seven or eight years ago?"

"Ten years," I responded.

Pete paused for a moment to collect himself, then said, "I remember. *I* carried the boy's body."

It was my turn to be shocked now, but I answered, "No, that was not my son; that was the other boy. They never found my son."

"That man," Pete continued, as if he hadn't heard me, pointing to the captain, "was captain of the boat that brought the boy's body back, and that," pointing to the boat in front of us, "is the boat on which the boy's body came back."

I could think of nothing to say, could only look at Pete. Ten years afterwards, with scores of fishing boats for rent in the area, and I find these two men and this boat.

Pete went back to talk with the captain once more and finally returned to say that the captain would take me, but only if the wind—coming from the north as always—was not too severe, since the winds had been very strong during the past two days. Pete promised that if the weather became dangerous today he would instead drive me to Punta Púlpito on another day and then take me around the point in a skiff.

I got aboard the cabin cruiser, and it pulled away from the dock. More light was showing along the horizon. The mate brought a folding captain's chair for me and placed it in the center of the lower deck, facing the wake of the boat, then climbed a ladder to the upper deck at the front of the boat, where the captain was operating the vessel.

We headed out of the harbor at Point Escondido in Baja Sur, then started to bear north. All around me I saw nothing but tall, sharp crags. Then the boat picked up speed, and a sea bird flew across our bow. The horizon was a pale yellowish silver, a few banks of clouds hovered south of us. Behind me and to my left in the far distance were cliffs—Carmen Island, I later learned, where the bodies of

Brenda and Tim had been found. The water beneath us looked dark, white foam trailing behind the boat.

We moved along at a good clip. Large drops of water flew across the back of the boat where I was sitting, and I felt the salt spray stick to my hands and face. The air was quite cool. My hands were cold, shaking slightly from the morning chill. I began to tape my impressions.

There's a fairly strong wind coming down from the north, and we're heading into sizable swells. I'm beginning to get a feel of what it's like to be out on the water of the Sea of Cortez. Even now, just at the start of this journey, it seems miraculous to me that six members of David's crew survived this sea ten years ago.

The cabin cruiser is beginning to rock from side to side, substantial swells around us. Water is flying across the deck, spraying over me. I'm finally starting to see open sea and that island again, to my left.

I suddenly sense I have company. I feel that David, Brenda, and Tim are sitting on the stern of the boat, grinning at me. In my mind comes the thought, seemingly from David, who turns to the other two and says to them (about my sense of their presence), "Not bad, huh? That's my pop."

The sun is starting to rise. I can see its arc now, behind the clouds: golden light, reflecting off the bottom of the southerly bank of clouds, some of the light filtering through them. Other cloud banks perch lower on the horizon. The sun's rays also are starting to glance off the slightly reddish cliffs along the coast. A strong wind continues to blow from the north.

Now the sun is well up, but the air is still quite cool. Every so often there are some sizable swells. A gull flies straight over the boat, from stern to bow, almost hovering right over me and then winging away. He is flying ahead of the boat now, as if leading us, then veers off toward the coast.

I guess one of the things I'm getting a feel for here is space. Huge stretches of water, towering cliffs. There is a great difference between looking at a map in Raleigh—trying to imagine Baja and the Sea of Cortez—and then actually seeing the vastness that is out here.

The first mate has just come down and has motioned me into the cabin to keep me from getting drenched. Water is washing across the windows facing the bow. Unfortunately, the captain and mate don't speak English, so I can't talk with them.

Ten years. Over 3,600 days I've lived since those events took place here. That's hard to believe. Well, David's gotten me to do a lot of things I wouldn't have done, except for him.

I guess this is a ritual journey of some kind. Still sadness and tears in me. A lot of love and compassion for the one who I was ten years ago. For George and Veronica, and for Krista and Eric, back there in that house in Raleigh in January of 1978. Totally helpless then, having no idea of what was out here or what was happening. Only now do I begin to sense the ordeal, the test, that those events posed.

The first mate—a thin, wiry, older man, with a white mustache and a ready smile—is standing in back of the open door to the cabin, arms folded, facing toward me, seeming almost like the guardian of the Sacred Mysteries, a high priest.

What kind of karma is being enacted out here? Maybe I'll find out some day.

Perhaps it's fitting that I couldn't get a boat yesterday. This is a new year, the first day of the new year, 1988, and it is—I hope—also a new life.

Why is it so important to see where David died?

I think of the tragedy, and yet I still have to remember the learning that has taken place in the last ten years: the people I've met, the places I've gone to, the lessons I've been given, the things I've discovered. Jean [a friend whose brother died] was right, though: you never get over it, the wound never heals completely. The center remains raw.

It's becoming pleasant outside. The sun is starting to burn away some of the haze. The glare on the water is quite sharp now. I would guess that we're running about a quarter of a mile from the shore. Hard to understand what kind of wind and waves and currents existed on January 24, 1978, that David and his crew couldn't make it to shore from a quarter of a mile out. And still the wind comes sweeping down from the north, pushing the waves ahead of it, the water pounding the boat.

The waves appear steeper now, and the captain has cut back the speed of the engine slightly. I see some whitecaps ahead of us. We're passing an area that appears to be simply sheer cliffs, with no place to land. I noticed as I drove along the coast yesterday that the only beaches were inside Conception Bay. The rest is very, very rugged.

Ten A.M. and still nothing but sheer rock that slides down into the sea along the coast. Only rock, no matter where I look. The sea is rougher now, with heavier swells and larger whitecaps, and the boat is rolling considerably. The coast veers off to the west, revealing a large bay, but the boat continues north.

Punta Púlpito may be up ahead. I see something in the distance that's like an enormous cliff, coming up out of the water, pushing out of a headland. I wish for the boat to move faster, but it doesn't.

The mate, who had left a while back, now returned and pointed to the rocky mass toward which the boat was moving. "Punta Púlpito," he said, then walked out of the cabin again.

As Punta Púlpito loomed ahead, I left the cabin and climbed halfway up the wooden ladder at the left that led to the upper deck. The captain, seated on the right, was steering the boat, with the mate to his left. Wind and sea water whipped across my face and body as I clung to the slick ladder with both hands, watching the rock of Punta Púlpito—like a mythological monster—rise up out of the ocean and tower almost 500 feet above me.

North of this great rock I saw another gigantic slab: longer, buff-colored, with a fairly flat face. Then a third huge cliff beyond that, and rocks and cliffs as far north up the coast as the eye could see. Jagged rocks jutted randomly out of the water, probably hidden during a high sea. Nowhere to land north of Punta Púlpito that I could observe.

The captain brought the boat surprisingly close to the point, and Punta Púlpito just hung above me, gigantic and dark—an ancient monolith. It was awesome. I can't describe my feelings at that moment.

After a few minutes, I motioned to the captain to take the boat further north of the point, and he reluctantly complied but then quickly turned the vessel south and started back around Punta Púlpito.

The previous afternoon I had tried to find some place to buy flowers to leave for David at Punta Púlpito, but to my distress found none in the local stores. However, in the back of the hotel I had noticed a plant with a few large yellow blossoms—roses, perhaps—and I had cut one off and had taken it to the boat with me.

As we went past Punta Púlpito again, I threw the yellow flower into the Sea of Cortez for David. I watched it dance on the waves in the sunlight as the boat pulled away from it, until it was lost from sight. It was only a small symbol of my love for David, but I wanted him to see it.

After we rounded the point, the wind vanished completely, as if by magic, and the Sea of Cortez was tranquil around us. The captain cut his engine and anchored on the lee side of Punta Púlpito, near the small, shallow beach that David's crew had tried to reach that day in January. The captain and mate then refueled, pouring gasoline from large plastic containers into the boat's fuel tank.

It was now 1:00 in the afternoon. Close to shore the cove we were in was sheltered, but when we had approached it from the south, quite a strong wind had come from the north across a little bridge of land reaching up to Punta Púlpito—which was probably why David's "tribe" had been unable to land there ten years ago.

It was a beautiful day, a beautiful sun. Looking at this peaceful scene, I had difficulty imagining how the terrible things that had happened here did happen. The captain finished refueling and started the motor again. As we began to leave Punta Púlpito behind us, I wondered if I'd ever see it again. I felt a little empty, as I had when I last saw David.

Four hours later we were still at sea. As I looked over the day, two thoughts entered my mind about this experience: one was the word "archetypal," the second was to think back to another rock like Punta Púlpito, I assumed from another life. Maybe I was part of a trans-temporal scenario that was connected with that, I thought.

As the sun started to set, I returned to the cabin. The swells were getting larger, and the air was becoming chilly. Although there didn't seem to be that much wind, the waves had become much higher and looked black, menacing. I suddenly noticed I was standing in about an inch and a half of water.

I went above to advise the captain about the water, although I don't know how, since I couldn't speak Spanish. The mate followed me down to the cabin and then started bailing unenthusiastically with a small blue plastic bucket. The bilge pump apparently was not working, and I sat there wondering, "Well, am I going to be joining David tonight?" But I kept tape-recording what was happening, thinking, "If the boat goes down, I'll put the tape in my pocket, and if they find me they'll know what happened." I didn't feel very nervous during all of this, since I had long ago accepted my own death.

The captain then started making strange maneuvers. First he cut back the speed of the engine, then he began to go around in circles—backwards. I had no idea what he was doing. I could see no life jackets or a raft on board, either, nor could I hear a radio. I later learned from the charter service that the boat did have a radio, but that it had also malfunctioned.

After about half an hour of these continuous gyrations, we came to a blinking signal light floating in the water near us, which I assumed meant we were near Punta Escondido. Then another blinking light appeared in the distance southwest of us, apparently on land, and the mate started flashing a hand-held light toward it, with no discernible effect. The moon was out by now and I could see the nearby shoreline clearly. Unless the water was too cold to swim, I felt I could make it to shore, though the coast was nothing but rocks.

I became aware that the moon was almost full. I remembered that someone in David's crew had said Tim had been quite startled when the moon had emerged from clouds on that evening of January 24, and I stared up at that cold disk of light in the sky, trying to imagine what it had been like there that night.

I began to wonder why this was happening to me, and I heard, inside myself, "Just a small taste of what they went through ten years ago." But *why?* No answer.

We eventually reached Point Escondido and safety. I was driven to my hotel in a ramshackle truck and a short time later was eating a very late dinner in the hotel's elegant dining room, feeling extremely disoriented to be alive and well in this setting after what had happened to me during the day.

I started driving back to Santa Barbara early the next morning, Saturday, and arrived home Sunday. Monday there was an article in the *Santa Barbara News-Press* describing how a local fishing boat had capsized in storm-tossed seas Sunday, killing one of the four aboard. The sixty-six-foot boat had encountered trouble during a storm that had generated high winds and large swells at sea. The crew had radioed the Coast Guard and reported that they needed a pump, since the boat appeared to be taking on water in its bilge—as my boat had.

What the article said to me was that I also could have drowned during the past few days. Maybe my experience on the Sea of Cortez was an example of Marian's statement that I was falling under the law of grace: I *could* have drowned but didn't. The deeper meaning of the previous week eluded me, though—perhaps I was only meant to experience the events, needed just to *go* to Baja, not understand why. Still, I knew that my trip to Baja and the Sea of Cortez was closure, that it had ended my search for David.

# conclusion

From darkness and from death Love was born, and with its birth, order and beauty began to banish blind confusion. Love created Light, with its companion, radiant Day.[40]

In India, when we meet and part we often say, "Namasté," which means I honor the place in you where the entire universe resides, I honor the place in you of love, of light, of truth, of peace, I honor the place within you where if you are in that place in you and I am in that place in me, there is only one of us.[41]

*Ram Dass*

By the end of 1981, the quest into which I had flung myself three years earlier seemed virtually finished. Most of the goals which I'd set in the aftermath of David's transition had been met. The only thing undone was the publication of David's journals, and I kept working on that. But as my journey had wound its way through time and consciousness, I had begun to feel vaguely uneasy at times. What did all this mean? And why was it happening to me? This uncertainty was followed by flashes of real panic when I thought, "What will I do with my life when this is over?—how can I let go of David?" Eventually I even teetered on the brink of a void: a pervasive fear that

I couldn't release the past because there was no future. David had been my future.

Then one day I noticed light flowing through my darkness—a darkness which must have been self-imposed, for, as David once wrote, light has always been available to everyone. That light, which had been there from the start, revealed to me that I was searching for something more than David.

This realization disturbed me, because I felt there *was* nothing more important to me than David. While I had been investigating and recording everything in this book, I had felt I was simply following the threads of David's story as they were being revealed to me, that I was just a reporter on the trail of an important—if personally relevant—story. I occasionally did sense that there was more to my search than this, but I rejected the insight. I wanted this to be David's story, not mine. David was my reason for existing now. Take away my focus on David, and I couldn't exist.

It was more than four years after David's death before I began to grasp that I was very much involved in this panorama of events, and another year before I was willing to admit that what I was searching for was my own self. This was somehow a painful and confusing admission to make. Here I had thought I was doing all this for David, and now it turned out that he was doing it all for me. An additional year had to pass before I could understand and accept Noreen's words that "the father is the mission" and that "the search only has to be within one's self—the right pages that will be in *his* writing will answer the questions he needs—the words will come from within himself." And the words did come!

Through those words—the words of these pages as I wrote them—I learned what illumination is: it is *understanding* what one only *knew* previously. I finally understood what I had only known for the last six years: that David and I are one. I recalled again the dream that I had had after David had died, in which I had repeated over and over, "David and I are one . . . David and I are one . . ." and had awakened with those words ringing in my mind. I also recalled what David had told Noreen: "Wisdom is sometimes a fallacy, because it is all around. It's awareness that is more needed than wisdom."

After more than six years, I was more aware—I understood. Since David exists, I can't cease to exist, for David and I are one; and of course David's story is also my story, for David and I are one; and of course David was helping me as I was helping him, for David and I are one; and of course David's search was my search, for David and I are one; and of course I'm moving into a New Jerusalem—a new state of consciousness, for David *is* in New Jerusalem, and David and I are one. Nor was I really searching for more than David, for David is part of the "more," and since David and I are one, I was searching for what is more in myself.

Still, what was I searching for? Like Oedipus, I could see outwardly with my physical eyes and rational mind but refused to use my inner sight or intuitive sense. For the knowledge of what I was searching for had always been inside me, waiting to be found. After my third or fourth meeting with Preston, she asked me, "Why do you seek me out?" After a moment's thought, my answer was, "I don't know, but it has something to do with love."

That was the message—loud and clear—coming right out of my own mouth, but once again I failed to understand.

I was still as blind as Oedipus, and as obstinate. More years had to pass before I began to realize there was a pattern to all this. I, who was fascinated by patterns in my clients' past lives, wasn't aware enough to understand the pattern in my own life. Yes, all right, this is about love, but—? Over time I've discovered it's very difficult to see what's happening to you as it happens. Often it takes years, if you even bother to try, to look back and see what your pattern is. I finally got it, though; I got it.

Edgar Cayce had said that all people choose the events and people in their lives—including parents, lovers, wives or husbands, friends and enemies—to help them learn. O.K., so what kinds of choices had I made before I was born? I had chosen parents who had seemed unloving, girls and women who seemed to abandon me either physically or emotionally, employers who didn't seem to give a damn about me, so during much of my life I *felt* unloved. Significantly, I also chose a damaged heart valve.

What else? I rarely had gotten emotionally close to anyone. Probably the first person who had really touched my heart was Carol, in life and in death, but it wasn't enough—I didn't open my heart very much to her, and her death was very painful for me, so I shut down my heart a great deal to avoid the pain. Then there had been Gail, but I had had the same sort of relationship with her as with Faith, most of it through letters while I was in the Army. Things had been as much on and off between us as they had been with Faith, and I eventually had committed a real spiritual blunder with Gail. One evening she said something which I took to mean that she was less interested in me than she was in being financially secure, and the moment she finished saying that I sensed a "click" in my chest. I knew nothing about metaphysics or chakras then, and it took twenty-five years for me to understand what had happened. That "click" was the heart-block that Faith had seen. I had simply closed down my heart again—not completely, but very tightly, all the same.

In 1967 I came down with bacterial endocarditis, an infection of the heart. It was diagnosed very late—I could have died—and I had five weeks in the hospital, plus several more weeks of recuperation, to think about the symbol and meaning of my "heart" condition. During that time in my life I was fighting with everyone on my job and was very unhappy with Veronica. I wasn't being loving to anyone, and I tried to solve problems cerebrally, which never seemed to work—because there was no heart in it. I understood the symbol of the heart but didn't know what to do about it—*wouldn't* do anything about it, is probably more correct. My infection was a wake-up call, but I didn't wake up.

However, every person and every event that comes into our lives is a mirror for us, if we take the trouble to look. What were people mirroring for me, then? That I wasn't being loving, wasn't caring, wasn't sensitive to people. Veronica and everyone around me also reflected my anger that my immediate world wasn't obeying my will. I refused to accept responsibility for any of this. It was everyone else's fault, not mine, and, as Ron Scolastico had said, I withdrew from the world more and more. Veronica, through the lens of her personality, intensely mirrored my spiritual withdrawal.

The universe has a step system, however. If you don't learn your lesson in step one, you're taken to step two, then step three, ad infinitum. At each step things get tougher, because the resistance of your ego keeps getting greater. For example, David and Krista had come to teach me about universal love—Krista *radiated* love when she was born. I was astonished, impressed, by this tiny baby's love, but I either didn't get it or ignored it, I don't know which. Since I wasn't willing to learn about love, the physical David was taken from me. That certainly got my attention and opened my heart, but I still wasn't "cooked." Hours of talking with Preston pushed my heart open a little more. Not enough. Then Faith came along and finished the job. The heart block wasn't completely gone, but now at least I had swinging doors.

Now, why did I always find people to love at a distance, either physical or emotional distance, often both? Why were women always more interested in a spiritual relationship with me than in a romantic one? Why did David die? It took me a long time to sort this out. All this was to teach me to love without attachment to the physical body of the person whom I was loving, to instruct me to practice love that was unattached, undemanding, non-romantic, without quid pro quo.

Then there was everything I had experienced during the last eighteen years. Would I have done all these things, met all the people I had met, if David hadn't died? Not a chance. I never would have joined all those organizations, taken all the training, met Faith, and so on. And why *had* I done it at all? Because I loved David. I did it for love, which is what I was supposed to do and did.

Why wasn't I allowed at first to know how David had died, and why wasn't David's body found? If I had known exactly how David had died and had his body been found, I probably would never have gone to the psychics, would never have started walking the spiritual road I've been trudging along. And Outward Bound? As with everything and everyone in life, O.B. had both a material and a spiritual role to play. O.B. *was* negligent and paid for being so, but O.B. was also a player on a larger stage, in a greater drama. I needed a villain to fight against, something to keep me from retreating into despair. Outward Bound was it.

But why me? Why this individual, this George Schwimmer? In David's story about Hope he had written, "Hope is a dumpy nymph with greasy hair. She is lazy, impatient, rude, ignorant, rebellious. Her morals are atrocious: she lies, cheats, and uses others. Gaea picks Hope because if the nymph succeeds in her mission, the victory will be overwhelming, whereas if a morally and aesthetically superior nymph were sent, the victory would be meaningless."

I wasn't as bad as Hope, but the parallel was there. I was unloving, distrustful, and suspicious. I could be rude, certainly impatient, sometimes lazy, definitely rebellious, silent, dysfunctional, a loner who wanted control. Would anyone expect a message of love from such a messenger? Hardly. So the fact that the message was coming from this vessel would in itself be significant.

There were a few other things I had always wondered about as well. Why had I been born in Hungary, then brought to the U.S.? Why was I born into a religiously indifferent family? Why was I torn away from my extended family, country, and religion when I was eight? The answer emerged into my consciousness only recently: I wasn't supposed to have any sort of roots—no normal attachments through family, local or regional community, country, or religion. That was why I have moved forty-three times during my life, resisted putting down roots. I wasn't supposed to get tied down. Like Thomas Paine and David, I had apparently chosen that "the world is my country, all mankind are my brethren. To do good is my religion." My loyalty and commitment were to spirit.

Equally significant was the fact that I experienced almost everything in this book myself. I had first-hand knowledge and could talk with authority about what I had learned. I also had academic credentials, if that mattered, and I had been taught—very well—to think and to write. My letters to Faith were the start of my writing, the start of my breaking out of my dysfunctional silence, the start of my being able to express in physical form what was inside me. Finally, it became obvious that the information I was being given was intended for mass dissemination. So I wrote articles, wrote this book, and eventually went to Los Angeles to study film and to write screenplays. The pattern of what my life was about became clear.

One last element was needed, though: jettisoning control of my ego. In Raleigh, one of my A.R.E. friends, Frances, often said to me, "Let go and let God." She said that to me all the time. After a while I was ready to throttle her. I would have, too, except that she was usually giving me a hug while she said, "Let go and let God." Hard to throttle someone when she's hugging you. Still, that statement seemed formulaic, and I also had no idea what it really meant.

After 1982 things got worse and worse for me. Nothing that I tried worked. Nothing. And nothing excited me any more. During 1983 I just about lost interest in living. I thought, "This is it—I'm over the hill. My life is finished." I finally hit what I thought was bottom for me. "I give up," I said to anyone listening. "I give up. I can't make my life work. Someone else will have to take charge from now on." The minute I gave up, things got better. As the saying goes, I was now "in the flow." I still had problems, but there had been a shift in my consciousness.

So, I surrendered my ego, understood that my main lesson in this life was love, and knew I was supposed to communicate what I learned to many other people. Except that I didn't really know what I was supposed to communicate. I still had a great deal to learn about this elusive creature called love, and during the following years—in myriads of ways, from inner and outer teachers—I was taught a number of critical things about love.

The first lesson I learned was that I was *never* unloved, was never unsupported. From the time of David's death to the moment that I'm writing this sentence, whenever I would hit bottom emotionally, someone always would be there at the bottom to offer me love: I would unexpectedly get a loving letter or phone call or visit from a friend or from family, or receive a sudden beam of love from a casually known co-worker or even a clerk in a store. And when I would stubbornly believe that no one loved me, I would become aware of David's love flowing through me, calming me. Slowly I began to see that what I needed—love—was *always* being given to me, although I often failed to see or accept that it *was* love.

I next was taught that love is *never* withdrawn. This was difficult for me to believe, because whenever I consciously reached out for love from a specific person during my life, that love eventually appeared to fade away. In particular, many loving people came into my life after David's death to help me with my search but then left almost as abruptly as David had. I was confused, upset, and often angry. Why did people always leave me? Why was love always withdrawn? What I failed to notice was that only *people* left, not love, for when one loving person vanished another one came into my life. Yet the parade of people receding from me continued. I felt I was taking a beating.

As this was happening, however, I discovered—with considerable surprise—that my greatest joy was loving someone, not trying to be loved. In fact, I had never known *how* to love until now and consequently had been trying to find the love I needed outside myself. It finally dawned on me that I was reaching outward for what already was inside me and that I should *never look for love, just give it!* Furthermore, I found that it was simple to love anyone, any time, as much as I wanted to: I controlled whom and how much I loved, whereas I had no control whatever over how much love I would get, or from whom, or when. The bonus I received in loving someone, moreover, was that the love I sent to that person first flowed through me! It felt great!

Then came the lesson, an overriding one, that I must learn to let go of people, which was symbolized by David's death. But how could I let go of the radiant love that David had always given me and everyone else? I had no choice in releasing the physical David, but how could I release the inner David? As new people appeared in my life and then left, I fought to keep them tied to me also. Why couldn't I let go of anyone? I eventually had to admit that the reason was fear—of losing or never again getting love from that "special" person.

After many experiences, although it has been a very difficult lesson to learn and one that I'm still learning, I've come to understand that *all* love is *one* love, and it doesn't need a special body to radiate from but can radiate from *any* body or anything: a man, a woman, a child, a cat, a bird, a tree, a breeze, a sunrise, a song. So, to let go of any particular individual, you open yourself to universal love, wherever it comes from, and you don't ask for love, you just give it. *Everyone* is special then, everyone is yours to love forever. *No one* can escape the love that *you* send them, and *that's* how you can release everyone.

Much of this knowledge became focused for me when a friend gave me a copy of *Love Is Letting Go of Fear* by Gerald G. Jampolsky. The book made me understand what I had been experiencing:

> Love itself remains constant: only the particular body from whom we sometimes come to expect it may change. . . . We have no interest in how Love will provide for us in the future. . . .
>
> Giving means extending one's Love with no conditions, no expectations. . . . Peace of mind occurs . . . when we put all our attention into giving and have no desire to get anything from, or to change, another person.[42]

The final illumination in my search was a meditation that I experienced while flying from Raleigh to New York one time, but which I didn't understand until a year later. It had seemed in my meditation that I projected my inner self to some higher plane of consciousness and there unexpectedly met Preston in the same form as I. I was surprised but happy to see her there and was drawn to her, when suddenly our two inner beings moved toward each other and merged. As I experienced this unusual state, David appeared beside us and also merged with our dual being, so that all three of us were now only one—though still three. Our energies were radiant, joyous, loving. We remained like that for a time, just experiencing and enjoying ourselves as part of a whole.

This meditation had great meaning for me. For what it ultimately made me understand was that if two can be one and three can be one, then—as David had written—when you touch anything in the world you find it attached to the rest of the universe. So if three of us are one, then *all* of us are one, and if *one* of us is love, *then we all are love.* And the love that I had searched for all of my life was not only already inside me, but *was* me. I—like every person—*was* love.

In his journals David had written of one hope dying and another hope being born, and this was indeed what happened in my life after David's exit from the material world. For when my hope of finding him alive died, the new hope of at least finding his body was born, and when that hope died, the hope of finding the spiritual David was born. Although that hope grew into a momentary form of reality, my hope that finding the spiritual David would solve my inner crisis also died after a time.

Many hopes have been born and have died since then, and it is now apparent to me that hope is only the earthly forerunner and herald of faith. For ultimately all hope must die, since hope implies some sort of future condition, whereas faith calmly states that everything one needs is here *now, always* has been here, and always *will* be here. Faith tells me that all I need to do is *open my heart*, and all that the universe has to offer is mine now, for the universe has but one thing to offer all of us, and that one thing is *love*: ourselves. The Light always has been with us, The Light always has *been* us.

So my search for love—for that is what David *is* and came to show us—has ended, because what I was searching for in the outer world has always existed in me in the inner world. Now I need only become more aware of what I know, more aware of who I am, and give to the outer world what the inner world gives me ceaselessly: love. Now I understand the purpose of my lifetime search, and now I understand the words of Ram Dass:

> When the despair is great enough, there is a turn around, and you start to go back to the One. The moment at which you look up, the moment at which you look in, starts the journey back. At that moment who you are starts to change, [and] a place within you starts to draw you as inevitably and irrevocably as a flame draws a moth. For a long time, maybe many, many lifetimes, you'll keep soaring in close and getting your wings singed. Now, whether your wing is being singed, whether the fire purifies you or destroys you, depends on who you think you are. The fire doesn't burn itself. And in truth, you are the fire.[43]

You and I are *light,* you and I are *love*, you and I are *one*.

Namasté!

# resources

Association for Humanistic Psychology
325 Ninth Street
San Francisco, CA 94103

Association for Past-Life Research and Therapies
P.O. Box 20151
Riverside, CA 92516

Association for Research and Enlightenment
P.O. Box 595
Virginia Beach, VA 23451

Patricia Hayes School of Inner Sense Development
P.O. Box 70
McCaysville, GA 30555

Spiritual Frontiers Fellowship International
P.O. Box 7868
Philadelphia, PA 19101

The Monroe Institute
Route 1, Box 175
Faber, VA 22938

For information about a past-life recall tape designed and narrated by the author, as well as about seminars in past-life recall or professional training in transformational guidance, please write:

George Schwimmer, Ph.D.
P.O. Box 6721
Beverly Hills, CA 90212

# notes

1. I later learned that Punta Púlpito *was* on David's right, and it *does* jut out from shore. We had bought David a green sweater for Christmas, which he took with him to Baja. It was not with his recovered personal belongings, so he may have had it on. Among David's belongings I afterwards found the following Dylan Thomas lines from "Fern Hill" written at the front of David's photo album: ". . . Time held me green and dying, though I sang in my chains like the sea . . ."

2. Actually, Holden had wanted to keep children from falling over the cliff. David had read *Catcher in the Rye* twice.

3. I later found the first stanza of this two-stanza poem: "The ships are lying in the bay,/ The gulls are swinging round their spars:/ My soul as eagerly as they/ Desires the margin of the stars." It was years before I recalled that an early title of David's novel *The Wilderness* had been *The Wandering*.

4. As I type this sentence, Krista is in Egypt, on her way to Jerusalem and the Sea of Galilee. There is no doubt in my mind that David is with her.

5. Words and music by Joe Brooks, copyright 1976, 1977 by BigHill Music Corp. Permission granted by Joe Brooks.

6. Words and music by Al Kasha and Joel Hirschhorn.

7. Words and music by Archie Jordan.

8. Looking back, this prayer appears to have been David's creed in life: "Lord, make me an instrument of your peace. Where there is hatred, let me sow love; where there is doubt, faith; where there is despair, hope; where there is darkness, light; where there is sadness, joy. O Divine Master, grant that I may not so much seek to be consoled, as to console;

to be understood, as to understand; to be loved, as to love. For it is in giving that we receive; it is in pardoning that we are pardoned; it is in dying that we are born to eternal life."

9. The readings included Revelation 3:12, "Him that overcometh will I make a pillar in the temple of my God, and he shall go no more out: and I will write upon him the name of my God, and the name of the city of my God, which is new Jerusalem."

10. Steven Foster with Meredith Little, *The Book of the VisionQuest* (Spokane, WA: Bear Tribe Publishing, 1983), p. 2.

11. I later found out that the North Carolina Outward Bound school had never lost anyone, nor had the Hurricane Island Outward Bound School, but the other Outward Bound schools all had incurred deaths.

12. Ruth Montgomery, *Strangers Among Us* (New York: Fawcett Crest Books, 1982), p. 101. Reprinted by permission of The Putnam Publishing Group.

13. Joseph Wood Krutch and Eliot Porter, *Baja California and the Geography of Hope* (San Francisco: Sierra Club, 1967), p. 4. Reprinted by permission of Sierra Club Books.

14. Peter Richelieu, *A Soul's Journey* (Garden City: Doubleday & Co., 1973), pp. 119-20.

15. *A Soul's Journey*, pp. 113-14.

16. Marcia Moore, *Hypersentience* (New York: Bantam Books, 1977), p. 135.

17. Marcia Moore, *Reincarnation* (York Harbor, ME: Arcane Publications, 1968), pp. 179-183.

18. The vibratory pattern of each complex of energies we call a soul is totally different from all others, just as no two snowflakes are alike. This pattern is the "signature" of the soul, and this is what a psychic "tunes in" to.

19. "Chakra" is a Sanskrit word meaning "wheel." In the human context, chakras are part of the human energy field: energy vortices which interpenetrate the body and act as transducers. There are seven major chakras, which are connected to the spine at different points—the first at

the coccyx and the seventh at the crown of the head. There also are a number of other, smaller chakras.

20. Marcia Emery, Ph.D., "Beautiful Dreamer," *Quarterly Journal of Spiritual Frontiers Fellowship International*, XXVI (Fall 1994), pp. 178-80.

21. Edgar Cayce, as quoted in *A Commentary on the Book of The Revelation* (Virginia Beach: A.R.E. Press, 1977), pp. 93, 75. Reprinted by permission of the Edgar Cayce Foundation.

22. Robert W. Krajenke, *Man Crowned King* (New York: Bantam Books, 1974), pp. 153-156. Reprinted by permission of the Edgar Cayce Foundation.

23. Violet Shelley, *Symbols and the Self* (Virginia Beach, VA: A.R.E. Press, 1976), pp. 6-19. Reprinted by permission of the Edgar Cayce Foundation.

24. *Symbols and the Self,* p. 18.

25. *Symbols and the Self,* pp. 9, 64-66.

26. Ad de Vries, *Dictionary of Symbols and Imagery* (Amsterdam: North-Holland Publishing Co., 1974), pp. 329-30, 473-4.

27. J.E. Cirlot, *A Dictionary of Symbols* (New York: Philosophical Library, 1963), pp. 37-38.

28. *A Commentary on the Book of The Revelation*, pp. 139, 143, 153, 159, 163, 201, 203.

29. The text of the drawing reads, "Dear People: I had a headache and thought that drawing would help. I still have a headache. The picture, though, comes from the sixth level of consciousness and should be taken literally. One must interpret from a Biblical, English, and mirror perspective. The tear is Pierre. He, no more than I, can speak to you. Greetings in the name of the beloved." The mirror text on the top is made up of both Hebrew and English characters, but no one has been able to decipher all of it up to this time. The top line translates, "It's strange," the next word—on the right of the second line—is "David," and the last word is probably "only." Please write to the author if you can decipher the rest.

30. Elizabeth W. Fenske, "The President's Corner," *Spiritual Frontiers Fellowship Newsletter*, December 1980, p. 2.

31. *Symbols and the Self*, p. 64.

32. Sir Oliver J. Lodge, *Raymond* (New York: George H. Doran Co., 1916), pp. 99 and 249.

33. James Joyce, *A Portrait of the Artist as a Young Man* (New York: The Viking Press, 1966), pp. 128-135. Reprinted by permission of Penguin USA.

34. *Symbols and the Self*, p. 17.

35. Joan Fleming, *A Daisy Chain For Satan* (New York: Ballantine Books, 1950), p. 182. Reprinted by permission of the Putnam Berkeley Group.

36. Reading David's journals, it seemed to me that David was also sometimes writing to his friends in his journals, subconsciously knowing the journals would be published. One person who read this book suggested that David was writing to me, as well.

37. Since this reading, Steve Forrest has published three books on astrology: *The Inner Sky; The Changing Sky;* and *Skymates.*

38. *Coastal Pilot*, p. 233.

39. From a news article: "Ocean kayakers have found that despite seas up to fifteen feet, they could handle large swells in the open sea with little trouble. It is closer to shore that they find trouble, when waves become steeper."

40. Edith Hamilton, *Mythology* (New York: Penguin Books, 1969), p. 64. Reprinted by permission of Little, Brown and Co., publishers.

41. Ram Dass, *Grist For The Mill* (Santa Cruz: Unity Press, 1977), p. 15. Reprinted by permission of Ram Dass.

42. Gerald G. Jampolsky, *Love Is Letting Go Of Fear* (New York: Bantam Books, 1981), pp. 8, 9, 36. Copyright by Gerald J. Jampolsky and Jack O. Keeler. Reprinted by permission of Celestial Arts, Berkeley, CA.

43. Ram Dass, p. 22.